Comparative Studies of Political Agendas

Series Editors
Christoffer Green-Pedersen, Aarhus University, Aarhus,
Denmark
Laura Chaqués Bonafont, University of Barcelona, Barcelona,
Spain
Arco Timmermans, Leiden University, The Hague, The
Netherlands
Frédéric Varone, Université de Genève, Geneva, Switzerland
Frank R. Baumgartner, University of North Carolina at
Chapel Hill, Chapel Hill, USA

The series publishes books on policy agenda-setting dynamics broadly understood. This includes for instance books dealing with the policy effects of agenda dynamics, the relationship between the political agenda, public opinion and the media agenda, and agenda dynamics in relation to particular issues. The series publishes both comparative books and books dealing with single countries if these single countries are placed in a comparative context. The books can be either monographs or edited volumes.

More information about this series at
http://www.palgrave.com/gp/series/14908

Miklós Sebők · Zsolt Boda
Editors

Policy Agendas in Autocracy, and Hybrid Regimes

The Case of Hungary

Editors
Miklós Sebők
Centre for Social Sciences
MTA Centre of Excellence
Eötvös Loránd Research Network
Budapest, Hungary

Zsolt Boda
Centre for Social Sciences
MTA Centre of Excellence
Eötvös Loránd Research Network
Budapest, Hungary

Comparative Studies of Political Agendas
ISBN 978-3-030-73222-6   ISBN 978-3-030-73223-3   (eBook)
https://doi.org/10.1007/978-3-030-73223-3

This Palgrave Macmillan imprint is published by the registered company Springer Nature Switzerland AG
The registered company address is: Gewerbestrasse 11, 6330 Cham, Switzerland

PREFACE

Over the past two-three decades, policy agenda research has become one of the most successful international collaboration in comparative politics and policy studies. Building on the trailblazing work of Baumgartner and Jones (1991) and Baumgartner, Breuning, et al. (2009), the Comparative Agendas Project (CAP—comparativeagendas.net) now counts more than two dozen country teams and the list is growing each year. The Hungarian CAP research team was established in 2013 as the first such research endeavor dedicated to studying policy dynamics in Central and Eastern Europe (Boda & Sebők, 2019).

By now our freely available datasets and corpora cover over 15 specific modules from media to parliamentary questions, from executive decrees to budgets (besides the international CAP site, our data can be accessed at cap.tk.mta.hu). Most modules cover multiple decades—in some cases over two centuries—and the project has become one of the major infrastructures for the empirical study of Hungarian politics and public policymaking. Research by the Hungarian CAP team has appeared in leading international journals, including East European Politics, European Political Science Research, Journal of Legislative Studies, Political Analysis, Politics and Governance, Policy Studies, and many more.

Based on these achievements we felt well-prepared to conduct a comprehensive analysis of Hungarian policy agendas from the mid-nineteenth century on. Such undertakings used to be the domain of historians, but the newly collected and analyzed data offered us a chance to revisit both old and new questions related to Hungarian policy history with a mixed-methods approach which equally relied on quantitative and qualitative social science methods.

We felt that the natural home for our manuscript would be the Comparative Studies of Political Agendas series at Palgrave. We thank Christoffer Green-Pedersen, Laura Chaqués Bonafont, Arco Timmermans, Frédéric Varone, and Frank R. Baumgartner as series editors for their unwavering support of our project and great insights regarding how to frame our contributions. Besides the extended time frame of analysis, one of the unique features of the Hungarian case is the high number of regime changes over the course of its modern history. This allowed us to investigate not just the general trends in policy agendas, but also the differences between information processing and decision-making in authoritarian, illiberal, or democratic regimes.

We thank the anonymous reviewers of the proposal for their helpful comments and the staff at Palgrave for their patience and professional cooperation in finalizing the manuscript. Our work benefited from the comments of participants at the annual CAP conferences, as well as EPSA, APSA, MPSA, SPSA, SWPSA, WPSA, and PSA. We are grateful for the grants provided to pursue our research agenda by NKFIH, the National Laboratory for Artificial Intelligence of Hungary, the H2020 projects DEMOS and OPTED, as well as the Bolyai Research Grant of Miklós Sebők. We are grateful for the ongoing support of our home institution, the Centre for Social Sciences in Budapest. We thank Csaba Molnár and Gábor Győri for their assistance with the manuscript, as well as Eszter Lancsár and András Tari for their help. Last but not least, we are indebted to all members of the Hungarian CAP team (many of them authors in this volume) and the over 50 interns who helped our work over the years. We hope that they found their association with the Hungarian Comparative Agendas team as rewarding, as we were grateful for their contributions.

Budapest, Hungary   Miklós Sebők
December 2020   Zsolt Boda

References

Baumgartner, F. R., & Jones, B. D. (1991). Agenda dynamics and policy subsystems. *The Journal of Politics, 53*(4), 1044–1074.

Baumgartner, F. R., Breuning, C., Green-Pedersen, C., Jones, B. D., Mortensen, P. B., Nuytmeans, M., & Walgrave, S. (2009). Punctuated equilibrium in comparative perspective. *American Journal of Political Science*, *53*(3), 603–620.

Boda, Z., & Sebők, M. (2019). The Hungarian comparative agendas project. In F. R. Baumgartner, C. Breunig, & E. Grossman (Eds.), *Comparative Policy Agendas: Theory, Tools, Data* (pp. 105–113). Oxford University Press.

Acknowlegdments

The book was supported by

- National Laboratory for Artificial Intelligence of Hungary (MILAB)
- National Research, Development and Innovation Office grant: "The dynamics of public policy in Hungary" (K-109303)
- National Research, Development and Innovation Office grant: "The Quality of Government and Public Policy: A Big Data Approach" (FK-123907)
- National Research, Development and Innovation Office grant: "Reactivity of the Hungarian Legal System between 2010 and 2018"" (FK-129018)
- National Research, Development and Innovation Office grant: "Populism in policy and law-making" (K-129245)
- János Bolyai Research Scholarship Grant of Miklós Sebők
- Observatory for Political Texts in European Democracies (OPTED) project funded by the European Union's Horizon 2020 research and innovation programme under grant agreement No 951832. Any dissemination of results here presented reflects only the authors' view. The Agency is not responsible for any use that may be made of the information it contains.
- Democratic Efficacy and the Varieties of Populism in Europe (DEMOS) project funded by the European Union's Horizon 2020 research and innovation programme under grant agreement No

822590. Any dissemination of results here presented reflects only the authors' view. The Agency is not responsible for any use that may be made of the information it contains.

Centre for Social Sciences—Hungarian Academy of Sciences Centre of Excellence.

PRAISE FOR *POLICY AGENDAS IN AUTOCRACY, AND HYBRID REGIMES*

"This important book, the result of a collaboration among a team of Hungarian scholars, unifies theories of governing regimes with policy process studies. It focuses on changing patterns of attention to policy issues across five major regimes that Hungary has experienced since 1867. Using a combination of quantitative and qualitive examinations of policy choices, along with intensive case studies in each regime, the authors test prevailing theories in the literature and generate some fresh thinking on policy change. The book will be essential reading in both policy studies and comparative politics."

—Bryan D. Jones, JJ "Jake" Pickle Regents' *Chair in Congressional Studies, Department of Government, University of Texas at Austin*

"The volume edited by Miklós Sebők and Zsolt Boda—with ten, mainly early career collaborators—offers an exceptionally careful analysis of a—mainly unsuccessful—century-long struggle of Hungary to combine liberalism and democracy. This case study of a small semi-peripheral country is of great theoretical interest to those who are interested in the worldwide spread of liberal democracy between 1970 and 2005 and its decline during the past 15 years. Warmly recommended for political scientists, economists an and sociologist."

—Ivan Szelenyi, William Graham *Emeritus Professor of Sociology and Political Science, Yale University*

CONTENTS

NOTES ON CONTRIBUTORS

Ágnes M. Balázs is a Constitutional Lawyer and a Political Scientist. She is an Assistant Lecturer of the National University of Public Service in Budapest. Her main research areas are policy-making, legislative studies, representation of minorities, the fundamental right to vote, and plural voting. She has been taking part in the Hungarian Comparative Agendas Project since 2015. She mainly works on the party manifesto database, but she also took part in the creation of the databases on legislation and media as well.

Tamás Barczikay is a Doctoral Candidate at Corvinus University of Budapest and Junior Research Fellow at the Centre for Social Sciences, Budapest. His main research interests cover methodology, statistics, and econometrics.

Zsolt Boda (Ph.D.) is a Research Professor and Director General of the Centre for Social Sciences as well as a part-time Professor of political science at ELTE University of Budapest. His academic work focuses on the problems of governance, public policy, as well as institutional trust, its social roots and its consequences for policy effectiveness. He is the Co-leader (with Miklós Sebők) of the Hungarian Comparative Agendas Project. He is also the Principal Investigator of DEMOS—Democratic efficacy and the varieties of populism in Europe, a consortial H2020 project.

György Márk Kis is a Statistician and Political Scientist. His recent work includes building statistical models and machine learning applications for supporting executive decisions in media and the creation of data collection schemas for business development. His interests are American politics, linear models, and quantitative text mining. He is also an external fellow of the Hungarian Comparative Agendas Project.

László Kiss (Ph.D.) is a Sociologist and Social Historian. He is a Research Fellow at the CSS-RECENS research group at the Centre for Social Sciences. He is a former Assistant Lecturer of Eötvös Loránd University and University of Pécs, Senior Lecturer of the Budapest College of Communication and Business, Researcher of Educatio Llc, and Research Methodology Advisor of the National University of Public Service. His main research interests are Hungarian social history of the socialist era and historical elite research.

Csaba Molnár is a Political Scientist. He is Junior Research Fellow of the Institute for Political Science, Centre for Social Sciences and Assistant Lecturer of Corvinus University of Budapest. His research mainly focuses on legislative studies and right-wing radicalism. He also serves as the legislative branch coordinator of the Hungarian Comparative Agendas Project.

Zsanett Pokornyi is a Junior Research Fellow at of Institute for Political Science, Centre for Social Sciences and a Ph.D. candidate at Eötvös Loránd University. Her research interests include taxation, tax compliance, tax morale and government regulation, executive and legislative agendas. She serves as the coordinator of the executive datasets in the Hungarian Comparative Agendas Project since 2017.

Orsolya Ring (Ph.D.) is a Historian and Research Fellow of the Centre of Social Sciences in Budapest. She is a member of poltextLAB where she works on the creation and classification of large-scale newspaper corpora. She is involved in the building of large-scale historical text corpora and its analysis with NLP methods in the Research Group on Computational Social Science (CSS-RECENS). Her research interests include social history and the history of socialist dictatorship and the application of text mining methods in historical research.

Eszter Sághy is a Student of University of Bath and a Research Assistant of the Hungarian Comparative Agendas Project.

Miklós Sebők (Ph.D.) is a Research Professor of the Centre of Social Sciences in Budapest. He serves as the Director of the Institute for Political Science at the Centre for Social Sciences, as Co-leader (with Zsolt Boda) of the Hungarian Comparative Agendas Project, and the Research Director of the Artificial Intelligence National Lab at CSS. His research interests include political economy and public policy and the application of text mining and machine learning methods in these fields.

LIST OF FIGURES

LIST OF TABLES

PART I

Introduction

CHAPTER 1

Understanding Agenda Dynamics in Non-democracies

Zsolt Boda and Miklós Sebők

The late 1980s, early 1990s constituted a watershed period in the global history of democracy. With the establishment of liberal democracy in post-communist Central-Eastern Europe, these years capped the third wave of democratization which had started in the 1970s with Portugal and Spain (Huntington, 1991). For many countries which were closed down to the world behind the erstwhile iron curtain, the collapse of the Soviet Union paved the way back to the Western path characterized by free and fair elections, liberal values (such as the respect for human rights) and market economies. Many tended to agree with Fukuyama (1989) that "an unabashed victory of economic and political liberalism" meant that humanity reached the "end of history." The enlargement of the European

Z. Boda (✉) · M. Sebők
Centre for Social Sciences, MTA Centre of Excellence, Eötvös Loránd Research Network, Budapest, Hungary
e-mail: boda.zsolt@tk.hu

M. Sebők
e-mail: sebok.miklos@tk.hu

3
M. Sebők and Z. Boda (eds.), *Policy Agendas in Autocracy, and Hybrid Regimes*, Comparative Studies of Political Agendas,
https://doi.org/10.1007/978-3-030-73223-3_1

Union with ten Eastern and Southern European states seemed to put the seal on the fate of Europe as a continent of democracies.

Yet two decades later, the state of democracy in the now enlarged Western world shows signs of distress. The rise (and fall) of right-wing populist leaders in established democracies started already in the 1990s with Jörg Haider in Austria, followed by, among others, Geert Wilders in the Netherlands and Marine Le Pen in France. This trend, however, only became ubiquitous in the second half of the 2010s with Brexit and the presidency of Donald Trump. These leaders and their political movements questioned the basic tenets of liberal democracy (or even core democratic electoral procedures per se, in the case of Trump and the 2020 elections).

By the Covid-plagued year of 2020, these developments looked certainly more than a brief detour from the teleological trajectory toward the end of history. More and more questions were reopened which the globalized, liberal elites of Western democracies had filed under "case closed." The free movement of people and capital, the separation of powers system, and a political culture of cooperation between rival democratic forces—all basic tenets of the prevailing consensus—were cast into doubt. Democratic backsliding replaced the processes of democratization and the projections of Fukuyama for the emerging superpower of China (the only remaining viable alternative to democracy and free market capitalism in 1989) that there "will inevitably be mounting pressure for change in the political system" proved unfounded.

Hungarian Prime Minister Viktor Orbán was one of the first elected leaders to sense that the winds had changed and the liberal order is less stable and invincible than what had been thought. Undeterred by claims of external constraints and the proverbial dependency new EU member states on fiscal transfers from Western Europe, he regained policy autonomy to a shocking extent and carved out an influence on the EU level that was utterly disproportionate to the population and economic clout of a country of less than 10 million people.

He gained notoriety as the first (and up until 2020 one of the few) EU member state leaders to declare that democracy need not necessarily be liberal. He often criticized Western liberal democracies not only for their allegedly extreme and oppressive liberalism, but also for their ineffective governance. In 2014, he stated that the financial crisis of 2008 was a turning point in history, as it revealed the fundamental weakness of liberal democracies:

We should take as a starting point the great reconfiguration of forces which happened in 2008 in terms of global finances, the global economy, the global trade, global power, including military power [...] it seems probable that the societies built on the liberal democratic principle of statehood will not be able to maintain their global competitiveness and will suffer a setback unless they manage to reform themselves substantially [...] today the leading idea is to better understand those regimes that are not from the West, are not liberal, not liberal democracies, maybe not even democracies, and still, make their nations thrive. Today the stars in international analyses are Singapore, China, India, Russia, Turkey.[1]

Whether Orbán's argument holds or not is one question. It seems to be a reformulation of the old Lee thesis, named after the Singaporean leader, Lee Kuan Yew, stating that democracy is not needed for the development of poor countries. On the contrary: it may even constrain economic growth (Barro, 1996). Nevertheless, several decades of international scholarship on the subject indicates that the Lee thesis cannot be generalized (Grindle, 2007; Knutsen, 2010). While there may be many viable strategies to effectively secure economic development and the case of Singapore undeniably represents a successful one, data proves that there is a positive and probably causal relationship between democracy and economic development. Two of the widely accepted mechanisms bridging them are effective institutions and effective governance (Robinson & Acemoglu, 2012).

Our book is not strictly about revisiting the Lee thesis and not because we are convinced that the question is settled for good. In light of the aforementioned developments in the history of the Western world, it would be ill-advised to make such bold statements. And of course, there is a good case to be made that liberal democracy is desirable for its normative value independent of the effectiveness of its governance. Still, the challenge of how best to organize our societies is eternal and so is the task of better understanding different coordination mechanisms (especially bureaucratic vs. market coordination, see Kornai, 1990), institutional arrangements, and styles of governance. In this sense, scrutinizing arguments like the ones made by Viktor Orbán, that is, revisiting the Lee thesis, is an endeavor that has a high potential to contribute to

---

[1] https://2015-2019.kormany.hu/hu/a-miniszterelnok/beszedek-publikaciok-interjuk/a-munkaalapu-allam-korszaka-kovetkezik.

the understanding of the democratic conundrum of the early twenty-first century.

The same applies to injecting policy studies with a sense of the underlying political and socio-economic structures. Traditionally, and not independently of its provenance in American academia, policy studies was a discipline focusing on policymaking in democratic polities (Baumgartner et al., 2017). In this book, we argue that this position is no longer tenable, and not just due to the inherent value in studying and comparing various political systems (which, obviously, something political scientists did going back to antiquity).

Needless to say, policy studies have come a long way from the late nineteenth century and now is a burgeoning field, which does investigate the effect of regime types on policymaking. However, when it comes to authoritarian regimes or procedural, "limited democracies" (Przeworski, 1999) many studies focus on socio-economic outcomes (Antonio, 2012; Deacon, 2009; Mulligan Casey & Sala-I-Martin, 2004). Or as Orbán put it: whether democracies or autocracies "make their nations thrive."

Outcomes are, of course, the final test of assessing the virtues of a given system of governance and as such, they are the legitimate focus of analysis. But we have a different agenda in this book: we study the processes behind the outcomes. The ambition of this volume is to contribute to a better understanding of governance—and, more specifically, the patterns of policymaking and policy agendas—in non- and partly democratic regimes. Just as policy evaluation should not only focus on the outcomes of policies, but also on outputs and processes (Vedung, 2000), analyzing the governance under different regimes should not be restricted to comparing outcomes solely.

What happens inside the "black box" of governance; how decisions are made; which actors have access to policy venues; what kind of discourses are framing policy decisions; and, in particular, how these and other factors shape the dynamics of policy change—these are among the classic questions of policy studies that we raise in the contexts of different political regimes. We believe these to be critical questions in need of answers—not just for the sake of policy studies but for the debates surrounding the deterioration in the quality of democracy all over the world.

Theoretical Framework

The general theoretical framework of our approach is based on the punctuated equilibrium theory (PET) developed by Brian D. Jones and Frank R. Baumgartner (Baumgartner & Jones, 1993, 2009) and the comparative study of policy agendas that this theory inspired. PET implies that although policy change is generally incremental, that is, policy subsystems are mostly in equilibrium, large-scale reforms also regularly happen and they are not necessarily provoked by external shocks, but the logic of policy agendas. PET depicts policymaking as a complex system of processing, weighing, evaluating, and selecting information, which ultimately influence policy choices (Jones & Baumgartner, 2005). The operation of the system depends on the interactions of multiple policy actors who try to advance their causes, make proposals, convince others.

The interactions of policy actors ultimately define the composition of different agendas: that of the public, the media, and political actors. If an issue becomes important, meaning that it happens to be present intensively on several agendas, that may elevate it on the level of macropolitics spurring action from the decision-makers—leading eventually to large-scale policy reforms. PET conceptualizes these large-scale reforms as punctuations that interrupt the periods of equilibrium. In sum, PET inspired the study of policy agendas: their dynamics and interactions signal and explain policy change. However, since the PET framework delineates a coherent theoretical approach by building the core concepts of policy studies, such as information, information processing, policy actors, agenda setting, policy change, etc., it has become one of the most influential theories of the field (Sabatier & Weible, 2014). It offers a useful vantage point for studying complex phenomena related to policymaking well beyond the question of policy dynamics.

The initial project of Baumgartner and Jones to systematically gather data on policy agendas in order to test and further develop their theory has soon grown into a major comparative database building endeavor called the Comparative Agendas Project (see comparativeagendas.net). Covering more than two dozen country and auxiliary projects (such as those on individual US states and the EU) it now offers the datasets and methods for a comparative analysis of policy agendas (Baumgartner et al., 2019). Furthermore, it provided fertile ground for longitudinal country case studies for Western Europe (Bonafont et al., 2015; John et al., 2013) and—in a concurrent timing with our project—for Turkey (Bulut & Yildirim, 2020).

This book follows in the footsteps of such country studies centered around punctuated equilibrium theory. For the first, we offer an extension of this paradigm to post-communist, Central-Eastern European countries. We also extended the time frame of analysis vis-á-vis most CAP research (with the notable exception of the US Policy Agendas Project). We investigate the policy agendas of different regimes through 150 years of Hungarian history with the assumption that differences in agenda dynamics signal deeper differences in the patterns of the policymaking process.

While over the past thirty years, the comparative study of policy agendas has become one of the fastest-growing subfields in policy research, the agenda-setting literature, similarly to policy studies in general, until recently focused almost exclusively on well-established democracies. This began to change with the groundbreaking articles by Baumgartner et al. (2017) as well as Jones et al. (2019) which set out the blueprint for studying policy agendas in regimes, which do not adhere to the principles of liberal democracy.

Baumgartner et al. (2017) analyze trends in budgetary data in four countries (covering Brazil, Malta, Russia, and Turkey) in both the democratic and autocratic periods and argue that policy punctuations are larger in authoritarian regimes. Jones et al. (2019) provide analytical categories in order to explain the differences in policymaking in democratic and authoritarian regimes. They discuss the role of information, incentives, and centralization in shaping the environment for public policy decision-making in various regimes (since this work serves as the starting point for our own analysis we return to it in more detail in the next chapter). A number of empirical scholarship followed this research agenda with a particular emphasis on China and Hong Kong (Chan et al., 2020; Chan & Zhao, 2016; Or, 2019; Wu, 2020; Xiao et al., 2020) and the military regime of Turkey (Bulut & Yildirim, 2020; Yildirim et al., 2020).

Building on our previous work (such as Sebők & Berki, 2018) and the new datasets of the Hungarian Comparative Agendas Project (Boda & Sebők, 2019), the present volume contributes to this developing literature by focusing on a hitherto less examined topic in comparative politics: the dynamics of policy agendas in partly free and hybrid regimes (besides purely autocratic and democratic ones). Our intention was to dig deeper into the policymaking patterns of non-democratic regimes and to extend the time frame of analysis, which allowed for a unique analysis of historical regimes in the PET framework. (We present our analytical perspective at greater length in the next chapter where we also formulate a number of expectations—if not falsifiable hypotheses—based on the regime-focused stream of agenda research.)

REGIME TYPOLOGY

In studies of the effect of regimes on public policymaking, the focus is inescapably on the institutional arrangements of the polity in question. There is a long-standing tradition in political science dividing the regimes in a dichotomous way into democracies and autocracies. However, over multiple decades a substream of this literature has devoted considerable space to regimes, which withstand such simplifications. Besides "traditional" cases of military juntas and electoral theocracies (such as Iran) from the late 1990s a new breed of regimes rose which was did not feature many traits of liberal democracies, but could not be associated with full-fledged autocracies either. This new breed was called hybrid regimes (also known as "competitive authoritarian regimes" (Levitsky & Way, 2002), "electoral autocracies" (Schedler, 2013), or "illiberal democracies" (Zakaria, 1997). A common attribute of these political systems is that they hold elections, but the elections are either not free and fair, and/or their results are not directly translated into effective governing power. In hybrid regimes, the freedom of the media is also curtailed and the protection of human rights is not fully ensured.

Hybrid regimes are not all alike; in fact, they are quite diverse. Calling a hybrid regime "electoral autocracy" or "defective democracy" (Merkel, 2004) therefore might be more than an issue of denomination: it may point to specific features of the polity in question. However, hybrid regimes share the characteristic of allowing more political freedom to social and political actors than full-scale autocracies do; and the power of the rulers depends at least partly on popular will. In more technical terms, the selectorate and the winning coalition are larger than in dictatorships (Bueno de Mesquita & Smith, 2011).

In this introductory chapter, we cannot dive deep into the ocean of regime theory—for the purposes of our research project we needed to simplify our explanatory variable, that is the types of regimes. We are fully aware of the fact that not only hybrid regimes, but autocracies and democracies also show considerable diversity. For instance, in Hungary, the hard dictatorship of the 1950s was quite different from the softer brand of autocracy of János Kádár in 1960s–1980s (see Chapter 7). In the 1950s, people were arrested and tortured for made-up charges and just for being suspicious (in fact, Kádár himself stood accused at a show trial). The ideological and administrative control on the society was very tight, the economy was highly centralized and practically any kind of civic autonomy was abolished.

From the 1960s, the control on society loosened: Stalinist totalitarianism gave way to a form of oppression of dissidents which was milder, the economy was partly decentralized, and first non-political, later, by the 1980s overtly political civic movements slowly emerged. Still, both regimes were autocracies, as the political power remained at the Communist (later: Socialist) Party and general elections had no role whatsoever in selecting decision-makers. Our conclusion is that there are differences within various kinds of autocracies and this may affect their policymaking practices as well (and we return to this issue in each period description in Chapter 3). Finally, democratic regimes are also manifold—see the different systems of government: presidential, parliamentary; majoritarian or consensual. Their institutional arrangements and norms obviously have a bearing on the patterns of governance and policymaking (Tsebelis, 1995).

Moreover, we have to emphasize that regimes should be evaluated in their historical context. For instance, democracy in the nineteenth century was very different from today's liberal democracy: its institutional setting was far less complex and the politically active citizens comprised only a small segment of society. The catalogue of human rights was considerably shorter, while the government was much more limited than today and it assumed less responsibility in providing public goods.

Readers of the period chapters should also bear in mind that the regimes studied there extend to a time span of 150 years. The key takeaway, then, is that differences between the patterns of policymaking in different periods may be explained just as much by the historical context as by regime characteristics. In those chapters, we made our best to untangle the factors that stem from the regime type in question and those which were defined by the socio-economic and political circumstances of the era, but further research may be needed to shed more light on these complex issues.

With all these complications—but also the limited number of our cases—in mind we use three categories for regimes types throughout the book: free (the liberal democracy of 1990–2010), partly free (the proto-parliamentarism of 1867–1918; the traditional authoritarianism of 1920–1944; and the illiberal hybrid regime of 2010–2018) and not free (the socialist autocracy of 1956–1989). Although the three partly free regimes feature limitations to the ideal type of liberal democracy, they are certainly not equivalent: the political regime of Dualism was closer to the democratic ideal type of the day than the Horthy era with its often hardline policies. In brief: context matters.

Having said that, in the next chapter we formulate expectations concerning the effect of regimes on policymaking and policy dynamics. The expectations are formulated in a context-free, generalizable manner— which obviously ties them to late twentieth century-early twenty-first-century Western liberal democracy. Chapters III.1–III.5 contextualize and translate them to the given historical period.

CASE SELECTION

This book presents a within-case study analysis of the policymaking of different Hungarian political regimes from the second half of the nineteenth century till the end of the 2010s, where the different regimes serve as the explanatory factors for the comparative investigation. Hungarian political history offers an ideal case to investigate the effect of regime changes on policy dynamics and agendas. Located in Central and Eastern Europe, it is a typical semi-peripheral "new" democracy. Over the 150 years in question, it experienced a rich variety of liberal, autocratic and semi-autocratic regimes.

Since Hungary was under communist/socialist rule from 1947 to 1989, our analysis will shed light on the policy dynamics of the communist/socialist regime which is a largely understudied area of research. More recently, under the governments of Viktor Orbán, Hungary has become a prime example of democratic backsliding (Scheiring, 2019; Sedelmeier, 2017) offering the possibility of studying *in statu nascendi* the policy implications of hybridization.

While full-fledged dictatorships are more and more rare, the number of so-called hybrid regimes is increasing. These trends make especially timely the investigations concerning the effects of political regimes on policy-making and the illiberal turn of many polities beyond Hungary (such as Poland, Russia, and Turkey) offer a fertile ground for testing the external validity of our results related to the Hungarian case.

THE OUTLINE OF THE BOOK

The rest of the book is divided into four large parts and several chapters. Part II presents the theory and methods behind our analyses. Chapter 2 gives more details on the theoretical considerations that informed our research: what PET says about policy dynamics under different regimes and what expectations can we formulate along the dimensions of policy content, process, and discourse concerning the patterns of policymaking in non-democratic polities vis-á-vis liberal democratic ones.

We introduce the concept of policy capacities for describing the mechanisms and actors which channel relevant information and knowledge about policy challenges toward decision-makers. We propose that illiberalism curtails policy capacities, that is, cuts informational channels from and toward to society resulting in higher policy punctuations and greater friction (along with the tendency of twenty-first-century hybrid regimes to centralized political communication and elevate the "leader" as the primary actor in these polities).

Chapter 3 gives an overview of the regimes studied in the book and their positions on the democratic–autocratic axis. The regimes scrutinized cover a century and a half, but we did not select all distinct systems of government for in-depth analysis. We study five different eras: the proto-parliamentarian regime of the Austro-Hungarian Monarchy (1867–1918), the partly free Horthy-regime (1920–1944), the autocratic socialist regime of János Kádár (1956–1989), the new liberal democracy after regime change (1990—2010) and the illiberal democracy of Viktor Orbán (2010—2018). Appendix A1 provides even more details on the full range of regimes in the period investigated including constitutional and party system features.

Chapter 4 present the databases of the Hungarian Comparative Agendas Project which undergird the empirical analyses of the book. Our collection covers more than a dozen individual modules from media and public opinion data through parliamentary speeches and laws to budgets. It also describes the methodology for assigning policy codes to large-scale textual and historical databases. The corresponding Appendix A2 details the relative merits of human coding, hybrid methods, and machine learning.

The parts of Part III are devoted to the presentations of different regimes from the pre-war era to the illiberal democracy of the post-2010 period. Each part provides a short introduction to the politics of the given era; a general description of the institutions of governance and the process of policymaking; a presentation of the composition of policy agendas; as well as same concrete cases of policy change and agenda dynamics. The cases point to typical or important policy issues of the regime in question and are meant to provide lively illustrations of the general patterns.

Part IV revisits the expectations formulated in Part II on the effects of regimes on policymaking. In doing so, it overviews the previous chapters and contributes with further qualitative and quantitative analyses to the discussion. We present new results related to the quantitative assessment of policy punctuations in different regimes. The association between different policy agendas as well as the diversity of agendas under different regimes are also analyzed. The chapter also discusses the possible explanations for some counter-intuitive results, and highlights the overwhelming importance of different historical contexts over the effects stemming from regime characteristics. This last chapter also suggests takeaways and avenues for future research.

CONTRIBUTIONS

Throughout its theoretical, methodological, and empirical chapters, our book offers a three-pronged contribution to our understanding of policy agendas. First, it advances the theory of policymaking in autocratic and partly democratic regimes, including a particular subset of the broader category of such partly free polities: illiberal-hybrid regimes. We test the hypothesis of larger policy punctuations in illiberal regimes and offer an explanation based on the idea of higher friction caused by truncated policy capacities and deficiencies in information gathering as well the preeminent (personalized) style of governance in these systems.

Second, the book's empirical contribution includes a comparative analysis of historical policy agenda data; the in-depth investigation of policy dynamics in a communist regime; as well as new insights into an emerging phenomenon (hybrid regimes) from a perspective (policy agendas) that has thus far not been studied in a comparative research design. Our new datasets over the various modules of the Comparative Agenda's Project offer the possibility of an exhaustive analysis and are freely available for further research and replication of our findings.

Third, the book makes methodological contributions as well as applies machine learning and other advanced quantitative methods of text analysis to political and legal texts from the regimes in the sample, offering a new, broadly applicable approach toward such research. Taken together, these contributions push forward the policy agendas literature in multiple promising directions and extend its scope in terms of time, space, and methods used.

REFERENCES

Antonio, M. J. (2012). Decreasing inequality under Latin America's "social democratic" and "populist" governments: Is the difference real? *International Journal of Health Services, 42*(2), 257–275.
Barro, R. J. (1996). Democracy and growth. *Journal of Economic Growth, 1*(1), 1–27.
Baumgartner, F. R., Breunig, C., & Grossman, E. (2019). *Comparative policy agendas: Theory, tools, data.* Oxford University Press.
Baumgartner, F. R., Carammia, M., Epp, D. A., Noble, B., Rey, B., & Yildirim, T. M. (2017). Budgetary change in authoritarian and democratic regimes. *Journal of European Public Policy, 24*(6), 792–808.
Baumgartner, F. R., & Jones, B. D. (1993, 2009). *Agendas and instability in American politics.* The University of Chicago Press.
Boda, Z., & Sebők, M. (2019). The Hungarian comparative agendas project. In F. R. Baumgartner, C. Breunig, & E. Grossman (Eds.), *Comparative policy agendas: Theory, tools, data* (pp. 105–113). Oxford: Oxford University Press.
Bonafont, L. C., Baumgartner, F. R., & Palau, A. (2015). *Agenda dynamics in Spain.* Springer.
Bueno de Mesquita, B., & Smith, A. (2011). *The dictator's handbook: Why bad behavior is almost always good politics.* Public Affairs.
Bulut, A. T., & Yildirim, T. M. (2020). *Political stability, democracy and agenda dynamics in Turkey.* Springer.
Chan, K. N., Lam, W. F., & Chen, S. (2020). Elite bargains and policy priorities in authoritarian regimes: Agenda setting in China under Xi Jinping and Hu Jintao. *Governance,* on-line. https://doi.org/10.1111/gove.12543.
Chan, K. N., & Zhao, S. (2016). Punctuated equilibrium and the information disadvantage of authoritarianism: Evidence from the People's Republic of China. *Policy Studies Journal, 44*(2), 134–155.
Deacon, R. T. (2009). Public good provision under dictatorship and democracy. *Public Choice, 139*(1–2), 241–262.
Fukuyama, F. (1989). The end of history? *The National Interest, 16*, 3–18.
Grindle, M. S. (2007). Good enough governance revisited. *Development Policy Review, 25*(5), 533–574.
Huntington, S. P. (1991). Democracy's third wave. *Journal of Democracy, 2*(2), 12–34.

John, P., Bertelli, A., Jennings, W., & Bevan, S. (2013). *Policy agendas in British politics*. Springer.

Jones, B. D., & Baumgartner, F. R. (2005). *The politics of attention: How government prioritizes problems*. University of Chicago Press.

Jones, B. D., Epp, D. A., & Baumgartner, F. R. (2019). Democracy, authoritarianism, and policy punctuations. *International Review of Public Policy, 1*(1), 7–26. https://doi.org/10.4000/irpp.318.

Knutsen, C. H. (2010). Investigating the Lee thesis: How bad is democracy for Asian economies? *European Political Science Review: EPSR, 2*(3), 451.

Kornai, J. (1990). The affinity between ownership forms and coordination mechanisms: The common experience of reform in socialist countries. *Journal of Economic Perspectives, 4*(3), 131–147.

Levitsky, S., & Way, L. A. (2002). The rise of competitive authoritarianism. *Journal of Democracy, 13*(2), 51–65.

Merkel, W. (2004). Embedded and defective democracies. *Democratization, 11*(5), 33–58.

Mulligan Casey, G. R., & Sala-I-Martin, X. (2004). Do democracies have different public policies than nondemocracies? *Journal of Economic Perspectives, 18*(1), 51–74.

Or, N. H. (2019). How policy agendas change when autocracies liberalize: The case of Hong Kong, 1975–2016. *Public Administration, 97*(4), 926–941.

Przeworski, A. (1999). Minimalist conception of democracy: A defense. *Democracy's Value, 23*, 12–17.

Robinson, J., & Acemoglu, D. (2012). *Why nations fail: The origins of power, prosperity and poverty*. Profile.

Sabatier, P., & Weible, C. M. (Eds.). (2014). *Theories of the policy process*. Westview Press, a member of the Persus Books Group.

Schedler, A. (2013). *The politics of uncertainty: Sustaining and subverting electoral authoritarianism*. Oxford University Press.

Scheiring, G. (2019). Dependent development and authoritarian state capitalism: Democratic backsliding and the rise of the accumulative state in hungary. *Geoforum*.

Sebők, M., & Berki, T. (2018). Punctuated equilibrium in democracy and autocracy: An analysis of Hungarian budgeting between 1868 and 2013. *European Political Science Review, 10*(4), 589–611.

Sedelmeier, U. (2017). Political safeguards against democratic backsliding in the EU: The limits of material sanctions and the scope of social pressure. *Journal of European Public Policy, 24*(3), 337–351.

Tsebelis, G. (1995). Decision making in political systems. Veto players in presidentialism, parliamentarism, multicameralism and multipartyism. *British Journal of Political Science, 25*(3), 289–325.

Vedung, E. (2000). Evaluation research and fundamental research. In R. Stockmann (Ed.), *Evaluationsforschung: Grundlagen und ausgewählte Forschungsfelder* (pp. 111–134). VS Verlag für Sozialwissenschaften.

Wu, Y. (2020). Dynamics of policy change in authoritarian countries: A multiple-case study on China. *Journal of Public Policy, 40*(2), 236–258.

Xiao, H., Wang, X., & Liu, C. (2020). Budgetary punctuations: A fiscal management perspective. *Policy Studies Journal, 48*(4), 873–895.

Yildirim, T. M., Bulut, A. T., & Ilter, E. (2020). Agenda dynamics and policy priorities in military regimes. *International Political Science Review.* https://doi.org/10.1177/0192512120923068.

Zakaria, F. (1997). The rise of illiberal democracy. *Foreign Affairs, 76*(4), 22–43.

PART II

Theory and Research Strategy

CHAPTER 2

The Effect of Political Regimes on Policy Agendas: A Theoretical Framework

Zsolt Boda

Policy dynamics refer to the patterns of stability and change of policies. Jones et al. (2019) argue that policy dynamics varies with regime types: policy punctuations, that is, large-scale policy changes are higher and more frequent in non-democratic (or: "unfree") regimes which they interpret as a sign of a deficiently adaptive system of policymaking. Adaptive policymaking refers to the ability to address relevant policy problems while avoiding "overly large and erratic shifts in policy commitments" (Jones et al., 2019: 9).

Both stability and change are needed in policymaking. Stability provides a reliable institutional background for policy actors—it is not desirable that laws and regulations change frequently because this would bring unpredictability for stakeholders. However, policies sometimes do have to be updated or even radically reformulated, because external circumstances change, technology develops, political preferences and

Z. Boda (✉)
Centre for Social Sciences, MTA Centre of Excellence, Eötvös Loránd Research Network, Budapest, Hungary
e-mail: boda.zsolt@tk.hu

© The Author(s), under exclusive license to Springer Nature Switzerland AG 2021
M. Sebők and Z. Boda (eds.), *Policy Agendas in Autocracy, and Hybrid Regimes*, Comparative Studies of Political Agendas,
https://doi.org/10.1007/978-3-030-73223-3_2

values evolve. Therefore, each government develops certain capacities embodied in institutional rules and practices to deal with the dual challenge of policy stability and change (Weaver & Rockman, 1993).

Jones et al. (2019) argue that policy dynamics measured in terms of punctuation is an indicator of the quality of policymaking. The empirical case of lower policy punctuation in democracies brings further evidence to those studies which uphold that democratic regimes provide better governance and more adaptive policies (Robinson & Acemoglu, 2012). The question is, which mechanisms realize the effect of the regime on policies.

Jones et al. (2019) present four basic mechanisms: friction, incentives/representation, centralization, and information. Friction is the institutional resistance to change and the authors advance empirical evidence that institutional friction in the policy process is higher under non-democratic circumstances (this finding is corroborated by many other studies, such as Sebők & Berki, 2018). But why is it lower in democracies than in autocracies? The thesis of "institutional efficiency" (Baumgartner et al., 2017) of non-democratic regimes looks just as convincing: the relevant policy actors are much less numerous in autocracies and the lack of political and institutional checks and balances render radical policy reforms easier to implement. Why do "efficient" autocracies still face larger friction? Incentives, centralization, and information provide the explanation.

Incentives are set by democratic accountability in a way that motivates decision-makers to address social problems in an effective way. In a democracy, politicians are under the constant scrutiny of the citizens who will decide at the end of the electoral cycle whether to trust them for yet another electoral period or to replace them. Therefore, democratic decision-makers have strong incentives to take signals about policy problems seriously, and to process and, possibly, solve them. Although a certain level of friction and policy punctuation is characteristic of the democratic policymaking process as well, these punctuations are more attenuated than in autocracies partly because of these incentives. Autocratic leaders are not subject to popular vote and are, therefore, less motivated to diligently react to the needs, demands, and expectations of the people.

Hybrid, or partly free regimes constitute an interesting problem. Evidence shows that friction is higher in hybrid regimes than in democracies, although lower than in autocracies—because in hybrid regimes, public opinion has more clout over political agendas. But the transmission from the identification of problems to the adoption of solutions is still more difficult in hybrid regimes than in democracies, in part because the accountability and the incentives of the decision-makers are weaker. Sebők (2019) points to another factor: that hybrid regimes often rely on poll-governed populist decision-making, focusing on a few, symbolically and politically important issues, while neglecting a large number of other problems. Spectacular, large-scale policies may be undertaken in terms of the former; no action may be initiated in terms of the latter, but if those problems fester, at one point they may also require significant changes. Both logic increases the likelihood of punctuations in hybrid regimes.

Jones et al. (2019) argue that centralization is another factor, which mediates the effect of political regimes on policy dynamics. Generally speaking, more centralized governments cause more severe policy punctuations. Data prove that this is true in democracies, and we may suspect that the stronger centralization of non-democratic regimes may be another factor, which leads to higher punctuation. Two mechanisms may be at work: first, as the authors argue, executives like to make changes. Centralization provides a fertile ground for taking major decisions and the power holders often use this opportunity. However, as we discussed above, in autocracies, they tend to follow their own agenda instead of the public agenda. Second, we suggest that political centralization increases friction. The features associated with political centralization—such as the relative weakness of autonomous political actors—the constrained policy venues as well as the hierarchically organized nature of government make it difficult for policy problems to ascend to the decision-making phase.

Finally, Jones and his co-authors argue that the lack of information in non-democratic regimes is also a factor that leads to more severe friction and punctuation. In non-free and partly free regimes, media is not operating unconstrained, the civil society is under control or oppressed, the political opposition (if any) has limited possibilities to influence the government. These actors and institutions might be considered as parts of the policy capacities of the society (Boda & Patkós, 2018), brokering information between society and the government. If they cannot fulfil their role, the flow of policy relevant information is restricted and cannot easily reach decision-makers. In other words, non-democratic regimes are struck by informational disadvantage (Baumgartner et al., 2017).

The argument about incentives states that in autocracies, decision-makers are not motivated to take policy problems seriously. The reasoning related to information implies that even if the rulers were interested in policy problems, the lack of available information would still hinder adaptive policymaking, therefore increasing the odds of policy punctuations. In this, one can argue friction is, in fact, caused by skewed incentives, centralization, and asymmetric information.

CONTENT, PROCESS, AND DISCOURSE

Jones et al. (2019) argue convincingly that (1) the likelihood of policy punctuations and institutional friction is higher in non-free and partly free regimes; and that (2) this is due to the lack of incentives, the higher level of centralization, and a shortage of information characteristic of those regimes. In the following, we further break down the above thesis and formulate a number of theoretical expectations concerning policymaking that we study in the forthcoming empirical chapters. We structure the arguments along three crucial dimensions of policymaking: content, process, and discourses.

Bartha et al. (2020) proposed an ideal type of liberal democratic policymaking along these dimensions. In terms of content, the ideal type is constructed of a reliance on a relatively coherent set of policy ideas; a central role of policy paradigms supported by area-specific expertise; majoritarian policy preferences constrained by the protection of minority rights; and—in line with Jones et al. (2019)—relatively low policy punctuations and rare large-scale reforms. In terms of procedure, it is characterized by a high level of institutionalization with a low level of leadership discretion; pluralism, that is, a variety of policy actors having access to the policy process; and public discussions on policy alternatives. In terms of policy discourses, it features competing policy discourses with mostly high and positive valence (Bartha et al., 2020).

Research in policy studies have been analyzing each of these elements and how they unfold and interact in producing specific policy-related phenomena, such as outputs, policy change, or policy stability (see Sabatier & Weible, 2014). Throughout its development over the past decades, the field of policy studies has produced increasingly sophisticated theories and empirical findings—without, however, moving out of the framework of the liberal democratic model of policymaking. Our aim here is to extend the external validity of such studies to non-democratic polities.

CONTENT

Policy content refers to the substance of policies under democratic and non-democratic conditions. Are there systematic differences in the composition of policy agendas and ultimately in the policy choices of different regimes? Selectorate theory implies that the size of the "selectorate," that is, the group of people which has an institutionally granted right or norm choosing the government, influences the substance of decisions made by the government (Bueno de Mesquita et al., 1999; Bueno de Mesquita & Smith, 2011).

In dictatorships the selectorate is small, typically including the leadership of the ruling party or the army. Since the longevity of the dictator's rule depends on them, he is inclined to make decisions that meet their interests instead of the society in general. Even worse, the dictator might be counter-motivated to make policies beneficial to the wider public, since emancipated, educated people represent a potential threat to his rule. Conversely, democratic rule is dependent on the decision (vote) of a large part of the society, therefore democratic governance tends to provide public goods that potentially increase welfare and the quality of life for many people. That is, the abovementioned democratic incentives mentioned do not only contribute to lower policy punctuations as suggested by Jones et al. (2019), but have an effect on policy agendas and the content of decisions.

Empirical findings are less straightforward than theoretical claims, but several studies have demonstrated that democracies do indeed spend more on the provision of public goods including education, health, sanitation, roads, and environmental protection (Bernauer & Koubi, 2009; Bueno de Mesquita et al., 2003; Deacon, 2009; see Lake David, 2001). At the same time, Lott (1999) and Mulligan Casey and Sala-I-Martin (2004) found no evidence that non-democracies would spend less on education. As a possible explanation, Lott (1999) suggests that autocracies may invest in education in order to indoctrinate the population.

An alternative hypothesis can also be advanced: autocracies cannot rely on input legitimacy in order to ensure the allegiance of their citizens, therefore they need to provide at least some basic outputs to people. An indirect support to this claim is given by Deacon's (2009) finding: the difference between democracies' and autocracies' performance is smaller in terms of providing safe water than in terms of providing secondary education. Clean water is certainly more essential than secondary education and even autocracies are compelled to secure it. The output legitimacy considerations might especially be important for soft autocracies and hybrid regimes as opposed to hard dictatorships in which rulers use more repression and brutality for maintaining their power.

Related to the problem of public goods is the spending on military and law enforcement (police, secret service, etc.). It is plausible to expect non-free regimes to devote more resources to those forces than democracies (see Brauner, 2015). Related to the distribution of public goods, some evidence suggests that the higher spending on public goods by democracies does not necessarily reach the poorest segments of the society (Keefer, 2005). Selectorate theory may offer an explanation to this through the concept of "winning coalition" defined as those members of the selectorate whose support is essential to keep the incumbent leadership in office (Bueno de Mesquita et al., 1999: 148).

A socially marginalized, politically passive part of society does not form part of a winning coalition: even democratically elected leaders need only the support of the majority of politically active citizens. Conversely, populist autocrats who rely on the poorer segments of the population may advance egalitarian social policies (see Montecino, 2012). At the same time, we should note that inequality is smaller in democracies (Dodlova & Gioblas, 2017).

The substance of policies includes not only the extensiveness of beneficiaries from policy decisions or allocation of attention between policy fields but the magnitude of policy changes as well as their quality. As for the formal, the typical pattern of policymaking in liberal democracies consists of incremental changes—although, as punctuated equilibrium theory shows, large-scale reforms also happen (Baumgartner & Jones, 1993, 2009). One of the main reasons for policy stability is the large number of policy actors involved in the decision-making process whose interests, preferences, and objectives counterweight each other and support the status quo. If so, one would expect higher policy instability in autocracies. Indeed, both Baumgartner et al. (2017) and Sebők and Berki (2018) found that policy punctuations are higher in autocracies.

Concerning the quality of the policies we assume that it is better in democracies—this is the argument of the "good governance" literature (e.g. Grindle, 2007; Kaufmann, 2003). This conclusion stems from the accountability argument (democratic leaders are more motivated to make good decisions) as well as from the wider informational basis upon which policies are based (see the next subsection).

In sum, it is a well-founded theoretical claim that democracies and autocracies make different policies in terms of their content. Democracies are expected to provide more public goods and services, to be better at reducing inequalities and to focus less on the military and the police; large-scale policy reforms are less likely while the quality of policies is better; and while the preferences of the majority have a large bearing on policy decisions, the rights and needs of minorities are also taken into account. Although the empirical evidence is somewhat less compelling, data also suggest that democracies follow different patterns in their choices of policies than non-democratic regimes.

At the same, it has to be emphasized that these differences are very much context dependent. For instance, communist dictatorships have prioritized more the provision of public services due to their radical left ideology. Partly free (hybrid) regimes may also scrutinize public opinion, since the popular vote does matter; and even autocracies must rely on output legitimacy, therefore they may provide at least basic public services to the people.

PROCEDURES AND ACTORS

By procedures and actors, we describe formally or informally institutionalized processes that channel policymaking from agenda setting throughout the whole policy cycle; the venues that provide policy actors access to the process; and the number and composition of policy actors having an influence on policy outputs and outcomes. Procedures employed under different regimes have spurred less academic interest than the content of policies until recently when a number of publications have treated the issue from different angles (Bartha et al., 2020; see Baumgartner et al., 2017; Boda & Patkós, 2018; Guy & Jon, 2019; Howlett & Tosun, 2019; Sebők & Berki, 2018).

Institutions and actors of the policy process influence the content of policies in a number of ways. If specific actors have access to the policy process, they may promote certain kinds of policies—for instance, the presence of green parties in a polity has a positive effect on environmental legislation and environmental quality (Bernauer & Koubi, 2009). Fairness and accountability of the government create trust which, in turn, help to accept even costly or unpopular decisions (Hetherington, 2005). That is, studying policymaking procedures under different regimes helps to better understand the differences in their policy choices and outcomes as well.

The most important—and most evident—feature of non-democratic policymaking procedures is the low level of involvement of different kinds of policy actors (Howlett & Tosun, 2019). The are many causes for this. First, in autocracies, the political activity of autonomous actors is, by definition, limited, if not plainly banned. Therefore, independent social actors, like parties, trade unions, NGOs, think tanks cannot flourish; independent political initiatives, such as protests, movements, campaigns, cannot freely organize. From a policy perspective, this means that potentially important information about social problems, preferences, needs, and implementation failures are not channeled into the policy process.

Second, in autocracies, the media and the public sphere are under control. Therefore, existing actors are censored—and self-censorship related to new initiatives is also often at work as a result of the fear of retaliation. One need not subscribe to an idealized Habermasian vision of liberal democracies to see that this is a major difference compared to liberal democratic policymaking in which policy ideas, arguments, and proposals can freely circulate in the public sphere. Free communication and the possibility of deliberation have a number of consequences on the policy process beyond the information providing function: they can contribute to the accountability of decision-makers, offer new insights about policy problems and solutions and increase the legitimacy of decisions (we return to the role of policy discourses in the next section).

Third, while in autocracies the "supply side" of policy advocacy and lobbying is limited, the "demand side" is also constrained: non-democratic decision-making procedures are lacking transparency and openness and are dominated by political leadership. That is, the number of meaningful policy venues is limited. Even if institutions and rules exist, they are emptied, purely formal and often circumvented by "real" decision-making processes. For instance, during the era of socialist autocracy in Hungary two parallel decision-making structures existed: the institutions of Potemkin parliamentary democracy and the State Party. While parliament did make decisions, the important questions were decided by the Party's leadership.

Howlett and Tosun (2019) suggest that two kinds of policy actors may nonetheless play an important role in autocracies: the bureaucracy and public opinion. Autocrats may use the state bureaucracy in order to implement changes and control society (see also Guy & Jon, 2019). This was certainly the case for the communist regimes of Eastern Europe where the bureaucracy had even some role in making decisions, beyond sheer implementation (Kulcsár, 2001). At the same time, especially in hybrid regimes, public opinion may exert some influence on decisions: as part of their output legitimacy autocrats may react to popular demands and avoid strongly unpopular reforms (Sebők, 2019).

The weakness of both the "supply" and the "demand" side of the policymaking process concerning inputs from policy actors has a number of consequences beyond a bigger likelihood of punctuations. Since autocracies are less open to bottom-up initiatives, their policy agendas are less influenced by other actors' agendas, such as the media or lobby groups. In liberal democracies, there are statistically significant associations between the composition of temporarily lagged different agendas as in the case of the media agenda and the symbolic policy agenda (Vliegenthart et al., 2016) or the agenda of interest groups and decisions (Gilens & Page, 2014). Researchers posit causality based on the temporal lags between the different types of agendas and the fact of successive thematization. However, as Boda and Patkós (2018) suggest, under illiberal conditions, such associations between agendas may be weak or even non-existent.

Partly free regimes (and even autocracies) may hold elections, although they are by definition not free and fair but distorted and rigged through both formal norms and informal practices. Still, if there are elections and parties, they are often accompanied by manifestos. Yet we expect party manifestos to be shorter and less diverse than in democracies on the one hand, and we expect a lower level of electoral pledge fulfillment as a consequence of limited accountability on the other hand. Finally, the presence of more actors in the policy process—as well as stricter institutional rules—slow down the pace of policymaking in democracies (which—as we discussed above—may have a positive effect on the quality of these policies).

To sum up, policy procedures and the involvement of policy actors in the policy process are expected to be different according to regime characteristics. In democracies, a high number of actors are involved in policymaking; there is responsiveness from decision-makers toward bottom-up initiatives; procedures are effectively institutionalized; and the policy cycle unfolds slowlier than in autocracies. In autocracies, the venues and procedures may be purely formal and often circumvented, while decision-making is faster, as rulers rely on governing by decree instead of laws.

DISCOURSES

By discourses, we wean policy frames, metaphors, narratives, and rhetorical strategies that policy actors use. Discourses have received a growing attention from policy scholars because of the varied role they may play in the policy process (Béland, 2009; see for instance Majone, 1989; Roe, 1994). Discourses have a cognitive, descriptive, and predictive function: they provide a specific understanding or interpretation of a situation (Schlesinger & Lau, 2000). However, the interpretation they provide is typically more than a neutral depiction: they involve emotions and values and likely have a prescriptive power as well, "accomplishing things with language" (McCloskey, 1985: 14). That is, discourses stabilize knowledge, persuade, create identities, or mobilize participants.

The role of discourses in policymaking and policy change is acknowledged by punctuated equilibrium theory as well. Baumgartner and Jones (1993, 2009) argue that policy frames and metaphors influence the way policy issues are perceived and evaluated. Therefore, changes in discourses may lead to changes in policies as well. We find two uses of policy discourses especially relevant for our topic: "discursive governance" (Korkut et al., 2015) and legitimation.

The former is related to communication regarding policy objectives even without taking any actual policy decisions. As discursive institutionalist research shows, ideas and discourses can play a formative role in institutional change (e.g. Béland, 2009). Discursive governance may influence people's attitudes, expectations and even their behavior. However, following Korkut et al. (2015), we expect discursive governance to be more prevalent in hybrid regimes and autocracies. In the democratic setting, policy decisions are channeled into formal rules and procedures; and the rule of law limits the widespread use of informal policy practices. People are constrained by the government to follow the law, but nothing more. Autocracies and hybrid regimes may rely less on institutionalized procedures and more on informal, ideological domination (even if this latter might be a meaningful concept in a democratic context as well—see Bloom & Dallyn, 2011).

The second important function is legitimation: value-laden discourses can help to make accept even difficult or costly decisions. Legitimacy, that is securing the allegiance of the population, is a central problem in any political system and both democracies and autocracies rely on the use of discourses that people find worth accepting or identifying with (see

Beetham, 1991). However, we expect democracies to use more discourses with a high and positive valence (Cox & Béland, 2013), while adversarial narratives ("us vs. them"), scapegoating and legitimation by crisis are communication tools typically employed by populist, extremist politicians and illiberal leaders (Bartha et al., 2020).

We also expect autocracies to make more use of general political ideas when legitimizing particular policy decisions and democratic policy discourses to stick more to the specific issue or field. For instance, during the period of socialist autocracy, the presentation of virtually any decision could invoke the global fight between Capitalism and Communism; while in a democracy, one expects more concrete arguments in favor of a policy measure.

We already referred to the important role of public debates in the policymaking of liberal democracies. In terms of discourses, democracies are characterized by a "marketplace" of competing policy ideas, frames, and metaphors. Why and how some discourses prevail over others is a million-dollar question of policy studies and policy practice. Potential factors range from the identity of the communicator (whether the person/organization conveying the discourse is seen as reliable, authentic, sympathetic, etc.), the size of the advocacy coalition advancing the argument, the power of arguments (affective value and/or factual references), the completeness of the discourse (whether it offers a comprehensive interpretation of events), the incidents of key events (like accidents or catastrophes illustrating the point), to the reaction of the media and other policy actors, as well as the social context.

Autocracies, especially hybrid regimes, struggle with similar problems: how to generate political discourses that are convincing, acceptable for large segments of society and which can successfully crowd out competitors. However, autocracies have less limited possibilities to convey their own messages while constraining competing discourses. Autocracies often spend large resources on communication and can spread intensively their messages through many different channels, including public broadcasting. Since competing discourses are suppressed and an ideological discourse is put forth through different channels, we expect less diversity in autocracies' policy-related discourses.

CONCLUSION

Policymaking is a complex process, which is defined by the institutional setting, the formal and informal rules of the polity; in other words, the political system. Extant research has addressed some policy consequences of different democratic systems (such as presidential vs. parliamentary systems), but, with notable exceptions, the policymaking of non-democratic regimes has not received much attention.

In this chapter, we reconstructed the arguments of Jones et al. (2019) on the factors that mediate the effect of regimes on policy dynamics. We argued that policy punctuations are larger in non-democratic regimes because institutional friction is also higher due to the lack of democratic incentives, to governmental centralization, and to the informational disadvantage of autocracies compared to democracies. Our empirical expectations concerning the effects of regimes on different features of policymaking concerned three dimensions: the content, the process, and the discourses of policies. We apply these concepts to the diverse empirics of the case studies of Part 3 and the discussion of Part 4.

REFERENCES

Bartha, A., Boda, Z., & Szikra, D. (2020). When populist leaders govern: Conceptualising populism in policy making. *Politics and Governance, 8*(3), 71–81.

Baumgartner, F. R., & Jones, B. D. (1993, 2009). *Agendas and instability in American politics.* The University of Chicago Press.

Baumgartner, F. R., Carammia, M., Epp, D. A., Noble, B., Rey, B., & Yildirim, T. M. (2017). Budgetary change in authoritarian and democratic regimes. *Journal of European Public Policy, 24*(6), 792–808.

Beetham, D. (1991). *The legitimation of power.* Palgrave Macmillan.

Béland, D. (2009). Ideas, institutions, and policy change. *Journal of European Public Policy, 16*(5), 701–718.

Bernauer, T., & Koubi, V. (2009). Effects of political institutions on air quality. *Ecological Economics, 68*(5), 1355–1365.

Bloom, P., & Dallyn, S. (2011). The paradox of order: Reimagining ideological domination. *Journal of Political Ideologies, 16*(1), 53–78.

Boda, Z., & Patkós, V. (2018). Driven by politics: Agenda setting and policymaking in Hungary 2010–2014. *Policy Studies, 39*(4), 402–421.

Brauner, J. (2015). Military spending and democracy. *Defence and Peace Economics, 26*(4), 409–423.

Bueno de Mesquita, B., & Smith, A. (2011). *The Dictator's Handbook: Why bad behavior is almost always good politics*. Public Affairs.

Bueno de Mesquita, B., Morrow, J. D., Siverson, R. M., & Smith, A. (1999). Policy failure and political survival: The contribution of political institutions. *Journal of Conflict Resolution, 43*(2), 147–161.

Bueno de Mesquita, B., Morrow, J. D., Siverson, R. M., & Smith, A. (2003). *The logic of political survival*. MIT Press.

Cox, G. W., & Béland, D. (2013). Valence, policy ideas, and the rise of sustainability. *Governance, 26*(2), 307–328.

Deacon, R. T. (2009). Public good provision under dictatorship and democracy. *Public Choice, 139*(1–2), 241–262.

Dodlova, M., & Gioblas, A. (2017). *Regime type, inequality, and redistributive transfers in developing countries*. World Institute for Development Economic Research.

Gilens, M., & Page, B. I. (2014). *Testing theories of American politics: Elites, interest groups, and average citizens*. Cambridge University Press.

Grindle, M. S. (2007). Good enough governance revisited. *Development Policy Review, 25*(5), 533–574.

Guy, P., & Jon, P. (2019). Populism and public administration: Confronting the administrative state. *Administration & Society, 51*(10), 1521–1545.

Hetherington, M. J. (2005). *Why trust matters: Declining political trust and the demise of American liberalism*. Princeton University Press.

Howlett, M., & Tosun, J. (Eds.). (2019). *Policy styles and policy-making: Exploring the linkages*. Routledge.

Jones, B. D., Epp, D. A., & Baumgartner, F. R. (2019). Democracy, authoritarianism, and policy punctuations. *International Review of Public Policy, 1*(1), 7–26.

Kaufmann, D. (2003). *Rethinking governance: Empirical lessons challenge orthodoxy*. Discussion Paper, The World Bank.

Keefer, P.-K., Stuti. (2005). Democracy, public expenditures, and the poor: Understanding political incentives for providing public services. *World Bank Research Observer, 20*, 1–27.

Korkut, U., Bucken-Knapp, G., Cox, R. H., & Mahendran, K. (Eds.). (2015). *Discursive governance in politics, policy, and the public sphere*. Palgrave Macmillan.

Kulcsár, K. (2001). Deviant bureaucracies: Public administration in Eastern Europe and in the developing countries. In A. Farazmand (Ed.), *Handbook of comparative and development public administration, public administration and public policy* (pp. 941–952). Marcel Dekker.

Lake David, B., Matthew. (2001). The invisible hand of democracy: Political control and the provision of public services. *Comparative Political Studies, 34*(6), 587–621.

Lott, J. (1999). Public schooling, indoctrination, and totalitarianism. *Journal of Political Economy, 107*(6, part 2), s127–s157.

Majone, G. (1989). *Evidence, argument and persuasion in the policy process*. Yale University Press.

McCloskey, D. (1985). *The rhetoric of economics*. The University of Wisconsin Press.

Montecino, J. A. (2012). Decreasing inequality under Latin America's "social democratic" and "populist" governments: Is the difference real? *International Journal of Health Services, 42*(2), 257–275.

Mulligan Casey, G. R., & Sala-I-Martin, X. (2004). Do democracies have different public policies than nondemocracies? *Journal of Economic Perspectives, 18*(1), 51–74.

Robinson, J., & Acemoglu, D. (2012). *Why nations fail: The origins of power, prosperity and poverty*. Profile.

Roe, E. (1994). *Narrative policy analysis: Theory and practice*. Duke University Press.

Sabatier, P., & Weible, C. M. (Eds.). (2014). *Theories of the policy process*. Westview Press, a member of the Persus Books Group.

Schlesinger, M., & Lau, R. R. (2000). The meaning and measure of policy metaphors. *American Political Science Review, 94*(3), 611–626.

Sebők, M. (2019). *Paradigmák fogságában—Elitek és ideológiák a magyar pénzügyi kapitalizmusban*. Napvilág Kiadó.

Sebők, M., & Berki, T. (2018). Punctuated equilibrium in democracy and autocracy: An analysis of Hungarian budgeting between 1868 and 2013. *European Political Science Review, 10*(4), 589–611.

Vliegenthart, R., Walgrave, S., Baumgartner, F., Bevan, S., Breunig, C., Brouard, S., & Chaqués Bonafont, L. (2016). Do the media set the parliamentary agenda? A comparative study in seven countries. *European Journal of Political Research, 55*(2), 283–301.

Weaver, R. K., & Rockman, B. A. (1993). *Do institutions matter? Government capabilities in the United States and abroad*. Brookings Institution.

CHAPTER 3

Hungarian Regimes and Their Institutional Characteristics

Csaba Molnár and Orsolya Ring

The wide variety of regime types featured in modern era Hungarian history makes it a suitable case for comparing regime effects on policymaking in general, and policy agendas in particular. For all but brief periods of interruption, from 1526 all the way to 1918, the Hungarian throne was continuously occupied by members of the Habsburg dynasty. This did not result in a complete abdication of the country's sovereignty, but it did limit it to varying degrees during this long period. Thus, the union with Austria (and Czechia) and the policies adopted as part of the joint state affairs fundamentally shaped the dynamics of Hungarian politics for centuries.

C. Molnár (✉)
Corvinus University of Budapest, Budapest, Hungary
e-mail: molnar.csaba@tk.hu

C. Molnár · O. Ring
Centre for Social Sciences, MTA Centre of Excellence, Eötvös Loránd Research Network. Corvinus University of Budapest, Budapest, Hungary
e-mail: ring.orsolya@tk.hu

M. Sebők and Z. Boda (eds.), *Policy Agendas in Autocracy, and Hybrid Regimes*, Comparative Studies of Political Agendas,
https://doi.org/10.1007/978-3-030-73223-3_3

33

It was not until 1848 that a modern political structure emerged in Hungary. It was the revolutionary transformation at the time that finally put an end to a form of feudalism (what was known as "estate dualism") that had persisted far beyond the age in which it was born and to which it was suited (Képessy, 2019). It was a system of government based on the division of powers between the sovereign and the representatives of the privileged strata (the estates—the aristocracy, clergy, bourgeoisie, and some smaller privileged groups) and the parliament elected by the latter (Asch, 2015: 359–361). The resilience of the regime is apparent in the fact that despite various attempts to impose absolutism on behalf of Austrian emperors, it never succeeded (Szijártó M., 2016: 14–19; Taylor, 1948: 14).

Moreover, the 1848/1849 revolution and war of independence laid the groundwork for a parliamentary democracy for the latter decades of the nineteenth century that was considered on par with the liberal parliamentarism of the age. Even though the aftermath of the revolution—which was jointly suppressed by two superpowers of the age, Austria and Russia—was hallmarked by martial law, the repression became untenable by the mid-1860s. Parliament retained a preeminent role with the Compromise between Austria and Hungary in 1867 and the uncodified "historical constitution" was once again in effect, up until 1949 (Bíró, 2019).

Therefore, the natural place to start an overview of comparable, modern era political regimes is 1867 and proto-parliamentarism of the pre-war era (see Appendix A2). The defeat in World War I marked the end of stability provided by this "belle époque." During the century or so that followed, Hungary experienced innumerable revolutions, coups, and regime changes. In 1918, the radical liberals and the social democrats clinched power. Less than a year later, in April 1919, they were followed by the communists, who in turn were ousted in August by right-wing forces. In March 1944, Nazi Germany set up a puppet government in Hungary, which was followed by a Soviet-controlled government in December of the same year—not before a German-backed national socialist coup in October, however.

In 1946, a more or less democratically elected parliament proclaimed the republic, which was then extinguished by the communist takeover in 1949. Although it managed to put an end to the Stalinist period, the 1956 Revolution lasted barely two weeks, and it was replaced by a new type of socialist autocracy, which mellowed to a state of post-totalitarianism after a period of reprisals. Hungary returned to a Western development path once again as a result of the regime transition in 1989/1990.

One contentious question is how these clearly distinct regimes can be classified in terms of the schemes offered by political science and international NGOs. Thus, for example, an intense debate is raging in Hungarian and international academic literature on how to characterize the period since the Orbán government took office in 2010 and how far the latter can be set apart from the political regime that prevailed in the initial period following the post-communist transition.

We will not undertake a review of all of these various political regimes as part of this volume. Indeed, it would be difficult to review such unstable, short-lived, and constantly changing political regimes as the Hungarian Soviet Republic of 1919, which endured for all of 133 days. Thus, our analysis will be limited to the five long-lasting and consolidated regimes during the past century and a half. We will analyze the Austro-Hungarian Dual Monarchy, which was in place between 1867 and 1918; the Horthy regime, which was in power between 1920 and 1944; the Kádár regime, which controlled Hungary from 1956 to 1989; and the period of post-communist democracy, which we break down to a liberal (1990–2010) and illiberal period (1990–2018).

Before turning to the examination of the policy agendas in the next chapters, here we provide a brief overview of the five regimes in question. Our key concern is the presence of the markers which are usually associated with democratic policymaking (see previous chapter). Table 3.1 features all the distinct regimes of the period in question as well as our assessment of their democratic qualities. In order to reach conclusions, of the few available classifications, we used the assessments of Polity IV, V-Dem and Freedom House as they cover fairly large spells of the 1867–2018 period. Of the political regimes we reviewed, Polity IV assigns the period of the Dual Monarchy and the Horthy era to an intermediate 'factional' category, while the Kádár regime—with the exception of the last few transitional years—is classified as "repressed." The regimes that have emerged since 1990 are then uniformly classified as falling at the other end of the spectrum, into the competitive category.

Although they used different designations, the experts at V-Dem arrived at very similar results: except for the respective transitional periods, the Dual Monarchy and the Horthy era were assigned to the ambivalent category, while except for the final years before its eventual collapse, the

Table 3.1   The classification of Hungarian political regimes (1867–2018)

Year/Period	Historical classification	3-value class
1867–1917	Austro-Hungarian Compromise(dualism)	Partly free
1918	Dualism/First Republic	Partly free
1919	First Republic/Soviet Republic/Horthy Regime	Not free
1920–1943	HorthyRegime	Partly free
1944	National Socialist Regime	Not free
1945–1946	Transitional Regime	Partly free
1947–1948	Second Republic	Partly free
1949–1952	RákosiRegime	Not free
1953–1955	Post-RákosiRegime	Not free
1956	Post-Rákosi/Revolution/Occupation	Not free
1956–1989	KádárRegime	Not free
1989	Late KádárRegime/Third Republic	Partly free
1990–2010	Third Republic(liberal democracy)	Free
2010–2018	Orbán Regime(illiberal democracy)	Partly Free

Kádár regime falls into the autocratic category. The post-1990 period—reviewed up until the elections of April 2018—by contrast, was assigned to the democratic category, except for the year 2018. Data from Freedom House is unfortunately only available from 1972 onwards. In parts, the findings of Freedom House differ from those of the other classification systems. They only classified the Kádár era as unfree until 1983, and they categorized most of the last decade under that regime as partly free. The period between 1990 and 2018 is then also assigned to the free category.

From these overviews, it is readily apparent that a democratic regime as we understand the idea today only emerged starting in 1990. Using a binary classification system, we find that prior to 1990, Hungary was not free, while the different political regimes that emerged after 1990 fall into the "free" category. We should also keep in mind, however, that even though in a binary classification based on current standards both were technically "not free," the Dualist and Horthy regime is fundamentally different from the Kádár regime, and as a result, we must distinguish between them and use a more nuanced system (where they would be assigned into the "partly free" category).

Given the fact that the emerging comparative policy agendas literature on the effect of regimes does make use of such a free/partly free/not free catalogue, we retain this approach and incorporate it into the analyses of this book. Therefore, since the two regimes that came before 1945 exhibit several features that are typical of democracies as we understand them today, we assign them to a distinct, partly free, category.

In the following, we will present a rough sketch of the institutional structure of the various regimes we examined, from the most repressive Kádár regime all the way to the "freest" liberal democracy and the three regimes that are positioned in the middle of this spectrum, including the pre-war era, the interwar period, and the illiberal Orbán regime. We also provide more detailed information on all the constitutional-government setups and party systems during the period covered in this book in Appendix A1.

THE PROTO-PARLIAMENTARISM OF DUALISM

Following the failed revolution and war of independence of 1848/1849, the Habsburg regime undertook a last-ditch effort to centralize its empire and to subject Hungary to an absolutist form of political rule. Ultimately, however, the Habsburgs failed because of military defeats and foreign policy fiascos, as well as on account of the passive resistance exhibited by the Hungarian population (Taylor, 1948: 85–94). Even though a substantial portion of the Hungarian elite sought to reduce relations between Hungary and Austria to the bare minimum—or sought to dissolve the bond between the two states altogether—they were ultimately forced to compromise.

The Dual Monarchy's (also referred to as Dualism) regime was the result of a compromise concluded between the sovereign, the Emperor (and King of Hungary) Franz Joseph I, and the Hungarian political elite (Frank, 2000). The concept of Dualism meant that the Habsburg Empire (of which Hungary was a distinct part with some degree of autonomy) was replaced by the real union of the two states that made up the Austro-Hungarian Monarchy.

One of the necessary functions of the accord between these players was to arbitrate the underlying conflicts between the parties that had risen to the fore in the 1848/1849 Revolution and the subsequent War of Independence. These conflicts boiled down to three essential areas. The first issue to consider was historical precedence, namely that since 1526, Hungary's throne had been continuously occupied by members of the Habsburg dynasty, who naturally strove to centralize the governance of their countries. At the same time, a distrust toward foreigners (primarily Austro-Germans) and a tradition of independence—with a strong Protestant streak—had been present in Hungarian political thought continuously throughout this extensive period, and it ran counter to the aforementioned efforts at centralization.

These two factors and their clashing impact resulted in a partial Hungarian autonomy, the varying degrees of which throughout the roughly four centuries following 1526 were heavily influenced by the respective strengths at any given point of the players involved. The third factor was that Hungary, as a result of the near continuous warfare with the Ottoman Empire through the fourteenth-eighteenth centuries, lost its ethnic Hungarian majority and became a multi-ethnic country. The conflicts between the ethnic Hungarians and the national minorities living in Hungary culminated in a civil war (against the Serbs, Croatians, and Romanians) right at the time of 1848/1849. Although subsequently these tensions eased substantially, the mid-nineteenth century was the time when the aspirations of the various national minorities for collective rights unfolded and collided with Hungarian efforts to secure independence from Austria (Hroch, 2016: 178–180).

The compromise with Franz Joseph finally entailed that, opposed to the views that sought to come to some sort of accord with the national minorities (and would thus have accepted some type of federation as a result), the leading role of the ethnic Hungarian community would be enshrined as long as it acquiesced to the accord with the Habsburgs, which limited the country's sovereignty. The emperor was also crowned the king of Hungary (as was traditional).

Theoretically, the Habsburg Empire consisted of two co-equal states: it was the real union of Austria and Hungary (it is important to stress that the Hungarian elite came to an accord with the sovereign rather than with the Austrian elite). In most areas, the two constitutive states operated independently of one another, but through the person of their joint sovereign, they were connected in their foreign and military policies, as well as in terms of fiscal policies, which covered the expenses of the former. They had a common military, diplomacy, monetary policy, sovereign debt, currency, foreign trade, and customs area. The costs of operating the Monarchy were covered by the two parties in line with an underlying agreement that was regularly reviewed (Péter, 2012b: 251–258).

Control over military and foreign affairs remained the sovereign's prerogative. He did not exercise these powers in person, however, but through the joint foreign and defense ministers. The Monarchy also had a joint minister of finance. All three ministers were appointed by the sovereign and they were accountable to him. Together with the prime ministers of Austria and Hungary, the three ministers made up the joint Ministerial Council (in order to forestall even the hint of any centralization, the Hungarian elite insisted that no joint government or parliament would be created, or that the actual bodies discharging such functions would under no circumstances be referred to by such designations). Apart from the head of state and the three joint ministers, the two states that made up the real union had no other joint institutions.

Furthermore, the Austrian and Hungarian parliaments each elected 60-member delegations, which deliberated separately from one another, did not convene as a joint parliament, and only communicated with one another in writing. These delegations were authorized to hold the ministers to account, but they did not have the authority to discharge them. Furthermore, they also had a right of veto with respect to joint fiscal matters (although in practice that veto was circumventable). Thus, by only allowing the creation of delegations with such weak authorizations and limited parliamentary powers, the Hungarian elite unwittingly ensured that when it came to the joint affairs of the two states, the lack of a potent counterweight to the sovereign's power resulted in an exceedingly high level of power concentration in the person of the sovereign as compared to what was typical in that historical period (Kozári, 2005: 65–80).

The king's role was not limited to managing the joint affairs. In Hungary, the sovereign was also invested with the authority to convene or to dissolve parliament—at the prime minister's initiative—or to reschedule its sessions. He appointed the prime minister, as well as the most important state officials and ministers based on the proposals of the prime minister or of the government, and he further also had the authority to issue decrees (although these were exceedingly rare and were mostly consigned to the period of the Compromise). Although theoretically the sovereign was not under obligation to consider the prevailing parliamentary majorities when appointing the prime minister, in reality, there was only a single instance when he actually exercised this prerogative (in 1905, after the electoral failure of the pro-compromise Liberal Party).

The sovereign further had the absolute right to veto any law, but he never availed himself of this authority. With respect to the process of legislation, his most important prerogative was the right of preapproval: based on a secret government decree of 1867, the government could only submit bills to parliament after having consulted the sovereign and affording him the opportunity to weigh in (Szente, 2011: 234–242). The right of preapproval was a crucial tool in the hands of the king because due to their lacking capacities in drafting entire laws, members of parliament refrained from writing bills themselves, and instead called on the government to draw up bills based on the policy proposals of MPs (Pesti, 2002: 60).

Apart from the aforementioned, Hungary in the age of Dualism featured a classical liberal constitutional structure. A centralized parliamentary regime was created. The first generation of human rights (e.g., the freedoms of speech, associations, assembly, and of the press) was widely respected and the range of such rights was continuously expanded during this period.

As far as the non-Hungarian population was concerned, at the individual level, they were given national minority rights (the use of their native language) which were generous for the age. At the same time, with the exception of the Croatians, they were not accorded any collective rights whatsoever. In the framework of Croatia-Slavonia, the Croatians were given their own parliament, government, and head of government, while their joint affairs with Hungary were regulated by a separate accord; Croatians were further also represented in the delegation on Austro-Hungarian affairs, as well as in the Hungarian government and parliament (see Kozári, 2005: 48–53 and 55–62).

A highly diverse and very influential press emerged in the era (Buzinkay, 2016: 177), while the informal powers of civic associations and lobbies were substantial. Parliamentary elections were regularly held during this period (for three and then five-year terms). Parties were free to compete in these elections, and political pluralism prevailed. Nevertheless, two key caveats prevent us from calling these democratic elections by today's standards. For one, suffrage was not universal, the right to vote was limited based on gender, wealth, and literacy, and as a result of the criteria thus imposed, roughly a quarter of the male adult population (around a tenth of the total population) actually had the right to vote (yet in European comparison, this was not a low ratio, especially in the early years of the period in question).

The other factor that became increasingly controversial—and would these days be deemed non-reconcilable with a liberal democracy—was the use of open balloting (Köpf, 2001). The reasons for allowing these factors to persist were rooted in the Compromise. The desire to maintain the underlying relations with Austria required that only political forces which acquiesced themselves to this regime would be allowed to govern. Since the rejection of the Compromise was especially prevalent among the Hungarian peasantry in Central and Eastern Hungary, in order to maintain the stability of the regime, a majority of them were excluded from suffrage.

The regime also limited the voting rights of the mostly uneducated or otherwise underprivileged national minorities. The so-called census that was applied to limit suffrage later also allowed for keeping socialist (agrarian socialist or social democratic) political organizations out of power. Although the electoral system was majoritarian, the district boundaries were often disproportional and there were substantial discrepancies in the population sizes of districts.

The cleavage that defined the party system of the age was based on the different views of the Compromise. The predominant political force at the time was the Sixty-Seveners (which alludes to the year when the Compromise was concluded, 1867, and also their support for it). They formed the Liberal Party which became the party of government for most of the period in question (the name of the party changed several times during this period).

Within the framework of the Compromise, and by abusing the defects of the electoral system and committing the odd act of electoral fraud, as well as by relying on their highly disciplined MPs, the ruling party was able to almost completely prevent any alternation in power during this period (the only exception were the years between 1905 and 1910). Although in line with the prevailing consensus of the time the governing party was dominated by national liberals (again, "liberals" by the standard of their day), it was also a heterogeneous catch-all party, which assimilated all sorts of political orientations.

The main force on the opposition side was the so-called Forty-Eighters (in allusion to the revolution of 1848), who stood on the other side of the paramount cleavage of the age. The Forty-Eighters strove to limit the scope of common affairs with Austria and the king's powers (they primarily wanted to remove monetary and customs policy, as well as military affairs, from the range of common policy areas). Several among them wanted Hungary to abandon the Austro-Hungarian Monarchy altogether.

By 1875, the moderates among them (the Center-Left Party) came to an accommodation with the Sixty-Seveners and the two forces merged into the Liberal Party (whose leader, Kálmán Tisza, came in fact from the ranks of the former Forty-Eighters). Due to the lack of alternation in power, the radicals among the Forty-Eighters (those in the Independence Party and its successors) often experienced frequent party splits and mergers.

Several attempts were made to overcome and bury the main cleavage of the time, but despite the emergence of new wedge issues and their growing importance, ultimately these proved unable to upset the dominance of the central constitutional debates. National minority parties as well as conservative parties were also continuously present at the political level during this period. Starting in the 1880s, anti-Semitic political forces also entered the fray, while in the 1890s another batch of new political orientations (Christian socialists, social democrats, and agrarian parties) emerged and saw their role increase.

The predominant party system also had a massive impact on the way parliament operated during this time. The exceedingly disciplined governing parties were consistently able to control the operations of parliament, and public policy was mostly decided by the conflict resolution mechanisms that played out within the heterogeneous governing parties. That was a major reason why the opposition—especially toward the end of the period in question—increasingly resorted to the instrument of obstruction (that is trying to paralyze parliamentary decision-making by initiating superfluous votes and filibustering the proceedings, delivering extremely long speeches). The governing side, for its part, sought to (mostly unsuccessfully) thwart these efforts by reforming the Rules of Procedure (Péter, 2012c: 128–130) and eventually breaking up obstruction by the use of force (in the process creating a precursor for the Parliamentary Guard of the illiberal period of the 2010s).

In line with the historical traditions, the Hungarian National Assembly remained bicameral. Of its two chambers, the lower house was elected, while the upper house was made up of members of the royal family; aristocrats; representatives of the Catholic, Reformed, Lutheran, Unitarian, Orthodox, and Jewish churches; certain public officials (e.g., high-ranking judicial leaders); the delegates of the Croatian parliament; as well as peers proposed by the government and appointed by the sovereign for life. As a result, the lower house was dominated by liberal forces, while the upper house was controlled by conservatives. Even though theoretically the two chambers were co-equals, in reality, the lower house, which enjoyed actual democratic legitimacy, dominated the legislative process (the details of which are detailed in Chapter 5; see also: Péter, 2012a: 321).

Even though this was not laid down in any legal provisions, the king adhered to the unwritten rule of appointing the leader of the party that boasted a majority in parliament as the prime minister. Parliament did not have the authority to reject the appointment of a prime minister or the program presented by the government, but it did have the right to take a vote of no-confidence in the prime minister, and if the motion was carried, then the prime minister was required to tender his resignation. Also, parliament could pass a resolution stressing its opposition when it came to items on the government's agenda of which the legislature disapproved especially strenuously.

The members of the cabinet were appointed by the king based on the prime minister's proposal. It is important to point out that ministers responsible for the common affairs with Austria were also members of the Hungarian cabinet (that is the Hungarian cabinet did have a minister for homeland defense and a minister "besides the king"—in today's diction, this would be the foreign minister). When it came to issues not expressly regulated by parliament, the government had the right to adopt decrees (except for taxes and restrictions on the rights of citizens), provided the king endorsed them (although the king almost always assented to the decrees adopted by the government). In urgent matters, the government also had the right to temporarily suspend or amend the application of laws, although prior to the World War I, it hardly ever availed itself of this authority.

THE HORTHY ERA: THE TRADITIONAL AUTHORITARIANISM OF THE INTERWAR PERIOD

Hungary's defeat in World War I ultimately led to the collapse of the regime of Dualism and to the end of the union with Austria. It also led to the loss of the territories inhabited by Hungary's national minorities, while many territories immediately adjacent to the new national boundaries that were inhabited entirely by ethnic Hungarians were also assigned to the successor states, resulting in some three million ethnic Hungarians living in areas outside Hungary proper (the population within the remaining territory of Hungary was roughly eight million). These territorial changes defined the subsequent two decades as the revision of borders became a constant rallying cry for major forces in Hungarian politics.

In the wake of the collapse of the Monarchy and with troops returning from a lost war, a period of turmoil ensued. From 1918 to the fall of 1919, there were multiple successive regime changes in Hungary. Although the Károlyi cabinet, which was made up of Forty-Eighters, as well as social democratic and radical liberal parties, had been appointed by Emperor Charles I (and the last king of Hungary) while the old regime was in the throes of disintegration, it swiftly proceeded to proclaim a republic.

The new government was accountable to the National Council, which was also newly formed by the parties of the parliamentary and extra-parliamentary opposition during the period of the Dual Monarchy (Föglein et al., 2003: 347–348; D. Szabó, 2008: 157–160). It failed to hold elections, however, and as it quickly lost its public support and could not cling on to power amidst the collapse brought by the defeat in war and the government's own insecure legitimacy (Eley, 2002: 155).

In March 1919, the Communist Party seized power by staging a coup (they took advantage of the fact that the social democrats lacked the courage to assume power all on their own in such an uncertain environment). This created the first communist regime in Hungary—and only the second one globally. It was during this brief totalitarian experiment that Hungary's first written constitution was adopted, which marked a clear break with the tradition of historical constitutionalism in Hungary.

As opposed to the Károlyi regime, the Soviet Republic proved capable of organizing an election (although it was a single-party election marred by fraud). It briefly operated a legislative body, too, but on the whole, the regime was characterized by instability (there were several changes, for example, with respect to the bodies that the members of the cabinet were accountable to, and even the number of officials at the helm of some ministries fluctuated). The regime sought to make up for its rapidly diminishing legitimacy by ratcheting up its use of terror. Finally, in the wake of foreign policy and military defeats against Czechoslovakia and Romania, and also in light of their lacking social support, the regime collapsed after only 133 days (Brown, 2010: 80–81; Révész T., 2003: 448–452).

The succession of revolutionary governments came to an end in the wake of the Romanian occupation and the "counter-revolution" launched by right-wing forces. The decisive role within the latter was played by the National Army led by Miklós Horthy, a former fleet admiral in the Austro-Hungarian royal navy (Tóth, 2011). Even as the new regime strove to draw the appropriate lessons from the collapse of the Dual Monarchy (thus, for example, it substantially expanded suffrage and extended the right to vote to women as well, while also introducing the secret ballot and involving left-wing, social democratic, and agrarian politicians in the government), it also took decisive action to prevent revolutions from recurring (the most important instrument to this end was violence and terror visited upon the presumed supporters of the revolution).

In the early years of the Horthy era, there was a debate whether the regime should move in the direction of a military dictatorship or some limited version of democracy instead; ultimately, the political elite opted for the latter. This also involved the dissolution of various right-wing paramilitary and terror organizations (Bodó, 2019: 73–80). The sensation of shock that the elite experienced in response to the revolutions led to the emergence of a consensus within this stratum that the monarchy should be retained. At the same time, however, the international situation rendered untenable the proposition that the Hungarian throne should be occupied by the Habsburgs once again.

To resolve this dilemma, in 1920 the elite reverted to the idea of installing a temporary head of state in the form of a "regent," a practice with precedence in Hungarian historical tradition. The person chosen to serve as regent was Horthy, thereby neutralizing the problem experienced in Poland, namely that unless he was integrated into the official power structure, a prominent and highly regarded person with command over a relatively substantial military force will sooner or later come to destabilize the entire political regime (Takács, 2019).

Initially, the regent was not invested with substantial powers. He was only allowed to draft decrees and bills with the endorsement of the government. He was only allowed to send bills back to parliament for reconsideration once (and he had no say in laws pertaining to the office of the head of state). Although it was not mandatory, it was expected that the government would present its legislative bills to him first before submitting them to parliament. Yet his power to dissolve parliament or to reschedule sessions was subject to major limitations.

He appointed the prime ministers (and the members of the cabinet based on the nominations of the former), but the cabinet remained dependent on parliamentary support. The regent's authority was especially pronounced with respect to his powers to directly control the military (Tóth, 2011: 119–124). The logic of the regime was geared toward preventing future revolutions, and hence several steps were taken to scale back the influence of political groupings that were regarded as extreme (whereby the regime sought to balance the impact of the reintroduction of the secret ballot in 1938).

The regent's powers were also gradually expanded over time. He was invested with the power of pardon, and his power to deploy the army, to dissolve parliament, and to reschedule its sessions became more expansive. As of 1937, the regent was given the right to return bills to parliament twice for reconsideration; he was no longer accountable for his performance in office; and he was given the right to make a recommendation as to who should succeed him.

Although by the end of this period the regent enjoyed a strong position as the head of state, and his office had become invested with substantial powers, he almost never availed himself of his actual powers. Instead, he ceded the actual exercise of power to the given prime minister who was able to muster a majority in parliament. And when he did exercise his powers, he generally tended to deploy them in the support of various prime ministers working under him (Péntek, 1996; Püski, 2006: 26–27).

Another instrument to prevent revolutions and the potential access to power of anti-system forces took the form of the restriction of civil rights. After 1920, the open ballot was restored outside major towns (the secret ballot was reintroduced nationally in 1938), press freedom was limited (but not eliminated), and the parties regarded as extremist (communists and national socialists) were regularly banned, their operations were impeded, and their members were persecuted (even though the social support and actual influence of the latter was marginal at best for most of the period—Püski, 2015: 465–472; Wittenberg, 2014).

To preempt the emergence of a vibrant social base that might serve as a breeding ground for potential revolutions, a limited land reform was introduced, and the second half of the 1930s also saw the adoption of social welfare legislation (although both were limited in their impact). There was at the same time an effort to increase the social influence of men who had served on the front, who were seen as reliable for the purposes of the regime. This was achieved in part by restricting the access to higher education of women and Jews through the Numerus Clausus Act of 1920 (which was substantially relaxed in 1926—Fenyves, 2011; Szikra & Tomka, 2009; Thompson, 2003: 842–843).

The party system of the Horthy era was basically reminiscent of the party system in the age of Dualism: a predominant governing party was facing off against a divided opposition. The governing party was an extremely heterogeneous conglomerate, which assimilated a wide variety of ideological outlooks. In the early stages of the Horthy era, it was dominated by conservatives (as opposed to the liberal predominance of the previous era, which was widely blamed by public opinion for the defeat in World War I), but then it gradually shifted toward the radical right. At the same time, from the time of its inception it also included liberal, agrarian, Christian streams; in the later years of the regime, it also became a home for far-right politicians. Unlike in the previous era, coalition governments were no longer out-of-the-ordinary events. In the early years, liberal, Christian, social democratic, and agrarian parties delegated ministers into the cabinets. The predominant party that emerged in 1922 also governed jointly with a Christian conservative party.

Within the divided opposition, the balance of power was shifting continuously. While initially the social democrats were the leading force of the heterogeneous opposition, they were later supplanted in that position by the agrarian parties, and later still by the national socialists. Although in the earliest phase of the new regime the Social Democratic Party had been involved in the government, it quit the cabinet in protest of the acts of terror that were used to consolidate the regime; as a result, the Social Democrats ended up boycotting the 1920 elections as well.

Their return to politics was made possible by the pact concluded between Prime Minister István Bethlen and the Social Democratic leader at the time, Károly Peyer. Based on their agreement, the Social Democratic Party was allowed to operate freely, although subject to some restrictions. The liberal, Christian, radical right, and agrarian opposition parties were loyal to the regime, their critiques were primarily aimed at specific policy areas (e.g., human rights, social policies, education, and agricultural policies).

The national socialists, by contrast, which gained strength in the second half of the 1930s and had emerged as the leading force within the opposition by 1939, continued to operate as anti-system parties despite some spectacular gestures that were meant to highlight their loyalty to the regime (e.g., their disingenuous proposal to elect Horthy king). The fact that they were allowed to remain involved in the political arena owed primarily to the pressure of Nazi Germany, although despite this outside support they were subject to massive repression on the part of the regime (Boros, 2008: 193–227).

Contrary to the previous era, between 1920 and 1926, parliament operated as a unicameral legislature. From 1926 bicameralism returned.

In 1920, the lower house was elected based on a majoritarian electoral system, while between 1922 and 1935, a proportional system was used to elect the members of parliament representing major urban areas, while in the rural areas a majoritarian single-member-district system was in place. In 1939, a mixed system (including both party lists and single-member districts) was used. In 1922, the relatively widely diffused suffrage (extending to roughly 40% of the total population) was restricted through a census, and was then restricted even further (to only ca. 30% of the population) in 1938 in exchange for the introduction of the secret ballot (Püski, 2015: 16–28).

The upper house was no longer an assembly reserved for aristocrats. It was made up of certain high-ranking representatives of public life (e.g., church and judicial leaders); the representatives of counties and major cities; the delegates of the most important economic, educational, scientific, and professional organizations (e.g., universities, the stock exchange, and banks); the regent's own appointees; and a limited number of representatives chosen by the aristocracy from their own ranks. The powers of the upper house were limited. It could return legislation to the lower house only twice for reconsideration. In 1937, this rule was amended and as a result, the upper house's second veto was no longer merely suspensive; upon the return of the previously rejected bill, the upper house was no longer compelled to adopt it. Instead, a joint session of the two chambers had to be convened, where all the members of both houses had one vote each, and they voted together on the underlying proposal.

Similarly, to the expansion of the regent's powers and the voting rights restrictions, this was introduced as a systemic safeguard against the potential electoral breakthrough of the national socialists (which was expected as a result of the plan to introduce the secret ballot in the elections). The upper house never actually exercised its right of veto, and there were only few occasions when it asked the lower house to amend the bills it had previously submitted to the upper house for approval. The upper house did not have the right to adopt amendments to the budget (except for its own budget), all it could do was to vote the budget up or down. There was no possibility of dissolving the upper house before the end of its term (Püski, 2000).

The government operated roughly in the same manner as it did in the age of Dualism, although the country's full-fledged autonomy, the more intense intervention of the state in the economy, as well as the growing importance of welfare issues did result in an expansion of governmental responsibilities. The cabinet's role was also reinforced as compared to those of its predecessors under Dualism. For one, it now had the authority to draft and adopt decrees without the approval of the head of state, and second, in response to the global economic crisis, parliament regularly gave the cabinet the temporary authority to regulate the economy through decrees; as of 1939, the same power was extended to military affairs in the event of a war (Püski, 2006: 167–168).

The fall of the regime was ultimately triggered by the distrust of Hitler's Germany toward the Hungarian elite (which was, incidentally, well-founded). In 1944, as the leadership of the Axis country, Hungary was jockeying to switch sides and join the Allies, it was occupied by the German army. The occupiers allowed Horthy to continue to serve as regent in order to legitimate their own rule (even as they tried to arrest Prime Minister Miklós Kállay and several members of his cabinet). After a few months of passivity, Horthy sought to use his actual powers to try to turn Hungary against the Germans and to switch sides in the war. As a result, the Hungarian national socialists staged a coup with German support, and for a period of roughly half a year, they established a polity that was modelled on the Nazi state. Their regime was ultimately overthrown by the arrival of Soviet occupation in the Winter-Spring of 1945 (Lee, 2008: 407–448).

THE KÁDÁR REGIME: SOCIALIST AUTOCRACY

In its own sphere of influence, the Soviet Union sought to set up "democracies" that formally complied with the democratic principles it had agreed to at the Yalta Conference. Yet these polities were nevertheless subject to Soviet imperial interests rather than being sovereign political regimes that would have allowed for actual democratic competition, political liberties, and the principles of representation.

In the first parliamentary election in Hungary after World War II, in late 1945, the Independent Smallholders' Party, a very heterogeneous but predominantly right-wing agrarian party won an absolute majority. However, the Soviets intervened in the process of government formation. The parliamentary balance of power was readjusted in the cabinet in favor of the communists, who were given key portfolios in the new government (they controlled both the police and the intelligence service).

In early 1946, the National Assembly adopted the law proclaiming the republic, which also regulated in detail the relations between the office of the president, the legislature, and the cabinet, as well as their respective powers. The conclusion that the Communist Party drew from the 1945 election was that the main challenge facing it was to "correct" the election results. Hence, their goal was to take apart the Smallholders' Party, which had been supported by almost 60% of the voters, as well as to discriminatively restrict voting rights.

At the parliamentary elections held in 1947, parties that were openly opposed to the communist-led coalition government were still allowed to compete, but at the same time, the new law governing suffrage substantially limited the range of persons who were allowed to vote. At the same time the electoral administration, which operated under Soviet influence, simply left hundreds of thousands of eligible voters off the voter roll. To achieve the desired results, outright fraught also occurred. The coalition led by the Hungarian Communist Party won an election victory, but it was not the sole political force (and even within the coalition, the communists did not have a dominant position), and the majority of voters continued to support right-wing parties (Romsics, 2001: 278–296).

The cabinet that was installed after the election still did not reflect the voters' preferences as expressed in the election. Despite having attained an absolute majority, right-wing parties were forced to enter into another coalition in which key portfolios (e.g., the interior ministry and the police) had to be ceded to the communists. Then several "bourgeois" parties (such as the Christian democrats) were either simply banned, merged into the communist party (this happened to the social democrats), or forced into a role of a satellite party (such as the agrarian parties).

The leader of the emerging Stalinist regime was Mátyás Rákosi, a veteran of the underground resistance (and political prisoner) during the right-wing authoritarianism of the interwar period. The Rákosi regime, which was in place with a brief intermission until 1956, was installed based on the 1949 Constitution marked a clear break with the historical traditions, and it was essentially a slavish emulation of the Soviet model. The emerging totalitarian regime eliminated all human rights guarantees and based its power on a significant extent of terror. All economic, social, and political autonomy of private actors were eliminated. Rákosi's rule was finally overthrown by the short-lived 1956 Revolution (Feitl, 1994; Földes & Hubai, 1994; Romsics, 2001).

The defeat of the Revolution at the hands of Soviet troops and the domestic forces aligned with the Party resulted in the installation of a new type of regime starting in November that year. It was led by the ruling party's first secretary, János Kádár (who had previously served as the minister of the interior but was also a prisoner of Rákosi). The new regime essentially adopted the same institutional structure as its predecessors without major changes, even as the fundamental logic governing its operations changed substantially. János Kádár's basic goal was to restore the pre-revolutionary—Soviet-type—regime, but in addition to the reprisals meted out to punish revolutionary activity, as well as the ongoing restrictions that the Hungarian public was subject to, Kádár also made concessions in order to achieve some level of social conciliation. As a result of these changes, by the mid-sixties, the previously totalitarian regime had morphed into a post-totalitarian, socialist autocracy (Brooker, 1995, 2014; Romsics, 2001).

The open terror that had previously extended to all social strata essentially ceased, and from that point on, rather than intimidating the population as a whole, the regime's repressive apparatus focused on its actual opponents. The previous mass mobilization and massive propaganda, as well as the cult of personality related to the party leader, were scaled back. Economic policy, which had been focused on deliberately keeping standards of living down while diverting resources toward preparations for a third world war and developing heavy industry, was replaced by a more balanced approach that provided a somewhat increased level of public welfare.

Still, there was no legal framework that would have allowed for any sort of political or social pluralism. Independent NGOs were banned and in their stead, the socialist party created its own legion of pseudo-NGOs. Control over the economy was centralized, although starting in the 1960s, extremely limited entrepreneurial activities were allowed in the agrarian sector, and in the 1980s, this option was extended to other sectors as well (Feitl, 1994; Rainer M., 2013; Romsics, 2001, 2007).

The key feature of the regime was the single-party state and the entanglement between the state and the state party (now renamed to the Hungarian Socialist Workers' Party). The state party and the executive operated two parallel and distinct systems in place, however, these two hierarchies were not distinct, they were intertwined and connected with one another at many points (Csanádi, 1997). For the most part, the previously existing institutions were formally retained, but their functions were altered fundamentally (see more on this in Chapter 7).

Even though elections were regularly held they could not function as genuine elections. An umbrella organization, the People's Front had the exclusive right to nominate candidates and it was only in the final moments of the regime that members of parliament were actually being recalled. High turnout was achieved with a mix of compulsion and intimidation.

The principle of the separation of powers was replaced by the principle of the unity of powers. Municipal autonomy was almost completely eliminated and supplanted by a centrally governed council system. The sessions of the unicameral National Assembly became rarer—on average, parliament met six to ten times a year—and the debates became shorter (even the debate and adoption of the budget took a few hours at most, often with only a few minutes of discussion in committee). The decisions of parliament were rendered unanimously, and the speeches given were pre-written and pre-reviewed.

Between the sessions of the National Assembly, the affairs were discharged by the Presidential Council of the Hungarian People's Republic (a body elected from members of the National Assembly and operated as a collective head of state), which also operated under the control of the ruling party. It was invested with most of the powers of the National Assembly and was allowed to adopt "decree laws" which were legally equivalent to laws. The Council of Ministers (the government) became the "most important organ of state administration." Its members were theoretically elected by the National Assembly and accountable to the latter, but in practice, it was never held to account (Feitl, 1994, 2019; Rainer M., 2013; Romsics, 2001).

Real power was concentrated in the hands of the governing party. It was the only legal organization of this sort and it had close to one million members in a country of ten million. It was surrounded by a network of pseudo-NGOs whose activities extended to all groups of society, including youth, religious, national minority, and women's organizations. The party's operation was governed by the principle of "democratic centralism": the decisions of the higher organs were binding for the official bodies operating at the lower levels, and engaging in horizontal cooperation was prohibited. The party was itself dependent on an external player as it was not allowed to take a position that ran counter to the decisions or strategy of the Communist Party of the Soviet Union, which it had to obediently.

In practice, the party's decisions had a binding effect even when they were not formally enshrined in legal statutes. The highest organ of the party was the Party Congress, which convened once every few years to adopt the party platform and elect the leaders. In between such Congresses, the Central Committee acted as the party's main decision-making body. And between two sessions of the Central Committee, the Politburo controlled and led the party. The Politburo was entitled to decide both matters of principle and practical policy; it drafted the party's policy positions while it also managed its everyday affairs.

Officially the first secretary's job was only to implement their decisions. In reality, however, the first secretary was the primary leader of the ruling party and thus of the single-party state. The party's organization, which thus operated alongside the parallel organizations of the state, enjoyed a primacy over the latter. It was only on November 22, 1988, that the Central Committee of the ruling MSZMP stated for the first time in a resolution that it would respect the National Assembly's exclusive authority to legislate, and it made the same concession with regard to the Council of Minister's independence and responsibility in the performance of its executive functions. Up to that point in time, the party had exercised direct control over these governmental functions (Németh, 1995).

In addition to the protection that the Soviet occupation forces provided for the regime, the party's leading role was also safeguarded by its own dedicated armed force (the so-called Workers' Guard), as well as the nomenclature system. There were some 20–30,000 jobs of special importance (starting with the members of the cabinet all the way down to school principals) that were filled with personnel selected or approved by the Party (Huszár, 2005; Romsics, 2001; T. Varga & Szakadát, 1992). The regime was able to operate as long as it had sufficient economic resources. As soon as the Hungarian economy was descending into crisis, the regime began to disintegrate (Barany, 1999; Csanádi, 2007; Rainer M., 2013).

A constitutional amendment in 1983 allowed for nominating two competing candidates in each single-member district in the elections for the National Assembly. Theoretically, the possibility had been given since the late '60s, but it rarely happened in practice. In the meanwhile, a chasm emerged within the party leadership as well, between those who were in denial about the crisis and those who were increasingly alarmed about its impact (Csizmadia, 2015; Rainer M., 2013; Romsics, 2013). All these trends combined to cause a crisis of the regime, and would eventually lead to its fall.

LIBERAL AND ILLIBERAL DEMOCRACY: THE POST-TRANSITION REPUBLIC AND THE ORBÁN REGIME

Ultimately, the Kádár regime was not brought down by its own internal opposition but by its inability to adapt to the changes in the global economy (especially the oil crisis) and the concomitant decline of the Soviet Union. After a while, the welfare system that provided the regime with legitimacy could only be financed by uncontrollable debt. The Hungarian elite (similarly to that of other communist countries) sought to find a way out of this quagmire by bringing back a capitalist economic structure. The collapse of the Soviet Union opened up the way to a return to Hungary's traditional Western orientation, while the crisis and the regime's loss of legitimacy provided the framework for a transition to democratic politics.

The new regime which emerged based on an agreement between ruling party and opposition politicians at the National Roundtable marked a return to parliamentarism. It adopted with immediate effect the modus operandi of Western liberal democracies, along with the relevant institutions. The standard array of first-generation civil rights prevailed once again (as a safeguard for the latter, the institution of ombudsman was introduced in Hungary, along with the creation of a highly active Constitutional Court which was invested with substantial powers even in international comparison). In the meanwhile, the multi-party system came back to life, along with media pluralism (Bozóki, 1993).

At the same time, media pluralism was hampered by the circumstance that post-communist and liberal forces were able to retain their control over the media even under the new regime. They were helped by their shrewd positioning during the economic transition and also exploited the fact that for several decades leading up to regime change only those who professed loyalty to the regime could work as journalists (although many prominent right-wing media personalities did play a role in the pre-1989 media landscape when they held more forgiving views toward 'communists'). The right-wing governments that ruled between 1990 and 1994 and from 1998 to 2002 failed to change this situation substantially. It was only Viktor Orbán's own media-building in opposition after 2002 and his subsequent return to governmental power after 2010 that made it possible to first deconstruct the left-liberal media dominance, and then to establish right-wing dominance in the media.

The regime that emerged as a compromise between the (now:) post-communists and the opposition in 1989 was a radical version of the separation of powers system with a myriad of veto points from super-majority requirements to strong local governments, opposition rights and a Constitutional Court which enjoyed unparalleled power. This state of affairs was turned to a majoritarian direction as a result of a deal between the right-wing Hungarian Democratic Forum (MDF), the biggest party after the 1990 elections, and the largest opposition party at the time, the liberal Alliance of Free Democrats (SZDSZ), which was virulently anti-communist back then. Based on this agreement, the number of policy areas requiring a two-thirds majority was cut, while ministers would be responsible to the prime minister rather than the National Assembly. Parliament would only be able to remove the prime minister through a so-called constructive vote of no-confidence, that is by electing another prime minister. In return for these concessions, SZDSZ got the right to nominate the first president of the republic as well as the top executives of the public media (at the time, Hungary did not have a commercial television channel or radio station, and thus this move essentially gave the opposition a media monopoly (at least for a few years—Arato & Miklósi, 2010: 365–368).

The Hungarian parliament became unicameral, and its members were elected in a mixed system in which candidates were either selected in single-member districts or from regional or national party lists (Benoit, 1996). Parliament was once again a forum where a wide variety of opinions were present, which was also reflected in the long and often vigorous debates. Public policy considerations and debates were also given room through a system of committees (which was considerably weaker than in the American system, however—Olson & Ilonszki, 2011).

Although the National Assembly re-assumed its historically central role, as—for the most part—the governments during the period boasted a stable majority, executive power emerged as the pivotal branch of government. Local autonomy also resurfaced in a state that otherwise followed long-standing Hungarian traditions in terms of the centralization of power.

Before 2010, the party system differed substantially from the party systems of earlier periods. The fragile unity of the former regime opposition had already frayed by 1989. In the years immediately following regime transition, the Hungary party system was divided into three major segments: a right-wing (Christian democratic, conservative, agrarian populist, and radical right-wing), a liberal, and a post-communist (which was transitioning toward a social democratic outlook) bloc. After 1994, the liberal bloc lost its previous relevance, and the party system gradually became bipolar, with the right-wing Fidesz and the left-wing Hungarian Socialist Party (MSZP) emerging as the major political parties, accompanied by a decreasing number of smaller parties (Enyedi, 2017).

The reasons behind the transformation of the post-transition regime roughly coincided with the reasons that had led to its emergence in the first place. The pact of 1990 failed to adapt flexibly to changing circumstances, and the increasing polarization in the party system led to a situation in which a growing number of necessary decisions could simply not be taken. Furthermore, the impact of the global economic crisis that began to unfold in 2008 was exacerbated by the previous crisis that had emerged in 2006 as a result of excessive government spending. The abundance of foreign exchange denominated mortgage loans taken out during the "roaring" 2000s turned sour leaving hundreds of thousands of families on the brink of eviction. Political infighting in the coalition between MSZP and SZDSZ led to a technocratic caretaker cabinet just one year before the 2010 elections which would become the watershed between the liberal and illiberal periods of post-regime change democracy in Hungary.

The difference between Viktor Orbán's illiberalism and the foregoing 20 years can be best captured by juxtaposing them with the changes that transpired as the post-1956 socialist autocracy set itself apart from the earlier totalitarian period. Despite the adoption of the new constitution, known as the Fundamental Law, the underlying political-institutional structure changed only slightly. What was transformed substantially, however, was the logic behind the way power was being exercised.

The foundation of the new regime was the emergence of a predominant party system in line with Hungarian historical traditions. On the one hand, there was now a ruling party, Fidesz, which was overwhelmingly positioned to the right of the political spectrum, although as a large political tent it did include some other ideological streams as well (The similarities with the Kádár era were reinforced by the various—workers, agrarian, Romani, etc.—"factions" within the party and the co-optation of many civil society and self-governing organizations which served either as mouthpieces—such as the Chamber of Commerce—or as funding bodies for the ruling party and its associates, for example see the formerly "Civic," now "National Cooperation" Fund). In the meanwhile, the predominant governing party was facing an extremely fragmented and substantially weaker opposition, consisting of social democratic/liberal, radical right-wing, and green parties.

Owing to the particularistic features of the Hungarian electoral system, Fidesz won a two-thirds supermajority of seats with around 50% of total votes in parliament in every election since 2010, which allowed it to amend any law as it saw fit. The operation of the governing party, with its vast majority and extremely disciplined parliamentary caucus, was extremely centralized: in practice, Viktor Orbán's will alone prevail in Fidesz for over a decade at that point (Körösényi, 2015).

As a result of this transformation, which Orbán called the "illiberal" turn (see Buzogány & Varga, 2018), the governing party gradually appointed its own cadres to the helm of all the independent institutions (cf., for example the Constitutional Court; the high court of Hungary, the Curia; the ombudsman's office; the prosecutor's office; and the media authority). This made it impossible for the separation of powers to prevail in practice. All the institutions of the political system came to be controlled by Fidesz politicians or by players with close ties to Fidesz. Moreover, the Fidesz caucus in the National Assembly could adopt any legal amendments to serve its momentary power interest or to overwrite unwelcome decisions by any institutional organ of the state.

From the very start, the new political structure was in the crossfire of opinion journalism and academic debates. Some scholars described the new regime as a "hybrid" one (Böcskei & Szabó, 2019; Bozóki & Hegedűs, 2018), others identified its emergence as democratic backsliding (Ágh, 2013; Greskovits, 2015), or as a paradigm shift in the constitutional and separation of powers system (Stumpf, 2017). Körösényi and Gyulai (2019) took an alternative view and identified it as a plebiscitary leader democracy.

In addition to occupying the formal positions of political power, Fidesz also put a distinct emphasis on controlling informal channels of power. That is why it built a media empire which secured a dominant position in the media system; networks of NGOs, think tanks, scientific and cultural institutions; all the while it furnished with capital a variety of entrepreneurs with ties to the governing party, starting with loyal small business owners all the way to such oligarchs as Lőrinc Mészáros, who became Hungary's wealthiest person within the span of just a few years.

Conclusion

The five political regimes reviewed above (including Orbán's regime as a distinct one from liberal democracy) are rather easily distinguished in terms of the substantive requisites of a late twentieth-century liberal democracy (which most of the comparative politics literature treats explicitly or implicitly as a benchmark for a "free" polity when comparing regimes). The Hungarian regime under the Dual Monarchy was considered democratic at the time when it came into being, but by today's standards, its democratic character had major defects. The limited suffrage based on the census, the persistence of the open ballot, and the sovereign's vast powers would not allow us to include it among the democratic regimes today. At the same time, because the government was accountable to a mostly freely elected parliament and because of the wide range of effective civil rights and liberties that prevailed, it cannot be regarded as fully repressive either; it falls into the category of partly free regimes.

During the Horthy regime of the interwar period, many civil rights were massively curtailed, and the political competition was also greatly restricted. Yet a diverse opposition was still allowed to operate (all legally, with the exception of the communists and from time to time the national socialists); the survival of the government in office was ultimately up to the discretion of parliament. The latter in turn was elected based on an electoral system which, although subject to restrictions, was at least partly free as well. Furthermore, public discourse in this era was also characterized by a plurality of opinions. Hence, this regime, too, classifies as partly free, although it was more removed from the free regimes than the political regime that prevailed prior to World War I.

The (for the most part) Stalinist regime of 1949–1956, and then the socialist autocracy of the Kádár regime did not possess such characteristics, however. It was devoid of pluralism, its elections were not competitive, all political arenas were dominated by the single ruling party, and civil rights protections were severely curtailed. This ranks the Kádár regime as one of the few decidedly unfree regimes of more than 150 years of Hungarian history.

Finally, the two regimes which emerged after the transition from socialist autocracy both featured governments that were accountable to parliaments, which were in turn elected in competitive elections with universal suffrage. Pluralism and civil rights also prevailed to different extends. Even as the level of several democracy indicators deteriorated in Hungary under the Orbán regime, up until 2018—thus the end of the period we examined—all the indices we consulted—apart from V-Dem's survey—continued to classify Hungary as a democracy. While the "free" nature of the liberal democracy between 1990 and 2010 is undisputed, the same cannot be said of the "illiberal" regime of 2010–2018 which we classified as "partly free."

References

Ágh, A. (2013). The triple crisis in Hungary: The 'backsliding' of Hungarian democracy after twenty years. *Romanian Journal of Political Science, 13*, 25–51.

Arato, A., & Miklósi, Z. (2010). Constitution making and transitional politics in Hungary. In L. E. Miller & L. Aucoin (Eds.), *Framing the state in times of transition: Case studies in constitution making.* United States Institute of Peace.

Asch, R. G. (2015). Monarchy in Western and Central Europe. In H. Scott (Ed.), *The Oxford Handbook of early modern European History, 1350–1750: Volume II: Cultures and power.* Oxford University Press.

Barany, Z. (1999). Out with a whimper: The final days of Hungarian socialism. *Communist and Post-Communist Studies, 32,* 113–125.

Benoit, K. (1996). Hungary's two-vote 'electoral system'. *Representation, 33,* 162–170.

Bíró, Zs. (2019). *Foundations of the uncodified historical constitution of Hungary.* Studia Iuridica.

Bodó, B. (2019). *The White Terror: Antisemitic and political violence in Hungary, 1919–1921.* Oxon.

Boros, Zs. (2008). Parlamentarizmus a Horthy-korban (1919–1944). In Zs. Boros & D. Szabó (Eds.), *Parlamentarizmus Magyarországon (1867–1944).* ELTE Eötvös Kiadó.

Bozóki, A. (1993). *Hungary's road to systemic change: The opposition roundtable. East European Politics and Societies, 7*(2), 276–308.

Bozóki, A., & Hegedűs, D. (2018). An externally constrained hybrid regime: Hungary in the European Union. *Democratization, 25,* 1173–1189.

Böcskei, B., & Szabó, A. (2019). *Hibrid rezsimek: A politikatudomány X-aktái.* MTA.

Brooker, P. (1995). *Twentieth-century dictatorships: The ideological one-party states.* New York University Press.

Brooker, P. (2014). *Non-democratic regimes.* Palgrave Macmillan.

Brown, A. (2010). *The rise & fall of communism.* Vintage Books.

Buzinkay, G. (2016). *A magyar sajtó és újságírás története a kezdetektől a rendszerváltásig*. Wolter Kluwer.

Buzogány, Á., & Varga, M. (2018). The ideational foundations of the illiberal backlash in Central and Eastern Europe: The case of Hungary. *Review of International Political Economy, 25*, 811–828.

Csanádi, M. (1997). *Party-states and their legacies in post-communist transformation*. Edward Elgar Publishing.

Csanádi, M. (2007). Party–state systems and their dynamics as networks. *Physica A: Statistical Mechanics and Its Applications, 378*, 83–91.

Csizmadia, E. (2015). The Hungarian democratic opposition in the 1980's. *Intersections: East European Journal of Society and Politics, 1*, 119–138.

Eley, G. (2002). *Forging democracy: The history of the left in Europe, 1850–2000*. Oxford University Press.

Enyedi, Zs. (2017). The survival of the fittest: Party system concentration in Hungary. In S. Jungerstam-Mulders (Ed.), *Post-communist EU member states*. Routledge.

Feitl, I. (1994). Pártvezetés és országgyűlési választások 1949–1988. In Gy. Földes & L. Hubai (Eds.), *Parlament képviselőválasztások 1920–1990*. Politikatörténeti Alapítvány.

Feitl, I. (2019). *Az államszocialista korszak álparlametje*. Országház Könyvkiadó.

Fenyves, K. (2011). When sexism meets racism: The 1920 Numerus Clausus Law in Hungary. *AHEA: E-Journal of the American Hungarian Educators, 1*–15.

Föglein, G., Mezei, B., & Révész, T. M. (2003). Az Országgyűlés. In B. Mezei (Ed.), *Magyar alkotmánytörténet*. Osiris Kiadó.

Földes, Gy., & Hubai, L. (1994). *Parlamenti képviselőválasztások 1920–1990: Tanulmányok*. Politikatörténeti Alapítvány.

Frank, T. (2000). The Austro-Hungarian compromise of 1867 and its contemporary critics. In *Hungarian Studies, 14*, 193–200.

Greskovits, B. (2015). The hollowing and backsliding of democracy in East Central Europe. *Global Policy, 6*, 28–37.

Hroch, M. (2016). National movements in the Habsburg and Ottoman empires. In J. Breuilly (Ed.), *The Oxford Handbook of the history of nationalism*. Oxford University Press.

Huszár, T. (2005). From elites to nomenklatura: The evolution and some characteristics of institutionalized cadre policy in Hungary (1945–1989). *Szociologiai Szemle (Sociological Review), 3*, 8–69.

Képessy, I. (2019). National modernisation through the constitutional revolution of 1848 in Hungary: Pretext and context. In M. Gałędek & A. Klimaszewska (Eds.), *Modernisation, national identity and legal instrumentalism (Vol. II: Public Law)*. Nijhoff.

Kozári, M. (2005). *A dualista rendszer*. Pannonica Kiadó.

Köpf, E. M. (2001). Electoral law in Hungary under the Dual Monarchy. *Hungarologische Beiträge*, 53–69.

Körösényi, A. (2015). A magyar demokrácia három szakasza és az Orbán-rezsim. *A magyar politikai rendszer—negyedszázad után*, 401–422.

Körösényi, A., & Gyulai, A. (2019). A hibridrezsim-fogalom korlátai és egy alternatív megközelítés: A plebiszciter vezérdemokrácia. In B. Böcskei & A. Szabó (Eds.), *Hibrid rezsimek: A politikatudomány X-aktái*. Napvilág Kiadó.

Lee, S. J. (2008). *European Dictatorships, 1918–1945*. Routledge.

Németh, J. (1995). *Az MSZMP központi vezető szervi üléseinek napirendi jegyzékei 1956–1962*. Magyar Országos Levéltár.

Olson, D. M., & Ilonszki, G. (2011). Two decades of divergent post-communist parliamentary development. *The Journal of Legislative Studies, 17*, 234–255.

Péntek, R. (1996). Istvan Horthy's Election as Vice-Regent in 1942, 23, 17–28.

Pesti, S. (2002). *Az újkori magyar parlament*. Osiris Kiadó.

Péter, L. (2012a). The aristocracy, the gentry and their parliamentary tradition in nineteenth-century Hungary. In M. Lojkó (Ed.), *Hungary's long nineteenth century: Constitutional and democratic traditions in European perspective: Collected studies by László Péter*. Brill.

Péter, L. (2012b). The dualist character of the 1867 Hungarian settlement. In M. Lojkó (Ed.), *Hungary's long nineteenth century: Constitutional and democratic traditions in European perspective: Collected studies by László Péter*. Brill.

Péter, L. (2012c). Ius Resistendi in Hungary. In M. Lojkó (Ed.), *Hungary's long nineteenth century: Constitutional and democratic traditions in European perspective: Collected studies by László Péter*. Brill.

Püski, L. (2000). *A magyar felsőház története: 1927–1945*. Napvilág Kiadó.

Püski, L. (2006). *A Horthy-rendszer*. Pannonica Kiadó.

Püski, L. (2015). *A Horthy-korszak parlamentje*. Országgyűlés Hivatala.

Rainer M. J. (2013). *A Kádár-korszak: 1956–1989*. Kossuth Kiadó.

Révész T. M. (2003). A szovjet típusú diktatúra első kísérlete: A Tanácsköztársaság (1919). In B. Mezei (Ed.), *Magyar alkotmánytörténet*. Osiris Kiadó.

Romsics, I. (2001). *Magyarország története a XX. században*. Osiris Kiadó.

Romsics, I. (2007). Economic reforms in the Kádár Era. *The Hungarian Quarterly*, 69–79.

Romsics, I. (2013). *Rendszerváltás Magyarországon*. Akadémiai Kiadó.

Stumpf, I. (2017). Separation of powers and the politics of constitutional reforms, including Judicial independence. *Constitutional Law Review*, 3–23.

Szabó, D. (2008). A magyar parlamentarizmus az Osztrák-Magyar Monarchiában (1867–1918). In Zs. Boros & D. Szabó (Eds.), *Parlamentarizmus Magyarországon*. ELTE Eötvös Kiadó.

Szente, Z. (2011). *Kormányzás a dualizmus korában. A XIX. századi európai parlamentarizmus és Magyarország kormányformája a kiegyezés után 1867–1918.* Atlantisz Kiadó.

Szijártó M. I. (2016). *A 18. századi Magyarország rendi Országgyűlése.* Országgyűlés Hivatala.

Szikra, D., & Tomka, B. (2009). Social policy in East Central Europe: Major trends in the twentieth century. In A. Cerami & P. Vanhuysee (Eds.), *Postcommunist welfare pathways*. Palgrave Macmillan.

T. Varga, Gy., & Szakadát, I. (1992). Íme a nómenklatúrák! Az MDP és a volt MSZMP hatásköri listái. *Társadalmi Szemle, 47.*

Takács, P. (2019). On state form of Hungary between 1920 and 1944: Applicability of the term "Monarchy without a King". *Journal on European History of Law, 10,* 139–148.

Taylor, A. J. P. (1948). *The Habsburg Monarchy 1809–1918: A History of the Austrian Empire and Austria-Hungary.* Hamish Hamilton.

Thompson, S. (2003). Agrarian reform in Eastern Europe following World War I: Motives and outcomes. *American Journal of Agricultural Economics, 75,* 840–844.

Tóth, A. (2011). Survey of important internal moments of the process of birth of the specific political system of interwar Hungary (1919–1922). *West Bohemian Historical Review,* 103–135.

Wittenberg, J. (2014). External influences on the evolution of Hungarian authoritarianism, 1920–44. In A. C. Pinto & A. Kallis (Eds.), *Rethinking fascism and dictatorship in Europe.* Palgrave Macmillan.

CHAPTER 4

The Data and Methods of the Hungarian Comparative Agendas Project

Csaba Molnár and Miklós Sebők

The research team of the Hungarian Comparative Agendas Project (CAP) has been developing its database on various public policy agendas in Hungary since 2013. In some cases, the time frame of the datasets encompasses more than two centuries. Besides data on policy agendas, we also collected several auxiliary datasets on metadata (such as the ministries of the government or the committee structure of parliament at any given time) that can be used in the analysis.

In this chapter, we first present how the datasets were collected and coded. Next, we describe in more detail the data on the policy agenda of various policy venues. Finally, we provide an overview of the methods used in this book. While the research design of the Hungarian CAP

C. Molnár (✉)
Corvinus University of Budapest, Budapest, Hungary
e-mail: molnar.csaba@tk.hu

C. Molnár · M. Sebők
Centre for Social Sciences, MTA Centre of Excellence, Eötvös Loránd Research Network, Budapest, Hungary
e-mail: sebok.miklos@tk.mta.hu

63
M. Sebők and Z. Boda (eds.), *Policy Agendas in Autocracy, and Hybrid Regimes*, Comparative Studies of Political Agendas,
https://doi.org/10.1007/978-3-030-73223-3_4

project was mainly based on the practice of the international CAP research network, in some cases, we added new topic codes or used innovative methodological techniques, which we also present in this chapter. In short, our goal is here to lay the foundation for following, substantive chapters on the policy dynamics of individual eras and regimes in Hungarian history.

DATA COLLECTION

The Hungarian Comparative Agendas project has developed fifteen comprehensive, comparable, and reliable datasets with a total of 446,534 observations. In some cases, such as interpellations in the democratic period (1990–2018), these cover the full population of items. In other cases (e.g., for media datasets), we analyzed a sample of the full set. While some modules cover more than 2 centuries, generally speaking, data is more extensive and detailed for the democratic era. Table 4.1 shows the different features and time frame of each of the modules of the CAP project.

THE CAP POLICY TOPIC CODING SYSTEM

In this section, we present some general features of the process of assigning policy topic codes to observations and we return to the specifics of each module below. We used both manual and computer-assisted methods of data collection and coding in our datasets. Machine learning was especially necessary in cases, which featured an extremely high number of observations (e.g., media database with almost 90,000 articles). Appendix A2 presents the artificial intelligence-enhanced (and for even more details see Sebők & Kacsuk, 2020). All data appearing in our database were validated by double-blind human coding, or by manually validated machine coding.

Our datasets contain both the text corpus of the investigated documents (e.g., the transcripts of the prime ministerial speeches) and a description of their content (notably the policy area). They also contain metadata on the documents (e.g., date or electoral cycle when they were presented). The unit of analysis varies between different datasets according to suitability and feasibility (e.g., we investigated party manifestos sentence by sentence, but decrees as a whole). All datasets and the related codebooks are publicly available on our website (cap.tk.hu/en).

Table 4.1 The datasets of the Hungarian Comparative Agendas Project

Dataset	Investigated period	Coding method	Unit of analysis	Number of observations
Public opinion priorities	1980–1989, 2004–2010, 2013–2014, 2017–2018	Manual	Question	2719
Petitions	1866–1867, 1874–1875, 1892, 1905, 1912–1913	Manual	Whole text	2336
Media	1990–2014	Manual and machine learning	Article	88,338
Party manifestos	1867–1944, 1990–2018	Manual	Sentence	41,839
Election results	1867–1944, 1990–2018	–	Result by party	234
Speeches of prime ministers	1867–1944, 1957–2018	Manual	Sentence (1867–1944, 1957–1988, 1998–2002, 2006–2009, 2010–2018) Paragraph (1990–1998, 2009–2010)	70,764
Speeches of first and general secretaries	1957–1989	Manual	Sentence	5011
Interpellations	1867–2018	Manual	Whole text	14,130
Laws and decree-laws	1790–2018	Manual	Whole text	9297
Decrees	1957–2018	Manual	Whole text	33,564
Secret resolutions of the executive	1957–1967	Manual	Whole text	4583
Party resolutions of the Socialist party	1957–1989	Manual	Whole text	334
Agenda items of cabinet meetings	1957–1989	Manual	Item	20,480
Agenda items of Politburo meetings	1957–1989	Manual	Item	19,843

(continued)

Table 4.1   (continued)

Dataset	Investigated period	Coding method	Unit of analysis	Number of observations
Central budgets and final accounts	1868–2018	Machine learning	Line item	133,062

Table 4.2   The major policy topics of the Comparative Agendas Project

1. Macroeconomics	8. Energy	16. Defense
2. Civil Rights	9. Immigration	17. Technology
3. Health	10. Transportation	18. Foreign Trade
4. Agriculture	12. Law and Crime	19. International Affairs
5. Labor	13. Social Welfare	20. Government Operations
6. Education	14. Housing	21. Public Lands
7. Environment	15. Domestic Commerce and other financial policy	23. Culture

The central element of these datasets is the codes revealing their policy content (see Table 4.2). For this purpose, we used a two-level codebook mainly based on the international Comparative Agendas Project codebook.[1] The 21 major topics of policy content (e.g., transportation) are also broken down to 219, more specific, subtopics (e.g., railroad travel). All observations get one code and one code only. Whenever an item covers more policy fields, such as an interpellation related to school shutdowns due to public health concerns, we coded for either the dominant or (in case of equal weight) the first-mentioned policy topic.

We also used fifteen additional major topic codes (e.g., death notices) and forty-two subtopic codes (e.g., traffic accidents) strictly in our media database. Furthermore, due to the specialities of the Hungarian politics, we modified the 219-element list of subtopics in some cases. First, we did not use many policy areas which are irrelevant in the Hungarian context (e.g., indigenous affairs). Second, we added some new policy fields which are important to understand Hungarian politics but had not been accurately captured by the original codebook (see Table 4.3).

---

[1] See https://www.comparativeagendas.net/pages/master-codebook.

Table 4.3   New and modified subtopic codes of the Hungarian CAP

Hungarian CAP subtopic	International CAP subtopic	Description of Hungarian CAP subtopic
219	299	Issues connected to autocratic regimes in general and former membership in secret police
336	323	Other health services and services not financed by social security
508	1308	Parental leave, child welfare
710	701	Pollution and protection of surface water reserves
1006	1002	Road transportation
1209	1201	Guns, arson, police abuses
1410	1401	Foreign currency-based mortgage loans and the financial crisis related to them
1921	1907–1921	Issues of all non-West European countries and regions
1930	1999	Ethnic Hungarians living in foreign countries, Hungarian diaspora

We provide a crosswalk for these specific policy topics on our website. A major advantage of this revised coding scheme is that it is independent of the context of any given regimes, yet it does capture some peculiarities of the era in question. In most cases, we can easily classify education-related laws of the feudal era, prime ministerial speeches of the interwar period, decrees of the socialist regime, or newspaper articles in the post-1989 democratic era according to these policy areas. This allows for tracking policy emphasis shifts over time as well as the evolution of the state and public policy from a minimal state of the early nineteenth century through the twenty-first century state covering all aspects of human activity.

The Description of the Datasets Used in This Book

We present our datasets in more detail according to their position in what Baumgartner et al. (2009) called the friction process of the public policy cycle. The three phases include inputs (which policy-makers use to make decisions), the policy process (during which the policy is formulated), and outputs (notably appropriations, budgets, and final accounts).

The Input Phase

Our dataset on *public opinion* focuses on the policy priorities of respondents. It contains 169 questions for the period 1980–1989, 2417 for the period 2004–2010, 93 for the period 2013–2014, 40 for the period 2017–2018: altogether 2719. The data on the 1980s is based on the collection of Open Society Archives Public Opinion and Media Research and the media quarterly "Jel-Kép" which published the historical analyses of the Magyar Közvéleménykutató Intézet (Hungarian Public Opinion Institute). Data on public opinion from 2004 to 2018 are based on polls by Medián Polling Institute. Entries in the dataset contain information on the policy topics of the questions in these polls and the importance of the given issues as assigned by respondents. They also include metadata (e.g., year of the poll).

The second dataset of the input phase contains information on a special instrument of direct involvement in politics: *petitions*. In the late nineteenth century, early twentieth century citizens, parties, NGOs (e.g., the Association of Feminists), local governments or groups of people (e.g., "socialist citizens of Hódmezővásárhely") could send petitions to the legislature. Often they were introduced by members of marginalized groups (e.g., ethnic minorities, women, members of sects, workers, or peasants). The policy content of petitions was defined manually. The petitions were collected from the website of the Hungarian National Assembly's Library.

In our analysis, we focused on five years' worth of petitions (1866–1867, 1874–1875, 1892, 1905, 1912–1913). During these periods, a total of 2336 petitions were introduced. Originally a form of individual initiatives, in later years, we can find evidence of the coordination of petitioning. For example, on December 13, 1912, the National Assembly's Committee of Petitions registered 194 petitions for a general and equal suffrage with secret-ballot voting. 13 of them were introduced by local governments, 6 by NGOs, 60 by participants of protests, 11 by local party organizations, and 90 by groups of citizens.

Our database on *media* consists of two distinctive parts. For the pre-1945 dataset, we used dictionary-based information retrieval from

Arcanum Adatbázis Kft's database. Although the Hungarian press was extremely plural and flourishing during this period, we could also analyze a subset of the available information. Therefore, we examined the content of, inter alia, liberal pro-Austria newspapers such as "Nemzet" (1882–1895), "Magyar Nemzet" (1899–1906) and 'Pesti Napló" (1867–1918) as well as "Budapest" (1877–1918), "Ellenőr" (1870–1881), "Magyar Újság" (1871–1874 and 1897–1899) which were critical of the Austro-Hungarian Monarchy. We investigated the interwar period with a similar methodology. There we covered the conservative "Budapesti Hírlap" (1920–1939) and "Esti Újság" (1938–1944), the pro-government radical right-wing "Függetlenség" (1933–1935 and 1939–1944) as well as many pro-Nazi, radical liberal and social democratic newspapers. With dictionary-based methods, we identified policy content in 5862 cases for the 1867–1918 and for 189,521 cases for the 1919–1944 period.

Although the list of newspapers investigated in the 1990–2014 period is much lower, their examination was much more systematic and all-encompassing. We investigated the content of all front cover articles of the left-liberal "Népszabadság" published between 1990 and 2014 and the conservative "Magyar Nemzet" published between 2002 and 2014. In this era, these were the most popular left-wing and right-wing daily news-papers, respectively. We coded manually all articles published on Tuesdays in "Népszabadság" and all articles published between 2010 and 2014 in both newspapers. All other articles were coded by a computer-based clas-sification method (see Appendix). The dataset contains 53,317 articles of "Népszabadság" and 35,021 articles of "Magyar Nemzet."

Our *party manifesto* dataset focuses on three out of the four high-lighted periods in this book: the 1867–1918, the 1920–1944, and the 1990–2018 eras (the exception was the one-party socialist era). The pre-1945 dataset investigates the strongest parties' electoral manifesto, while the post-1989 dataset includes all parties which have been able to form parliamentary group in more than one electoral cycle (for better compara-bility, in some cases we also investigate party manifestos from years when their publisher did not get into parliament). It is important to mention that before 1944, especially prior to 1918 it was uncommon to prepare a new party manifesto for each election. Parties usually published an elec-toral program when they were founded, and they published new ones only after serious changes of the socio-economical-political context.

From the pre-war era, we investigated the party manifestos of the governing pro-Austria liberal "Deák Party" (1867), Liberal Party

(1875), National Party of Work (1910), and many opposition parties, including the anti-Austria, liberal Independence Party (1867, 1872, 1874, 1891, 1895), and the conservative Constitution Party (1905). As for the interwar period, we primarily focus on the party manifestos of the governing conservative Unity Party (officially Catholic-Protestant Peasant, Farmer and Civic Party; later renamed to Party of National Unity (1932), and then to the Party of Hungarian Life (1939)). We also examined several Catholic, agrarian, and social democratic parties, as well as the national socialist Arrow Cross Party (1939). The unit analysis for the 72 party manifestos were quasi-sentences (which many times coincided with actual sentences). The database contained 41,839 manually coded lines.

Although it is not a central element of our research design, in keeping with several articles in the CAP literature, we incorporated data on *elections* into our research. During the investigated periods, competitive elections were held between 1867 and 1918, 1920 and 1944, and 1990 and 2018, but no competition occurred during the socialist regime. Hence, our dataset contained information on 28 general elections and 234 party-election year results.

The Policy Process Phase

Speeches of Hungarian prime ministers were coded systematically from 1957. All speeches of prime ministers in the legislature were investigated. Sentences were the unit of analysis for the 1957–1990, 1998–2002, 2006–2009 and 2010–2018 periods, and—more suitable—paragraphs for the 1990–1998 and 2009–2010 periods. Data were collected from the website of Hungarian National Assembly and Library of National Assembly. A total of 12,926 sentences and 2083 paragraphs were analyzed (although not all of them contained policy-related content). We also coded 54,395 sentences of speeches by prime ministers delivered outside parliament for the period between 2010 and 2018.

We have not coded all prime ministerial speeches for the pre-1945 period. Instead, we focused on inauguration speeches in the legislature for a slew of prime ministers with a major historical role. This dataset contains ten inauguration speeches with 1360 sentences. We chose five speeches from the pre-war and five from the interwar era. These include Gyula Andrássy, the first prime minister after the Austro-Hungarian compromise (1867–1871), the second longest-serving prime minister, Kálmán Tisza

(1875–1890), the first government of the first non-noble prime minister Sándor Wekerle (1892–1895), the second government of Sándor Wekerle (1906–1910) which was inaugurated after the only electoral victory of the coalition of anti-Austria parties as well as the second government of István Tisza (1913–1917), the most important Hungarian of the era.

From the interwar period, we chose Károly Huszár (1919–1920), the first prime minister of the Horthy regime and István Bethlen (1921–1931), the most important and influential politician of the era. Our dataset also includes a speech by Gyula Gömbös (1932–1936), a former radical right-wing opposition politician, who tried to establish an overtly autocratic regime. As for the years leading up to World War II, we selected the inauguration of Kálmán Darányi (1936–1938) who implemented the most important constitutional and economic reforms of the period, and Béla Imrédy (1938–1939) who made a stillborn experiment to adopt a corporatist state structure. All data were collected from the website of the Library of the National Assembly and were coded manually.

During the years of socialist autocracy following World War II a "party state" was established in which party organs were the primary venues for decision-making. Thus—besides speeches by the prime ministers—we investigated the *speeches of the first secretary* (from 1985: secretary general) delivered before the congresses of the Hungarian Socialist Workers' Party (1959, 1962, 1966, 1970, 1975, 1980, 1985). Each sentence of these speeches was coded yielding 5011 lines. The corpus was collected from the official newspaper of the Socialist party (Népszabadság) and observations were coded manually.

Besides speeches by the executive and party leaders, much of policy discourse was centered around the work of the National Assembly. Throughout history, several kinds of parliamentary questions were available for members of parliament. The most important among them is the institution of interpellation. *Interpellations* are followed by a short debate between the MP and the interpellated minister, and as a conclusion, those present at the plenary session vote whether they accept the ministerial answer or not. Our database includes all interpellations between 1867 and 2018 (14,130 cases) collected from the website of Hungarian National Assembly and Library of National Assembly. The unit of analysis is the full text of interpellation; observations were coded manually.

Our database includes information on the key form of rendering policy decisions: primary and secondary legislation. Our dataset includes all laws published between 1790 and 2018. We also added the so-called decree laws which were adopted by the Presidential Council of the People's Republic during the socialist regime (1949–1989). They were identical in effect to laws and were subject to an ex-post confirmatory vote by the full house of parliament. We investigated a total of 9297 laws and decree-laws, all of which were coded manually.

We also collected the various forms of executive decrees for the period between 1957 and 2018. The 33,564 such observations were assigned policy codes by human annotators. Even as most democracies regularly adopt classified decrees, as a general rule law-making is conducted in a transparent manner. Non-democratic ones generally eschew this (almost) full transparency. Such was the case of the socialist one-party state which decided on a slew of secret resolutions. We could include such documents for the period between 1957 and 1967 as they had been declassified during our research project. We collected this corpus from the database of the "Hungaricana Közgyűjteményi Portál" archive. The complete text was used as the unit of analysis; we coded 5228 such units manually.

The last group of datasets related to the policy process phase were related to socialist autocracy. Despite the fact that they were did not constitute official "state" documents, we analyzed the *resolutions of the Communist Party* due to their obligatory effect for party members who controlled all fields of public life. We investigated 334 Party resolutions for the period 1957–1989. We also perused the agenda of the Party's *Politburo meetings* as this was the most important policy venue of the era. We used the collection of the National Archives of Hungary which covers 19,843 observations for the same period as party resolutions. Finally, we investigated the agenda of cabinet (Council of Ministers) meetings as well. Once more, we used archival material for a dataset, which covers 20,480 such agenda items for over three decades starting in 1957.

The Output Phase

The most important outputs of the policy process are financial decisions in most cases rendered in the form of appropriations, budgets and final accounts. Besides laws our financial datasets—which cover budgets and final accounts—are the most extensive ones, covering the period between 1868 and 2018. The sources for the composite dataset include the website of the Hungarian National Assembly and documents provided by the Hungarian National Bank as well as the Ministry for National Economy. Our database contains 133,062 observations where the unit of analysis was line items. This dataset was also one of the machine-coded ones, for which we used dictionary-based methods (for more details, see Sebők & Berki, 2018).

METHODOLOGY

We conclude this chapter with a brief description of the social science methodology used in this book. Most chapters equally rely on quantitative and qualitative data. In this, our approach is decidedly one mixed-methods. The case studies detailed with respect to the periods in Part 3 were selected based on the frequency distributions of policy codes. This descriptive statistics of the amassed database can be considered to be the primary tool for the research presented in this book.

Time and time again, we also used historical, institutional, and other types of qualitative analysis. We also relied on advanced quantitative techniques, especially in Part 4. Finally, we extensively relied on text mining and machine learning for the policy coding of various corpora which effort underpins all topic coding based analysis in the book. We provide more detail on our machine learning-based methods in the Appendix.

REFERENCES

Baumgartner, F. R., Breunig, C., Green-Pedersen, C., Jones, B. D., Mortensen, P. B., Nuytmeans, M., & Walgrave, S. (2009). Punctuated equilibrium in comparative perspective. *American Journal of Political Science, 53*(3), 603–620.

Sebők, M., & Berki, T. (2018). Punctuated equilibrium in democracy and autocracy: An analysis of Hungarian budgeting between 1868 and 2013. *European Political Science Review, 10*(4), 589–611.

Sebők, M., & Kacsuk, Z. (2020). The multiclass classification of newspaper articles with machine learning: The hybrid binary snowball approach. *Political Analysis, 29*, 1–14. https://doi.org/10.1017/pan.2020.27.

PART III

The Dynamics of Policy Agendas in Four Regimes of Hungarian History

CHAPTER 5

The Pre-war Era of Proto-parliamentarism (1867–1918)

Csaba Molnár

The Dual Monarchy (or Dualism), between 1867 and 1918, was the first sustained period in Hungarian history in which the political system featured a vigorous form of parliamentarism and interparty competition. On the whole, the regime was democratic, at least by the standards of the era in question. The emergence of Dualism after 1867, following the so-called Austro Hungarian Compromise, was a seminal moment in Hungarian history as it marked the end of the earlier regime which had been based on the direct and personal power of the king/queen (in a personal union with the Austrian emperor/empress). The short-lived absolute monarchy of 1849–1867 was replaced by a consolidated, modern parliamentary system.

C. Molnár (✉)
Corvinus University of Budapest, Budapest, Hungary
e-mail: molnar.csaba@tk.hu

Centre for Social Sciences, MTA Centre of Excellence, Eötvös Loránd Research Network, Budapest, Hungary

© The Author(s), under exclusive license to Springer Nature Switzerland AG 2021
M. Sebők and Z. Boda (eds.), *Policy Agendas in Autocracy, and Hybrid Regimes*, Comparative Studies of Political Agendas,
https://doi.org/10.1007/978-3-030-73223-3_5

77

The emergence of the new regime did not imply a comprehensive break with previous periods, however. Even though the nascent constitutional structure was predominantly reflective of the goals and achievements of the 1848 Revolution—in which Hungarians had fought for a modern democratic regime and for their independence from Austria—the fundamental relationship between Austria and Hungary continued in the form of the joint ruler and the joint institutions. Nevertheless, the underlying arrangement was overhauled and legally restructured in 1867, thereby transforming the respective positions of the political forces involved.

The main cleavage of the era was centered around the constitutional issue: the relationship between Austria and Hungary. Two major movements took a different approach to this question (and organized into a wide range of parties and coalitions—see below). The Sixty-Seveners (taking their name from the year of the Compromise) supported the Dualist regime, thus the common foreign and defense policy with Austria. For the most part of this period (between 1867 and 1905 and from 1910 to 1918), they dominated the Hungarian cabinet. On the other hand, the Forty-Eighters (commemorating the suppressed revolution of 1848) were the main opponents of the regime: they campaigned for an independent Hungarian army and a personal union between Austria and Hungary (or, depending on leadership, reinstation the full sovereignty of the Hungarian Kingdom).

While the pre-war era cannot be well described by the dominance of a single charismatic figure, many important leaders stand out who shaped the course of public policymaking. The Compromise was struck between Franz Joseph (in his position of King of Hungary) and Ferenc Deák, a liberal politician who, despite the fact that he did not participate in any cabinets, became the leader of the Sixty-Sevener Party (which was also named after him until his death in 1876). Besides them, a father and son duo of the governing party made a mark on the policy agendas of the era. Kálmán Tisza, who governed between 1875 and 1890, is the second longest-serving Hungarian prime minister in Hungarian history (after Viktor Orbán). His son, István held the position of prime minister (twice between 1903 and 1905, and from 1913 to 1917) and was generally responsible for the rigidity that hallmarked the last two decades of Austria-Hungary.

An investigation of this period allows us to gain an insight into the policy decision-making of a regime in which a limited democratic operation was subject to both external and internal constraints. An external factor in this context was the fact that, as part of the Austro-Hungarian Monarchy, Hungary enjoyed only limited sovereignty in certain policy areas (similarly to the relationship that prevails between the European Union and its member states today). Among the internal factors that apply to this situation, certain institutional elements must be highlighted, such as limited, censitary suffrage, an unelected upper house of parliament, and the king's right of veto. In this chapter, we review how the policy agenda was set during this time and how the dynamics of policy decision-making evolved.

THE POLICY AGENDA OF THE DUAL MONARCHY

The most striking feature of Hungarian domestic politics in the age of Dualism may be that the central cleavage defining the political divisions of the time was not based on the divergent assessments by the major parties of some contentious policy issue or some matter of high symbolic relevance. Instead, it was based on their conflicting ideas about the preferred constitutional arrangement (Vida, 2011: 22).

The major parties of the time were organized around the question of whether they accepted the Austro Hungarian Compromise of 1867 (where acceptance also implied that they more or less rigidly insisted on it, too) or whether they rejected it either in part or comprehensively. Partial acceptance here entailed that the parties in question wanted to restrict the scope of jointly governed policy areas, by insisting on an autonomous Hungarian monetary policy or by simply demanding a personal union, for example. Other political forces, which organized themselves around ideals that did not neatly map on this cleavage, failed to break through politically during this period. Correspondingly, one would expect that the relationship with Austria would occupy a prominent role on the policy agenda of the period in question.

As was already discussed in Chapter 3, which laid out a basic overview of Hungarian regimes, the Dual Monarchy failed to arrive at a widely accepted solution to the key issues of suffrage and national minorities. At the same time, it should be noted that widespread dissatisfaction with the prevailing rules governing voting rights was not unusual at the time. Even though an expansion of voting rights was a common corollary of the rise of democratic regimes in the second half of the nineteenth century (Przeworski, 2008), the process of extending full universal suffrage was not fully realized until the middle of the twentieth century in Western Europe, either (see France: 1944; Switzerland: 1971).

Although in the beginning, the Hungarian regime under the Dual Monarchy was relatively generous in international comparison in terms of extending the right to vote to comparatively wide swathes of the population, the limited suffrage was not appreciably expanded thereafter until the final years of the regime (although no actual elections were held based on the new suffrage rules). Despite the relative immutability of the rules governing voting rights, the issue of expanding suffrage remained on the policy agenda throughout this period.

The third topic that our review must extend to is the question of national minorities. During the period of Dualism, roughly half the Hungarian population was made up of persons who were affiliated with the various national minorities e.g., Romanians, Germans, Slovaks, Croatians, Serbs, and Rusyns (Marácz, 2012). Already in the early years of the regime, these groups began to publicly promulgate their elaborate demands and manifestos aimed at asserting their rights as national minorities.

Legislation regulating the rights of national minorities (the scope of which was unprecedented at the time in European comparison) was adopted relatively quickly in the year following the Compromise, and regional autonomy was extended to Croatia-Slavonia. Nevertheless, the national minority parties continued to be actively involved in politics, and questions surrounding the rights of national minorities were among the major issues on the policy agenda of the period. An important factor driving this was that even though censitary suffrage led to a substantial underrepresentation in parliament of national minorities—on account of the educational and financial requirements on which the right to vote was made contingent—representatives of national minorities were nevertheless continuously present in the National Assembly (Iudean & Popovici, 2011) throughout the entire period. In some cases, they represented their own distinct minority parties, while in other cases, they were affiliated with mainstream Hungarian parties. Just to cite one example, Zsivkó Bogdán (in Serbian Živko Bogdan), an ex-mayor of Nagykikinda (now Kikinda in Serbia), and an ethnic Serb was elected as an MP of the Sixty-Sevener National Party of Work in 1910.

The Dual Monarchy created the modern Hungarian state, along with its key subsystems, such as the market economy, modern public education, and some basic pillars of the welfare state. Already in the first half of the nineteenth century, the Hungarian elite had designated industrialization as a vital goal for Hungary (Janos, 2000: 126–127), but the process only gained traction under Dualism. This has increased the importance of industry, anti-trust legislation, and transportation infrastructure and they all played a major role in the policy agenda.

Another important long-term policy goal of the period was the elimination of illiteracy, along with the creation of a modern education system. It is thus no coincidence that several key political figures of the period were in charge of the Ministry of Religion and Public Education (e.g. József Eötvös or Ágoston Trefort; see Bölöny and Hubai (2004: 224–246). Thus, it should come as no surprise that education, too, took a prominent place on the policy agenda at the time.

Although the process was largely only completed in the second half of the twentieth century, the creation of a social safety net and a welfare state in Europe began much earlier, in the second half of the nineteenth century (on the early welfare states of Central Europe, see Saxonberg & Sirovátka, 2019: 149). The financially most underprivileged strata had no parliamentary representation during that period, but as we shall see in the following, they still had some influence on the policy agenda. This led to the issue of the welfare state to appear frequently on the policy agenda of that period.

Although Dualism mostly coincided with the long peace period following the Congress of Vienna (1814–1815), it did ultimately lead up to World War I, and as a result in the final years of the regime, the issue of defense funding had moved to the fore on the policy agenda. Examining defense policy is also instructive because, unlike the previously discussed subject matters, this issue was managed jointly with Austria, and as a result understanding its presence on the agenda will improve our understanding of how the Austro-Hungarian Monarchy worked (Péter, 2006).

Rather than homing in on some other major public policy area, at the end of our chapter, we focus on certain specific features of policymaking during this period. Thus, we first analyze what impact distinct parties and stakeholders had on the policy agenda. In this context, we take a closer look at the efforts by the People's Party, which represented the interests of the Catholic Church, to thwart secularization. We also investigate how the regime reacted to an exogenous shock. To this end, we will review the presence on the agenda of the phylloxera epidemic that decimated vast tracts of the vineyards across Europe, Hungary included.

In explanation of the aforementioned topic emphases, it is important to point out that since the Dual Monarchy was in place until 1918, numerous policy areas either did not exist at the time (e.g., nuclear energy or space research) or became more relevant only later (e.g., the environment and energy policy, which were continuously present on the agenda already back then but only exerted a marginal impact). Another important limitation of intra-era comparison is that Hungary did not operate as a fully sovereign state at the time since certain policy areas (e.g., defense and foreign policy) were (overwhelmingly) governed by institutions that the Hungarian regime operated jointly with Austria.

Some policy areas (e.g., customs and currency policy) were governed based on mutual agreements between Austria and Hungary (which the National Assembly had the power to approve or reject, however). In terms of these issues, and notwithstanding the lack of independent Hungarian jurisdiction over these policy subsystems, the texts of the petitions, party manifestos, interpellations, and prime ministers' speeches during this period regularly reflected on them. We also found some legislative efforts that focused on these issues (the reason is that the Hungarian state had to contribute its share to the upkeep of the joint military and that the National Assembly had to ratify international agreements).

The absence of jointly governed issues is most striking in the Hungarian budgets. Foreign policy expenditures were nigh completely absent from the Hungarian budgets until 1912 (and even thereafter they only played a negligible role), while for the most part the military was not funded through the Hungarian budget, either with one qualification. It was marginally present in the budgets throughout the entire period because of the Hungarian *Honvédség* (which literally translates as homeland defense; this is the designation used for the Hungarian military to this day) and its small number of active-duty personnel. The relative unimportance of defense as a topic was also reflected in the fact that the military expenditures in the Hungarian budget barely budged even during World War I (that is they remained at the same levels as during the pre-war period). Military expenditures were funded from the joint budget of the Austro-Hungarian Monarchy, and they took up over 90% of its spending (Hungary typically contributed between 6 and 12% of its own budget to the operation of the Monarchy).

Decision-Making and Information Processing in the Era of Dualism

Counter to the neo-absolutist attempts in the preceding era, the Hungarian regime under the Dual Monarchy developed comparatively effective mechanisms for collecting policy information. By holding regular and competitive parliamentary elections in Hungary after the Austro-Hungarian Compromise of 1867 (Köpf, 2001), the public policy process incorporated robust institutionalized feedback mechanisms, as well as avenues for the grassroots expression of values and interests. This was true even if the right to vote was still limited by the census (roughly a quarter of adult males had the right to vote) and even though elections were often accompanied by pressure and manipulation exerted by the governing party—especially through the use of the open ballot (Pál, 2014).

Despite the presence of such problems, there was genuine political competition in the elections (although in this predominant party system, control of the government only changed hands as a result of election outcomes twice, in 1906 and in 1910 (Stone, 1967)). The competing parties stood for real alternative ideals and goals, and the electoral success (which did not necessarily imply an election victory) achieved by these parties through their distinctive manifestos and initiatives generally resulted in reshaping the policy agenda.

One example that will be discussed below is that of the People's Party, which represented Catholics, while another interesting case is that of the National Anti-Semitic Party. Its electoral gains did not result in policy changes that reflected the goals of the party; its temporary successes in the 1880s, which demanded anti-Jewish measures, in fact, proved to be an own goal. The end results led to the emancipation of Hungarian Jews with full and equal rights, along with the equal recognition of their religion (see Hartman, 2000: 167–168).

Since the majoritarian electoral system used at the time forced every representative in parliament to be personally accountable to their electors, the mechanism for enforcing voters' expectations was relatively straightforward. The second method whereby pressure from below could be brought to bear on the political elite was the very diverse and free press of the period (Buzinkay, 2016: 177). Although most newspapers were openly committed to some political course, for the most part, this did not imply that they operated as flat-out party outlets. Thus, for example, the conservative *Magyar Hírlap* allotted space equally to the National Party and the Constitution Party.

The political positions of the newspapers occasionally shifted independently from those of the political parties. Thus, while *A Hon* initially supported the Forty-Eighters, in the 1870s it gravitated toward the Sixty-Seveners, all the while the *Pesti Napló* followed the opposite trajectory (Buzinkay, 2016: 202). At the same time, however, the role of the press as an independent source of control with a distinct impact on the policy agenda was somewhat limited by the fact that several prominent journalists of the era also assumed political roles, with some serving as MPs (such as the famous novelist, Mór Jókai).

The final element that needs to be highlighted on the input side was petitions (Pesti, 2002: 66). The Standing Order of the Hungarian parliament during the period of Dualism allowed for any citizen (thus not only those who had the right to vote) to file petitions with the National Assembly through any member of parliament (municipalities like counties and major towns, however, were allowed to turn directly to the speaker). Once the petition had been processed by the Petitions Committee, its substance was debated by a specialized committee, which answered the petitioner and simultaneously forwarded the petition to the state agency that was responsible for handling the given issue.

The only restrictive filter that applied to these petitions was the legally enshrined responsibility of the member of parliament to make sure that a petition presented would not contain any expressions that were "derogatory of the constitution, the laws, the dignity of the house, or of public morals" (The Standing Order of the House of Representatives, 1868). Petitions could also be filed with the House of Peers, through any member of the upper house. Only in the 1880s was a new rule added to the Standing Order, which provided that a petition would not be put on the agenda if a decision on the underlying matter had already been taken during the given session of parliament (The Standing Order of the House of Representatives, 1887).

Petitions thus provided a constant and institutionalized instrument for the members of the public to indicate their preferences to the legislature, and citizens frequently availed themselves of this possibility. And as a matter of fact, petitions often led to actual policy decisions. Thus, for example, industrialists in the southern Hungarian town of Versec (today Vršac in Serbia) and the western Hungarian town of Nagyszentmihály (today Großpetersdorf in Austria) jointly petitioned for an amendment of the social security law in December 1912, which parliament ended up adopting in June 1913.

This highlights the fact that although the various actors in the policy-formation process were obviously unequal, the range of actors who had some measure of relevant impact was nevertheless relatively broad, and this added to the democratic character of the regime. Those who had the right to vote also played an important role owing to the institutional structure. Although the political parties of the era were cadre parties (that is they had a tiny membership and were passive outside campaign periods), it was precisely on account of their loose organization and extremely limited party discipline that they allowed for the active involvement and input of local elites in politics.

A network of lobby groups and NGOs emerged, some of which (e.g., the Chamber of Commerce and the Chamber of Architects) were involved in institutionalized forms of collective bargaining (Strausz, 2011: 31 and 33), while trade unions also appeared on the scene (Lénár, 2011: 52). The policy influence of social organizations is readily apparent in the fact that numerous preeminent politicians assumed a leading role in such organizations, and many lobbyists of the respective organizations owed their appointment to a seat in the upper house of parliament to their engagement in NGOs (e.g., Konrád Burchard-Bélaváry as the influential representative of the mill industry, or Leó Lánczy, who played the same role for banks). Another key player was the previously mentioned press. Finally, although their role was less prominent, virtually every citizen, local government, social organization, or societal group could play a role, primarily by using petitions.

Looking at the second phase of policy decision-making—the legislative process—it is worthwhile to start with a discussion of one of the most powerful tools at the disposal of individual members of parliament, namely interpellations, which can be used to influence the policy agenda. In the Hungarian system of parliamentarism, interpellations constitute the most potent form of parliamentary questions. Their power lies in the fact that once the minister who was thus questioned has had the chance to respond, the National Assembly votes whether to approve their answer (Sebők et al., 2017).

Although this institution had not yet been introduced in the Standing Order adopted by the Hungarian parliament in 1848—the first modern Hungarian parliamentary Standing Order as we understand them today—as a matter of practice, the representatives frequently availed themselves of this instrument. Its first formal regulation occurred in 1868, but at the time it was not yet enshrined in the rules that the member of the cabinet who had been subject to the interpellation was required to answer the question.

The first detailed regulation of interpellations occurred in 1875, and from that point on, the interpellated person had 30 days to react (a substantial latitude that they rarely abused, however, as they almost always provided substantial answers within a reasonable timeframe that was commensurate with the complexity of the question). The response by the minister was followed by a brief debate in which the representative was given the option to respond to the minister's initial reaction, while the minister, too, was allowed to offer a rejoinder. The representative was also allowed to ask for a second rejoinder, which the National Assembly approved without fail; starting in 1913, the right of a second response was extended to members of parliament without the need for a vote by the plenary. Up until 1875, interpellations were presented as part of the parliament's regular agenda, but after 1875 they were scheduled after the regular agenda (Kozári, 2005: 106).

Nevertheless, the most important function of the National Assembly was legislation. Although bills could be submitted to parliament by representatives, in reality only the government's own bills were adopted as laws (Pesti, 2002: 60). The bills were first debated by groups of representatives that were drawn by lot, but over time these randomly constituted committees (the so-called "classes") would be supplanted by the increasingly important specialized standing committees. Once they had been reviewed in committee, the bills were forwarded to the plenary, which first voted on the amendments proposed (mostly initiated by the representatives) and then on the bill itself.

All bills had to be approved by the House of Representatives (the lower house of parliament) as well as the House of Peers (the upper house); the latter operated very similarly to the lower house, albeit its procedures were far more informal. The promulgation of laws also required royal assent (Péter, 2012a: 321). Apart from the laws, the most important statutes were decrees, which were mostly issued by the ministers. Thus, it is readily apparent that the most important domestic policy venues were parliament, the government, and, to a limited extent, the court of the king. For this latter, the official policy venues included the bodies handling the joint affairs between Austria and Hungary, i.e., the delegations, the joint

Council of Ministers, and the king himself. Among the non-official policy venues, the leadership of the governing party needs to be highlighted.

The most serious impediment to the operation of parliament was obstruction. This was a widespread problem in Europe at the time, as the parliamentary oppositions sought to counterbalance their minority position and the resulting exclusion from power by trying to prevent the adoption of decisions they opposed by proffering needlessly long and excessive numbers of speeches, which was made possible by the absence of restrictions on speaking time (Müller & Ulrich, 2014: 316–317). The Hungarian opposition's predilection for obstruction was massively exacerbated by the predominant party system and the lack of alternation in power (Péter, 2012b: 128–130).

The instrument of obstruction was mostly used by the opposition Forty-Eighters to prevent military conscription; to reform the homeland defense forces; related to amendments of the Standing Order aimed at eliminating obstruction itself; the adoption of the budget; as well as the usage by Croatian national minority representatives for enforcement and expansion of the rights of ethnic Croatians. As we shall see below, the major waves of obstructionism (1872, 1889, 1898, 1903–1906, 1908, and 1912), all ended up crippling the operation of the legislature, while they also brought down the incumbent government at the time (about changes in government during this period, see Bölöny & Hubai, 2004). The fact that the opposition had the possibility to retard, successfully avert, or substantially alter the process of legislation by way of obstruction speaks to the democratic character of the underlying regime.

Obstruction proved most effective as a political instrument when it successfully thwarted the adoption of budgets that had been submitted for parliamentary approval at the output end of the public policy cycle. The method for adopting the budget was more or less the same as that for adopting laws: an affirmative vote by the two chambers was followed by the necessary royal consent. Especially during the time of escalating obstruction, the government occasionally found itself compelled to ask parliament to vote on a so-called indemnity, which meant that affairs continued to be managed based on the previous year's budget. There were four occasions when the opposition successfully prevented parliament from adopting indemnities (1899, 1903–1904, 1905–1906, and 1910), which led to what we would call a government shutdown today, when both the levying and collection of taxes were on halt and only the most pressing state expenditures continued to be paid (Pesti, 2002: 69).

Overview of the Databases

The biggest obstacle in the way of analyzing the Hungarian policy agenda prior to World War I is the dearth of data, as well as the raw, unprocessed nature of the data that are actually available. Since no national opinion surveys were conducted prior to 1945, we know very little about the preferences of the public or the issues that interested them, and what we do have are merely indirect indications of these preferences and interests (Henn, 2018: 151).

That does not imply, however, that we are completely in the dark in trying to gauge said preferences. The previously discussed institution of petitions allows us to capture at least those issues which the politically active segment of the public—the individuals, organizations, and bodies, which could publicly articulate their interests—considered the most important issues of the day. The number of petitions submitted to the National Assembly was humongous. Despite the fact that our chapter analyzes only five years of such submissions, even in this short period, 2336 petitions were filed.

Although the Hungarian press was flourishing and diverse in the period between 1867 and 1918, their output has not been processed in academic studies, at least not based on the CAP methodology. Nevertheless, in our chapter, we drew on the contents of several print titles published in that period and performed a dictionary-based analysis of their articles. The range of publications thus reviewed included the most prominent Sixty-Sevener and Forty-Eighter publications, as well as the newspapers affiliated with the electorally less influential conservative, Catholic, social democratic, and radical parties.

The third input element we reviewed were elections and the manifestos of the parties that competed in them. It is important to stress that we had to narrow the scope of our analysis because of the vast number of parties, and hence we ended up focusing on all Hungarian (i.e., non-minority) parties that won more than a single seat in the elections of this period with available party manifesto. One characteristic feature of this period is that the parties of the time—which were usually cadre parties—did not release new national manifestos before each election. Typically, they would publish a manifesto (and it would not be uncommon for such a manifesto to be a speech by the party chair) at the time of their election, but they would only release a new one thereafter when the political situation changed substantially (the source for the party manifestos: Mérei & Pölöskei, 2003).

Thus, the governing Sixty-Sevener party released a manifesto in 1867, in which it set out its stance on the Austro-Hungarian Compromise. It followed up with another platform in 1875, when it merged with the moderate segment of the Forty-Eighter opposition, and a new one in 1910, on the eve of the election concluding the single term in the government of the Forty-Eighters during the entire period of the Dual Monarchy. The speeches given by party leaders early in the terms of the newly elected National Assemblies, the proposals for the response to the king's speech, as well as the governing side's legislation during the foregoing term of parliament were often viewed as party manifestos. This left us with a total of 19 party manifestos to analyze in our study, and of the 1030 sentences in these texts, roughly half had some policy relevance.

Initially, the terms of the National Assembly spanned three years, but after 1887 their length was extended to five years. Nevertheless, on several occasions, it became necessary to diverge from that timeframe. Thus, early elections were held in 1896, 1905, 1906, and 1910. Furthermore, the term of the National Assembly elected in 1910 was extended due to the World War, and thus no elections were held in 1915 (Szabó, 2008: 156). Overall, therefore, a total of 14 elections were held during this period, including the National Assembly elected in 1865, which laid the constitutional foundations for the coming era.

Having looked at the input side, let us now turn to the process segment of the public policy cycle. The various governments' goals and preferences are well captured by the speeches of the prime ministers upon taking office. In the present chapter, we will review five such inaugural speeches by prime ministers in the National Assembly during this period. Gyula Andrássy was Hungary's prime minister between 1867 and 1871 (and then went on to serve as the foreign minister of the Austro-Hungarian Monarchy for another eight years), and it was during this time that the foundations of the Hungarian regime under the Dual Monarchy era were laid.

The longest-reigning prime minister of the period—and second after Viktor Orbán in all of Hungarian history—was Kálmán Tisza. In addition to his long term in office, Tisza is also worthy of a more detailed examination because he launched the predominant governing party of the period. It is also essential to examine the first terms as prime minister of Sándor

Wekerle since it was during his time in office between 1892 and 1895 that Hungary's secularization was completed, and the country transitioned to the Gold Standard. We will also examine another of Wekerle's three terms in office, namely the second, which began in 1906 and ended in 1910. This term was unique in the period of the Dual Monarchy since Wekerle led a government supported by a coalition of former opposition parties. Finally, we examined the inaugural speech of the second term as prime minister of the defining politician of the period, István Tisza, who served as the head of government again between 1913 and 1917.

At this stage of the policy decision-making process, another instrument of interest is parliamentary questions put to the government. We found that of the various types of parliamentary questions, interpellations were most prominent in Hungary in the period investigated, with a total of 3371 being asked. Laws constitute the second type of the units of obser-vation that can be examined in the mid-section of the policy cycle. In addition to laws, our examination also extended to decrees. While 2115 laws were passed during the period in question, 12,490 decrees were adopted.

On the output side of the policy cycle, we looked at Hungarian national budgets (we only refer to the joint budgets of the Austro-Hungarian Monarchy in passing). Initially, budgets were adopted for the calendar year, but in 1914 (before World War I broke out) a change was enacted to the effect that the budgetary year would span the time from the second half of the given calendar year to the first half of the subse-quent calendar year. The various methods of obstruction deployed by the opposition were primarily aimed at preventing the budget from being adopted. On four occasions obstruction was successfully used to prevent even the indemnity from being adopted, thereby causing an extra-legal situation in which Hungary operated without an effective budget. Our database lacks data for the years 1910, 1915, and 1918.

An Empirical Description of the Agenda During the Period of Dualism

The General Features of Individual Policy Arenas

The range of societal actors who could submit petitions was extremely diverse. It included private persons, elected bodies (the local govern-ments of counties or towns, for example), various social groups (e.g., the "socialist citizens of Hódmezővásárhely"), and individual protesters all the way to NGOs or business associations (e.g., the Budapest Coffee Industrial Society or the Association of Feminists). Petitions were often submitted by the members of marginalized groups (such as for example national minorities, members of religious sects, workers, peasants, or women). As time progressed, the issues addressed in the petitions began to reflect a level of coordination.

Thus, for example, on December 13, 1912, the National Assembly's Petition Committee processed 194 petitions demanding universal, equal, and secret suffrage. Thirteen of these had been filed by local governments, six by NGOs, 60 by demonstration participants, 11 by local party organizations, and 90 by groups of individuals (a petitioner was allowed to submit more than one petition on the same issue). During the five years we analyzed, public affairs predominated in the petitions from the very start, but the share of petitions focusing exclusively on private matters (e.g., petitions requesting individual pension hikes) declined massively during the entire period, from 32% in the beginning to 9% in 1875 and 1% at the turn of the century.

Among the petitions we examined, the most frequently raised questions pertained to government operations (24.8%), civil rights (17.9%), and agriculture and land ownership (9.4%). The environment and immigration, by contrast, were totally absent (an explanation for the latter may be that even though the issue of Russian Jews was generally on the agenda during this period, in the years we focused on it was not a major issue).

Since we do not have a comprehensive overview of the media agenda during this period, we only used data on media in the case studies of the present chapter. Such a limitation did not apply to our analysis of the party manifestos, however. The length and substance of the various manifestos differed substantially. While in 1891 the Independence Party presented itself to the voters with a manifesto featuring 171 sentences, the manifesto of the Centre-Left Party in 1868 was a mere three sentences long.

The average manifesto was 54.21 sentences long, but the standard deviation was rather substantial (48.44). The impact of the few massively long manifestos is apparent in the low median value of 31 sentences. The policy content of the manifestos also differed substantially. Thus, only 34% of the National Party of Work manifesto in 1910 had policy relevance, while in the same year 95% of the National Farmer Party manifesto revolved around policy-related matters. The issues touched upon most often in the party manifestos were government operations (34.3%), macroeconomics (19.7%), and national defense (10.4%), while the environment and energy policy were completely absent.

In the elections investigated, the governing Sixty-Seveners Party generally won around 60% of the seats (there were only few occasions when it did substantially better than that) throughout the entire period with the exception of the term from 1905 to 1910. Apart from the governing party, a constant presence in parliamentary life were the opposition Forty-Eighters, who won roughly 20% of the seats except for the elections before 1875 and in the period between 1905 and 1910 (in the earlier period, their share of the seats ranged between 30 and 40%, while in 1905 and 1906 the coalitions they led actually won the election).

Apart from these, there was also a Sixty-Sevener opposition with a more conservative outlook throughout most of the period in question, and it tended to win between 10 and 20% of the seats in the elections in which it actually competed (thus between 1875 and 1896, and from 1905 to 1906). Relatively enduring, albeit less relevant, players on the scene were the national minority parties, which represented the non-Hungarian population (after 1867, their share of the seats was consistently below 10%) and the Catholic People's Party, which held around 5% of the seats from 1896 on.

Apart from the aforementioned, there were also several marginal players, a variety of small parties that won a few seats here and there but their role was negligible. In any given election, the number of parties that would win seats ranged between three and nine. It is important to stress that because of the censitary suffrage, other ideological streams that could otherwise draw on significant support in society—such as the social democrats, the Christian socialists, the farmers' parties, and the national minority parties—were either not represented at all or were massively underrepresented (Vida, 2011: 22–25).

The lengths of the five prime ministers' speeches increased steadily and without fail; Andrássy's speech at the beginning featured a mere 17 sentences, while István Tisza's oration at the end of the period in question consisted of 113. At the same time, although the trend was not as strictly linear, the share of contents without policy relevance followed the opposite trajectory, declining over time. In the case of Andrássy, 70.6% of his speech did not touch on policy issues, while only 22.1% of the sentences in the speech delivered at the start of Wekerle's second term were devoid of such contents; but at the beginning of István Tisza's second term, the corresponding figure increased again, to 34.5% (which is still a lower value than the one we saw in the speeches of Andrássy or Kálmán Tisza, however). The policy issues most often touched upon in the speeches we analyzed were government operations (30%), macroeconomics (15.6%), and civil rights (12.2%). In the meanwhile, environmentalism, energy policy, immigration, housing, and cultural policy were completely absent.

An average of 240.8 interpellations was presented per term, but at 206, the median value was lower. This indicates that some terms featured an extraordinarily high number of interpellations. The standard deviation was 156.8, and part of the discrepancy is explained by the fact that the terms of parliament differed in length: Prior to 1887, they lasted three years, while subsequent parliaments were elected for five-year terms. That is why it makes sense to analyze interpellations in an annual breakdown. This reveals that an average of 64.8 interpellations was presented per year, while the median value was 57 and the standard deviation was 36.2, which makes the relative standard deviation significantly lower in the annual breakdown than in the breakdown by terms.

The fewest interpellations were presented during the term from 1905 to 1906 (1 interpellation) and in the year 1905 (2 interpellations). The reason for these low figures was the aforementioned crisis. The Austro-Hungarian monarch, Franz Joseph, did not want to call on the opposition coalition led by the Forty-Eighters to form a government, but with their parliamentary majority, the opposition was able to paralyze the operation of the Fejérváry cabinet appointed by the king. Parliament virtually stopped operating entirely during this term, which was ultimately cut short.

The highest number of interpellations were presented during the term from 1910 to 1918, but the reason was not that the representatives were substantially more active during this period: among the ten years with the highest number of interpellations, only two, 1911 and 1916, fell into this term (the latter year came in tenth), but since no elections were held on account of the World War, the term ended up spanning over eight years. In annual breakdown, the highest number of interpellations were presented early in the period investigated, between 1869 and 1873, and then during the crisis of the constitutional model (1903, 1907–1908, and 1911).

Looking at the trends, we find that the number of interpellations was exceedingly high between 1870 and 1873, around 1897, in 1903, between 1907 and 1908, in 1911, and between 1916 and 1918. At the other end of the spectrum, the relevant figures were exceedingly low between 1885 and 1889 and from 1899 to 1901, in 1905, and between 1912 and 1915. The reasons behind the fluctuations varied over time. As part of the reform of the National Assembly's Standing Order in 1872, interpellations were regulated far more strictly than previously (although no explicit restriction on their number was introduced), as a result of which their number dropped substantially.

In 1899, 1904, 1908, and 1912, the Standing Order was amended with the explicit goal of suppressing obstruction, to reduce the number of opposition speeches and the range of opposition activities in the house. The low point in 1905 can be explained by the previously discussed interruptions in the operation of parliament. It is apparent therefore that the occasional bursts in the number of interpellations were typically "reined in" by amendments of the Standing Order.

Interpellations were predominantly presented by members of parliament who were affiliated with the opposition parties, typically, 70–80% of all representatives who interpellated. Apart from a few brief periods early in the era, the exception to this general trend was only the term from 1906 to 1910. As a solution to the crisis of 1905/1906, the former Sixty-Sevener governing party, the Liberal Party, was dissolved prior to the 1906 election, with the result that only opposition representatives ran in the election, and the coalition of parties that ascended to power after the election won 90% of the seats. As a result, the small number of opposition representatives, consisting mostly of national minority members of parliament, could not dominate the interpellation agenda, even though at 33.8% their share of interpellations in this period did far exceed their share of seats in the legislature.

The main arena for interpellations was the lower house of parliament; only 2.3% of interpellations were presented in the upper house during the period investigated, and there were two terms when none at all were presented in the upper house. And that is hardly surprising—the Habsburg princes, aristocrats, senior church figures, leading state officials, and prominent peers appointed to the chamber most probably found it undignified to spend their time holding the government accountable.

Juxtaposing the share of interpellations presented by each party with their respective share of seats, we find that the share of interpellations by the Forty-Eighter parties was generally two to three times higher than their share of seats, while in the case of the Sixty-Sevener parties, the corresponding ratio tended to be between a quarter and a fifth. The polit-ical parties whose outlook did not conform to the defining cleavage of the period were also highly active; this included the socialist and Farmer Party representatives, as well as the members of parliament for the Catholic People's Party.

As for the representatives of the national minorities, except for two highly active periods (1869–1875 and 1901–1910), they were typically more subdued when it came to the use of interpellations. Only in one term—from 1906 to 1910—were Croatian members of parliament over-represented among those who submitted interpellations; that was because they engaged in obstructionism during this period. In terms of the policy areas that were most likely to be the subject of interpellations, govern-ment operations (17.8%), civil rights (11.2%), and defense (9.7%) were the most important, while the environment (0.1%), energy policy (0.3%), and housing (0.4%) were raised least frequently.

Turning now to legislative production, the high number of laws adopted during the period in question is an indication of the substan-tial role played by parliamentarism in Hungary at the time. The average number of laws adopted was 152 per term, while the median figure was 157. With a standard deviation of just 75.5, legislative production was relatively steady over time. Yearly fluctuations are even smaller. The average annual number of laws adopted was 40.7, with a standard devia-tion of 15.9. As a result of the previously discussed crisis in 1905/1906, not a single law was adopted in the year 1905 or in the term from 1905 to 1906. The term in which the highest number of laws was adopted was that from 1910 to 1918 (for the same reason as higher than average interpellations: the protracted length of this term).

The legislature was most active in the first decade and a half of the Dual Monarchy, and then in the years leading up to World War I. The number of laws adopted was below average from 1877 to 1878, in 1885, 1903, 1905, and between 1909 and 1911, which largely coincides with the years when interpellations (and obstruction) were used most actively. The policy areas that saw the most legislative output were transportation (19% of all laws), government operations (15.7%), and macroeconomics (13.8%), while the policy areas with the least legislation were immigration (0.05%), environment (0.1%), and energy and culture (0.2%, respectively).

We also found relatively stable figures over time for the numbers of decrees adopted. The major inflection point was the outbreak of World War I. Before the war, the average annual number of decrees was 202.6, but with the onset of the hostilities, it soared to 593 (with median values of 197 before the war and 636 during the war). The standard deviation was relatively low in both periods (56.4 and 125.2, respectively). The difference between the two periods, and specifically the growing influence of the executive in this emergency situation, was obvious in this context, too—even the lowest annual number of decrees during the war was higher than the highest corresponding annual figure in the period of peace preceding it. At the same time, it is vital to point out that the surge in executive activity did not imply that the legislature's work had dried up; there was barely any change in the rate of parliamentary activity, which was a key difference to the trend we observed in the context of World War II (see Chapter 6).

The official initiator of the bills was always without fail the government. In the absence of an appropriate apparatus to assist them with the process, individual representatives generally did not even try to sponsor bills in parliament. Instead, they presented their policy initiatives either in the form of parliamentary speeches or as proposals for resolution. In the event that the latter was adopted, the National Assembly called on the government to draft law(s) with the specific content proposed.

Thus, our examination also needed to consider how often a representative would not use an interpellation to hold the government to account but to advance policy proposals. Anywhere between 20 and 40% of interpellations tended to proffer some initiative, and interpellations by government party and opposition representatives were similarly likely to feature some type of policy proposal (but the relevant figures for representatives affiliated with the government exhibited a greater volatility, while they were relatively stable over time for opposition members of parliament). The interpellations that referred to some type of initiative most often concerned government operations (16.2%), transportation (11.8%), and civil rights (9.8%), while they were least likely to focus on the environment (0.2%), energy (0.3%), and housing (0.6%).

Finally, the average length of the budgets we examined was 834 line items (the median value was 829.5), and the standard deviation had a middling value of 353.6. The shortest budget was that of 1868 (161 items), while the longest was 1913 (1571 items). As of the turn of the century, we found a rising trend in the number of line items in the budget.

Fulfilling Electoral Promises and Policy Responsiveness in the Dual Monarchy

We analyzed five inaugural speeches by prime ministers during this period to gain a better understanding of the decision-making process under Dualism. The speeches in question can be clearly assigned to one of two distinct categories. The 1867 speech by Gyula Andrássy and Kálmán Tisza's 1875 address were succinct to the extreme, they merely outlined the rough contours of the principles they wished to follow during their terms, and hence the speeches included few promises and touched on but a few policy areas. The speeches by Sándor Wekerle and István Tisza form the other group with their greater emphasis on specific pledges and policies.

Andrássy used a mere 17 sentences to highlight the principles he wished to follow, while Tisza used 22. A common feature of both speeches was that portions of them overlapped not only with the governing party's agenda but also with the manifestos of the opposition parties. Almost the entirety of Andrássy's speech was devoted to the Compromise, and for the most part, it was devoid of policy content, featuring a mere five sentences that went beyond rhetorical pronouncements. As part of the limited policy content he discussed, he promised to lay the foundations for local self-governance and parliamentarism in line with the manifesto of the moderate Forty-Eight-leaning Center-Left Party, as well as to uphold the union with Austria and a separate constitutional Hungarian state within the latter, in line with the program presented by his own Deák Party. The desire for local self-governance was also manifest in the petitions submitted to the legislature. During his four-year term, Andrássy ended up realizing the relatively vague promises he made in his inaugural speech.

The 22 sentences in Kálmán Tisza's 1875 speech are also few and, moreover, only 11 of them had public policy relevance. The latter also mostly pertained to the Compromise, primarily its economic dimension. Thus, in line with the pertinent petitions, as well as the manifestos of the Sixty-Sevener Liberal Party and the Forty-Eighter Independence Party, Tisza mentioned the proposal to set up a Hungarian central bank (without making a firm commitment to do so), and, echoing the manifestos of his own party and of the conservative Right-wing Opposition, he pledged to uphold the customs union with Austria. He promised to preserve the political system created by the Compromise, in line with the manifesto of the Right-wing Opposition.

In light of the global economic crisis of the time, his decision to forge unity and follow the petitions and various party manifestos—those of the Liberal Party, the Independence Party, and the Right-wing Opposition (hence all the relevant political players of the period) makes sense. Like Andrássy, he largely kept the promises he made; only the separate Hungarian central bank did not come into being at the time (although he had not unequivocally committed himself to its creation anyway), and it took a while, until 1880, to make good on another of his pledges and for the budget to become reliably nearly balanced in the long-term.

The speeches by Sándor Wekerle and István Tisza form another distinct group. They were far longer (Wekerle's 1892 address consisted of 41 sentences, while his 1906 speech went on for 77, and István Tisza's 1913 speech featured 113) and they mostly consisted of policy-related text (75.6% of the sentences in Wekerle's first speech featured policy content, and this was true of 87.9% of his second speech and 64.6% of István Tisza's, too). As compared to the previous group, their speeches were far more detailed and touched on more policy areas, proffering specific proposals concerning the areas they addressed.

In his 1892 speech, Sándor Wekerle promised to deliver on several initiatives that had been proposed in petitions, including the regulation of veterinarian medicine and expanding Hungary's military capabilities. In outlining his promises, he could not draw on the governing party's manifesto, since no new manifesto had been published. He did end up incorporating several elements of the opposition parties' manifestos into his own speech. In line with the platform of the Forty-Eighter Independence Party, he promised to emancipate the Jewish religion (that is he promised to include it among the religions recognized by the state and to ensure its representation in the Upper House of parliament), the introduction of civil birth and marriage registries, and the free choice of religion for children.

The expansion of Hungary's military capacities was also initiated by the Independence Party, although this move had also been requested by several petitions submitted to parliament. Industrial development and the reform of the Hungarian high court, the Curia, had been urged by both the Independence Party and the conservative National Party. In line with the manifesto of the National Party, Wekerle's promises included government support for agriculture. He fulfilled all of these promises without fail during his tenure as prime minister. In some areas (e.g., agriculture), the spending increases were distinctly small, but the change did go in the direction which the prime minister had laid out in his inaugural speech. Wekerle also made several promises that reflected his own initiatives. He kept a majority of those promises, too. The budget remained balanced and the spending on remedying the massive damage wrought by the phylloxera epidemic—which will be discussed below—was slightly increased; a police unit was introduced to guard agricultural lands; the pace of expanding railway and water transportation infrastructure was accelerated; and water management expenditures were increased. The municipal system was reformed; the legal status of civil service employees was regulated; criminal procedure was codified; and Hungary entered into new commercial agreements, especially with Eastern countries.

In line with the commitments laid out by Wekerle, the country's foreign policy alliances and the Austro-Hungarian compromise remained in place. However, contrary to his promises, he failed to reform or nationalize public administration; he did not take action to rein in electoral fraud; and the operation of administrative courts, disciplinary proceedings in public administration, and the legal status of civil servants were not codified.

Although Wekerle's speech at the beginning of his second term as prime minister in 1906 was similar in these respects to the speech that marked the start of his first term, the cabinet that set out to implement these was backed by a far more volatile, extremely unstable majority coalition in the National Assembly. From the various demands advanced by petitions, Wekerle's government only committed itself to the idea of creating a distinct customs area, and even that promise went ultimately unfulfilled.

Of the parties in the coalition, the Catholic People's Party and its manifesto appear to have exerted the greatest impact on the government's platform. The cabinet adopted the People's Party's—ultimately unrealized—calls for the autonomy of the Catholic church; the streamlining of public administration; the adoption of a new election procedure law; the creation of stricter worker protection laws; and the increased support for small and medium-sized enterprises. Although in line with the manifesto of the People's Party, a form of industrial representation for workers was ultimately realized, and there was a slight improvement in the situation of agricultural laborers, ultimately the law concerning the latter—which critics derisively referred to as the "canning law"—was the subject of intense and varied criticisms.

It was denounced by workers and their representatives because of the restrictions on their free movement during the agricultural season and the decision of the lawmakers to retain the possibility of administering corporal punishment at work (although at the same time the law did also impose increased social obligations on the landowners toward their laborers and it improved working conditions for children and women, while it also introduced mandatory rest days and made it easier to switch jobs). Of the policies proposed in the brief and vague manifesto of Wekerle's own conservative Constitution Party, the government adopted the promise of returning the budget-making process to parliament and the pledge to approve the Hungarian contribution to the Monarchy's joint budget, which were all fulfilled.

As for the promises that did not feature in any of the party manifestos, emigration was regulated; health and accident insurance schemes were introduced for workers in the commerce and industry sectors; the civil and criminal codes were reformed, as were the tax system. Public education (with a greater emphasis on teaching Hungarian language), the Curia, and the land registry system were revamped; railway construction continued; the pending financial agreement with Croatia was ratified and Croatian autonomy was preserved; and, finally, an order was issued to draft new recruits into the joint military of the Monarchy. In line with Wekerle's promises, spending on industrial development and healthcare was increased, and there was also a small uptick in the budgetary outlays on agriculture and social policy.

However, his government failed to realize a significant portion of the pledges it made. Hence, it failed to implement currency reform or the reform of church funding; it did not introduce a social security scheme for pensioners; no unions were established to represent agricultural workers and no credit system was created for agriculture. Universal suffrage remained elusive as did the possibility to cast vote in every settlement instead of only constituency centers. The population sizes of electoral districts were also not adjusted to make their distribution more balanced. There was no reform of public procurement or of the efforts to combat corruption; rural cultural centers were not shored up; priority development was not provided for water transportation; the position of local governments was not strengthened; the vocational training system was not overhauled; and industrial arbitration was not introduced.

There was also no currency reform; the more extensive public use of the Croatian language was not authorized; nor was there a land reform dividing up parcels of land to distribute among at least some of the landless agrarian population. Furthermore, in the spirit of the compromise reached with the sovereign, even before taking office, the government abandoned one of its most important pledges, namely the promise to reorganize the military along national lines, to symbolically strengthen its Hungarian characteristics. It came as no surprise, then, that the coalition quickly lost its majority in parliament. By 1909, the coalition had collapsed, the Independence Party split, and ultimately the Constitution Party joined with former members of the Liberal Party to create a new Sixty-Sevener governing party, the National Party of Work. Thus, in the early elections held in 1910—four years into the five-year term—the share of seats held by the former opposition parties dropped from 90.3% in 1906 to a mere 27.1%.

As the last inaugural speech in our sample, we looked at the address by István Tisza as he embarked on his second term as prime minister in 1913. This was the longest among the speeches examined, and its structure was roughly similar to Wekerle's inaugural addresses. Because of World War I, Tisza would fail to deliver on most of his promises. At the same time, his speech gave more room to outside initiatives than any of the others we analyzed. Among the petitions examined was the call for adopting a new Civil Code; the reform of the notary's office and of press regulations; as well as the expansion of voting rights. The government eventually implemented these promises.

Among the petitions that reached the National Assembly was the— ultimately realized—call for the creation of a workers' insurance scheme (which was also part of the manifesto of the National Farmer Party), while in line with the manifesto of the leading party of the government, military spending was increased and the conflict with Austria was smoothed over. The promise of retaining the Monarchy in an unchanged form was also kept. Nevertheless, despite pledges to that effect, no new universities were established, the autonomy of the Catholic church also went unrealized, as did the reform of rural public administrations, and a new regulatory scheme governing urban investments.

Although the promise to overhaul the public administration of Budapest was not present in any of the other documents we examined, it was nevertheless implemented. At the same time, the government did not deliver on several issues. Thus, it failed to come to an agreement with the national minorities, especially the Croatians; to increase and make more consistent the state funding for protestant denominations; to regulate labor strike laws; to reform public elementary and secondary education as well as legal education; to reform criminal law and criminal procedure; to reorganize county-level public administration; to implement new regulations governing the appointment of public administration officials; as well as the implementation of centralized state control over the police.

In conclusion, we need to stress that our analysis was not comprehensive. We only examined five of the 19 governments during this period, although the total time these five cabinets spent in office spanned 29 years, over half of the entire in-period question. It nevertheless clearly emerges from our data that all these governments without exception took into consideration the proposals in the petitions—which were the best tool they had for surveying the needs of the public—they had received, and that they adopted proposals from the platforms of both the parties supporting the government and the opposition forces. It is apparent that a substantial proportion of outside proposals and proposals that overlapped with the demands of other actors on the one hand, and the government's own initiatives on the other, ended up being implemented.

We found the highest share of unfulfilled promises in the case of the second Wekerle cabinet, which makes the subsequent electoral defeat of his coalition unsurprising. What is noteworthy is that István Tisza's second government managed to deliver on a major portion of his promises (albeit still only a minority) despite the fact that only the first year of his term coincided with the pre-World War I peace period, and for the remainder of the term, the Tisza government had to operate as a war cabinet. The high level of responsiveness on the part of the government unequivocally highlights the democratic principles underlying the regime's operation despite its apparent shortcomings when it comes to a universal suffrage or free and fair elections (by secret ballots) in the twenty-first-century sense.

CASE STUDIES: IMPORTANT AND CHARACTERISTIC POLICY AREAS OF DUALISM

The Constitutional Debate: An Unresolved Structural Conflict

As we noted previously, one of the main debates during the period of Dualism in Hungary was the issue of relations with Austria (Vida, 2011: 22). This broader issue implicates aspects of several codes of the Comparative Agendas Project (CAP) policy codebook. Because of the joint central bank, it partly concerns *macroeconomics*; the issue of relating to previous political regimes partly concerns *civil rights*; the joint military touches on *defense*; the customs union on *foreign trade*; joint foreign operations on *international affairs*; while the issues concerning the political structure also allow for including some of the units of observations with the code for *government operations*. This issue was continuously present on the parliamentary agenda of the period in question covering 5–10% of interpellations and bills before parliament. We only observed exceptionally high values in the early years after the emergence of the Dual Monarchy, and for the aforementioned reasons, the issue was not reflected in the Hungarian budgets of the period.

At the same time, a review of the petitions, party manifestos, and inaugural speeches of the prime ministers yields divergent findings. Although the issue was constantly present in the party manifestos, it only played a preeminent role at the time when the new regime was launched and only moved to the fore again when the regime was in the throes of crisis in 1905 (in these two periods, the presence of the constitutional issue on the agenda exceeded 40%). Outside these two periods, it was always below 25% (although for a constitutional issue, this is still a very high value).

Since the Compromise was reached only in 1867, the issue did not figure in the petitions before the Andrássy government assumed office, and subsequently, its share continued to remain under 20%. As the 1905 crisis set in, however, it jumped to 49.2%, which was followed by its near total disappearance by 1913. Its share of mentions in prime ministers' speeches was typically not high, the exception being the inaugural address of Kálmán Tisza in 1875; that exception is hardly surprising, however, since as the former leader of the moderate Forty-Eighter opposition, Tisza had to commit to the basic principles of the Sixty-Seveners.

Voting Rights: The Unresolved Tension Between Liberalism and Democracy

The expansion of suffrage was a central issue on the European policy agenda, including the Hungarian agenda, starting in the nineteenth century all the way to the mid-twentieth century (and in some places even further—Przeworski, 2008). We examined it by drawing on the CAP codes related to voting rights. Our findings show clearly that there was continuous pressure from society during this period to extend suffrage to larger swathes of the population; this was also manifest in the high number of petitions concerning voting rights. Over time, this desire took on an organized form, and the increased social coordination was reflected in the fact that in the year before Prime Minister István Tisza's second term in office, the National Assembly addressed 368 petitions concerning voting rights (although not all of these called for universal suffrage).

At the same time, the issue did not figure prominently in the prime ministers' speeches before the turn of the century. Among the inaugural addresses we examined, only Sándor Wekerle's and István Tisza's second speech at the launch of their respective terms in office reflected on suffrage, although they both talked about it at some length. Among the party manifestos, that of the Independence Party addressed the issue most intensely; of the 21 mentions in the various party manifestos, 16 were in the documents published by that party.

It was also obvious that this was a topic that concerned the opposition forces throughout this period. The Sixty-Sevener Deák Party only addressed the issue of voting rights before it took office in 1867, its subsequent manifestos did not allude to it, and neither did those of its successor parties. But it was present in the conservative National Party's 1891 manifesto, as well as in the manifestos of the Catholic People's Party in 1895 and of the Farmer Party in 1909. It was also continuously present on the agenda of interpellations, with an overall share of that agenda that was roughly balanced over time. And although several bills concerning voting rights were adopted during this time, universal suffrage was not in fact introduced during the period of the Dual Monarchy. However, the right to vote was massively expanded in 1913 and in 1918 (although no elections were actually held based on these new laws).

The National Minority Issue: Lacking Responsiveness

One of the most vital and contentious problems during the time of the Dual Monarchy in Hungary stemmed from the fact that roughly half of the population back then did not belong to the ethnic majority group, i.e., the Hungarians (Marácz, 2012). Using the CAP codebook, we can capture this issue through codes 201 (minority rights, ethnic discrimination, and racism) and 2001 (local governments—filtered here to reflect the issue of Croatia-Slavonia).

Although census voting as practiced in Hungary typically resulted in the underrepresentation of the less educated and financially worse-off national minorities, the National Assembly nevertheless continuously featured national minority representatives throughout the period investigated (Iudean & Popovici, 2011), sometimes as representatives of their own national minority parties, and sometimes as the representatives of other nationally organized non-ethnic parties. The share of seats held by distinct national minority parties never exceeded 6%, however. Nonetheless, in part on account of the national minority politicians in parliament, and in part due to those in the Hungarian political elite who evinced a sensitivity toward this issue (which did not necessarily imply that they supported granting minorities greater rights), the issue of national minorities constantly figured on the agenda of interpellations.

The same cannot be said of the National Assembly's legislative agenda; apart from a few major laws, no distinct regulations on the subject were adopted by parliament. Consequently, the share of budget spending on this issue also did not change substantially during this period. The notion of collective rights did not feature in the policy debates of the time, which focused on first-generation human rights, and thus the institutions associated with the exercise of collective rights were not given budgetary funding. The treatment of the Croatian minority was one of the exceptions to this general trend, since they were given regional autonomy.

The other exceptions were the recognized Greek Orthodox churches affiliated with the Serbian and Romanian national minorities. In the prime ministers' speeches, the issue of national minorities tended to come up toward the final years of the Dual Monarchy, and, in the speeches we reviewed, it was most often mentioned by István Tisza. Prior to 1912/1913, it only cropped up sporadically on the agenda of the petitions. At that point, however, the issue gained massive traction (although this was not the result of the activities petitioners affiliated with national minorities or advocating on their behalf but of the efforts of those who saw a threat to Hungarian supremacy in the aspirations to extend more generous voting rights to national minorities).

The Issues Related to Flourishing Capitalism

Already in the first half of the nineteenth century, the industrialization of Hungary emerged as an important objective for the Hungarian elite (Janos, 2000: 126–127). That is why the issue of industrialization is also crucially important in the period we investigated. We used the observations falling under the CAP codebook's codes 108 (industrial policy), 10 (transportation), and 1520 and 1521 (corporate management and small businesses) to analyze it. We found that although industrialization was never a major topic in the party manifestos of the period, it was nevertheless continuously present as an issue.

This was true, even as in the prime ministers' speeches it was only addressed by Sándor Wekerle. This is hardly surprising given that he was the only economic expert to occupy the office of prime minister among the four heads of government whose inaugural speeches we analyzed. Paradoxically, however, the opposite dynamic prevailed when it came to petitions; no industrial policy-related petitions were filed in the years prior to the entry into office of the Wekerle cabinets, while in the other three years before the entry into office of the new cabinets were analyzed, there were large numbers of such petitions.

With respect to the interpellation agenda, we found that the issue was heavily present before 1872/1873, but thereafter its presence on the agenda dropped to a level of around 5%, and only started rising again after the turn of the century. A similar dynamic played out with respect to budget spending on such priorities, except that the decline experienced between 1870 and 1877 was followed by a steadfast trend of incremental growth all the way to the start of World War I.

The reason behind the decline in the 1870s was in all likelihood the economic crisis that had previously emerged and was still ongoing at the time (see Good, 1978). In contrast to the trends we observed in the abovementioned policy arenas, industrial development played an inconstant but on the whole major role in the legislation adopted during this period, especially with respect to railway construction (at this time, the building and launching of new railways lines were still regulated by laws).

Education: The Creation of Modern Public Education

The elimination of illiteracy and the creation of a modern system of education were designated as important long-term objectives during this period, and we used CAP code 6 to track the role of this policy area. It is no coincidence that several major Hungarian politicians in the period of the Dual Monarchy served as Ministers of Religion and Public Education (e.g. József Eötvös, Ágoston Trefort and Loránd Eötvös; see Bölöny & Hubai, 2004: 244–246).

The issue was also heavily represented in the petitions filed during this period (most prominently in 1912 through 1913, when 152 education-related petitions were submitted). Interestingly, however, for a long time, it did not feature in the inaugural addresses of the prime ministers. Only toward the end of the period analyzed did it appear on those agendas, too. However, at that point, it became the object of substantial attention in these speeches. Similarly, the issue of education was only sporadically present in the party manifestos and its role only became more pronounced toward the end of the period.

Nevertheless, it was very much present on the agenda of the National Assembly all throughout the era, as a large number of interpellations were presented on the subject while every few years the legislature also adopted bills pertaining to education. It is also important to point out that up until World War I, the share of education spending in the budget increased steadily, rising from 0.6 to 0.7% at the beginning to 5.9 and 6.1% toward the end.

Creating a Social Safety Net: The Seeds of a Welfare State

Although the better part of the process of crafting social safety nets and building welfare states in Europe fell into the second half of the twentieth century, this process actually began much earlier, in the second half of the nineteenth century. Our analysis of this issue was not limited to CAP code 13 (social welfare) but also comprised 3 (health) and 5 (labor). The data show clearly that on the input side of the public policy cycle, the number of relevant petitions was continuously high and rising. By contrast, social welfare issues appeared only sporadically in the party manifestos before 1909.

With respect to the activities of the National Assembly, we found that the issue was more or less consistently and rather prominently featured on the parliamentary agenda, and among the interpellations specifically, its share increased over time. We also observed a slow and incremental increase in budget spending on social issues, with the result that while such outlays made up only 2% of all expenditures in the early phases of the period investigated, their share had grown to around 4% by the end.

National Defense: From Constitutional Debate to Gearing up for the World War

The issue of national defense was obviously of vital importance in the run-up to World War I, but for the purposes of our analysis, it also serves as a useful illustration of how the institutional framework can explain the varying presence of a given issue on different agenda arenas (Péter, 2006). A significant portion of the petitions addressed this issue (although these mostly served to express the petitioners' rejection of the joint Austro-Hungarian army) and there were also a great many interpellations on this issue; laws regulating defense were continuously being adopted, and both party manifestos and the inaugural addresses of prime ministers alluded to the issue.

Yet, despite this massive attention, the share of defense in the budget expenditures barely budged throughout this period. The reason was the institutional setting that we previously discussed: The joint military of the Austro-Hungarian Monarchy was financed through the joint budget of the Monarchy, which meant that military expenditures on the joined forces with Austria did not show up as a distinct spending item in the Hungarian budget. An examination of the role of national defense on the agenda nevertheless provides a compelling test of the relevance of our data. The count of interpellations and petitions concerning this issue began to increase after the turn of the century, and their surge in these arenas was especially pronounced during the World War as well as during the series of uprisings and Russo-Turkish War between 1876 and 1878, which ended up redrawing the map of the Balkans (Yavuz & Sluglett, 2011).

Anti-secularization: The Role of Issue Owners

The case of anti-secularization offers insights into the potential impact of issue advocates who have little public support but are neverthe-less prominent and widely recognized players in public discourse. While roughly two-thirds of the Hungarian population were Catholics and only a third were Protestants (also considering national minorities, the ratio was 60–22%), the latter group was massively overrepresented within the Hungarian elite (thus, for example, between 1884 and 1918, there were more Protestant than Catholic members of parliament among those representatives whose religious affiliation was publicly known).

At the same time, the Habsburgs, who nurtured close ties with the Catholic church, were able to limit the influence of Protestants in public life up until the time when the Compromise between Austria and Hungary was concluded. The Compromise and the competitive politics that emerged and took roots during the era of the Dual Monarchy proved to be a massive boon for the political influence of the Protestant elite. As a result of this new trend, which was exacerbated by the rising dominance of liberal thinking at the time, the Hungarian elite of Dual Monarchy considered the separation between the Catholic church and the state— which had been strongly intertwined before, primarily through the person of the monarch—as a self-evident proposition.

Many interpellations in parliament featured anti-Catholic or anti-clerical (although not atheistic) outbursts. As a backlash of sorts against the aforementioned anti-Catholic trend, there was a short-lived attempt already in the 1870s to organize a Catholic party. Ultimately, this effort proved unsuccessful, however (Vida, 2011: 64). The breakthrough for political Catholicism came with two papal encyclicals, the Quod Multum, penned in 1886 against Kálmán Tisza's "pagan" rule, and the 1893 Constanti Hungarorum, which rallied Catholics against the first Wekerle government's secularization policies. These developments catalyzed the emergence of the People's Party, the organized expression of Catholic thought and interests (Vida, 2011: 98–99).

Although the manifestos published by the People's Party were known for their level of detail and addressed a wide variety of issues as compared to what was typical of manifestos at the time, among the large number of issues they focused on (such as for example the openness toward national minorities, social policy demands, and the desire for expanding suffrage), our analysis will focus on the one particular issue that was the party's raison d'être: its calls for anti-secularization and the defense of Catholicism.

The party faced a hostile reception on the part of the liberal polit-ical elite (thus, after its first electoral run, procedural laws were changed to preempt the recurrence of a widespread phenomenon in the 1896 campaign, when Catholic priests used their pulpit to threaten those who planned to vote for other parties with eternal damnation, especially in the country's northern and western regions). As late as 1912, István Tisza would inveigh against universal suffrage by arguing that it would lead to a substantial expansion in the support of the People's Party. Nevertheless, the People's Party ultimately successfully integrated itself into Hungarian public life and became part of the governing coalition between 1906 and 1910, and then again from 1917 to 1918 (Vida, 2011: 98–99).

It is important to stress that the issue of secularization featured especially prominently on the agenda of the legislature during the terms immediately following the Compromise. By the 1880s, however, its relevance had faded. At the same time, state funding for the churches generally tended to decrease or stagnate. Around 1890, another wave of secularization set in, which was also reflected in the interpellation agenda: In the term from 1884 to 1887, there had been only two interpellations concerning the churches, but in the next term, from 1887 to 1892, their number increased from two to nine, and between 1892 and 1896 it surged to 22.

At the same time, new laws concerning recognized churches and secularization were adopted (thus, the Jewish religion was given equal rights with other recognized denominations, and a civil birth and marriage registry was introduced, along with the freedom to choose the child's religion). From the perspective of the churches, another major grievance was that between 1892 and 1896, the funding they received from the state budget dropped by 30% as compared to the foregoing term.

Even the mere parliamentary presence of the People's Party, which had been founded as a reaction to this trend, was enough to counter it to some extent. For one, the party's representatives were extremely active in shaping the parliamentary agenda, which was also reflected in the fact that in the term from 1896 to 1901, half the interpellations involving church-related issues were presented by their small caucus. In each of the four terms (in which the National Assembly was fully operational and not paralyzed by crisis), state funding for the churches increased substantially (by 70–80% as compared to the respective previous term).

The People Party's influence is also reflected in the fact that even World War I did not halt the pace of increased budget support for the churches. The highest rate of growth was achieved during the sole term when the party was in government for the entire duration of the term, between 1906 and 1910, while the second-highest pace of growth was achieved between 1910 and 1918—despite the war—when the People's Party was in office for the second time at least for a part of the term (although during that period, the rate of increase in state funding for the churches was barely lower than during the People's Party's first term in the National Assembly).

The successful operation of the People's Party was another illustrative example of the Hungarian regime's policy responsiveness during the time of the Dual Monarchy: The presence of a party with such a distinctive ideological outlook and with such a pronounced impact on the agenda was liable to effect substantial policy changes even though the party's public support was rather limited on the whole (even at the height of its electoral success in 1906, the People's Party won only 8% of the seats in parliament). In addition to the party's extraordinarily high level of engagement, ultimately it was also necessary for it to be acceptable as a coalition partner and to thus gain access to government positions; as a result, budget support for churches increased from 0.1% in the term from 1891 to 1896 to 1.1% by the final term of the National Assembly under the Dual Monarchy, from 1910 to 1918.

The Phylloxera Epidemic: Reaction to an External Shock

Besides the strategic moves of domestic and Viennese decision-makers, the Hungarian policy agenda also reflected external shocks on a regular basis. The grape louse (phylloxera) is an insect, which is native to America but appeared as an invasive species in Europe in the nineteenth century (it was first detected in 1866 in France, and in Hungary, its presence was first publicly recorded in 1875). It rapidly decimated the native grape species in Europe: the area of French vineyards dropped to half the pre-phylloxera levels, while in Hungary they went down to 57% of their original size (Beck, 2005: 17–18; Gale, 2003: 70–71). Needless to say, this caused widespread condemnation in a nation known for its traditional wine culture.

Although the epidemic only reached Hungary in 1875, the press outlets we reviewed as part of our research had already started reporting about its European spread in 1870 (initially, phylloxera was rarely mentioned, but the coverage devoted to the issue increased over time). Although the National Assembly passed a bill that was aimed at arresting the spread of phylloxera in the year following its appearance in Hungary, at that point the issue had not yet made it onto the mainstream of the policy agenda. The year 1879 was the turning point, and once phylloxera did enter the interpellation agenda, it immediately drew three questions, while its mentions in the press also surged (to 154).

In the following years, the state took more concerted action to scale back the epidemic: Four decrees were adopted to fight phylloxera in 1880, to be followed by two more in 1881, one in 1882, five in 1883, two in 1884, one in 1885; four laws were also passed between 1880 and 1883. Starting in 1881, the budget also allocated funds to scaling back phylloxera and restoring the destroyed vineyards.

By 1883, the media's interest in the issue had declined substantially (phylloxera was only mentioned 109 times as compared to the 174 mentions in the previous year), but then the issue kept surging again until 1890 (to a high of 409 mentions). Public attention on phylloxera peaked in 1890. In addition to receiving the highest number of media mentions in that year, 1890 was also the year when there were once again more than one phylloxera-related interpellations in parliament. Furthermore, between 1887 and 1892, 21 decrees were adopted concerning the epidemic.

The trend in the related budget expenditures also aptly reflects the attention on the issue: looking at the relevant budget data with a year's delay as compared to the other agendas (since the applicable budget during any given year was either completed or drafted in the foregoing year), we found that budget spending always grew most significantly (by one-third of the previous value annually) in the years when the media attention was most intense. The decline in media attention after 1890 led to a halt in the growth of phylloxera-related expenditures, and then to their stagnation. Still, in line with the pledge by Prime Minister Wekerle in his inaugural address, their share of overall spending did not decline.

Phylloxera then began to gradually fade from the press agenda. By 1903, its annual number of mentions had dropped to under 100, and after the outbreak of World War I, it was mentioned fewer than ten times a year. The last interpellation on the subject was presented in 1896; the last decree dates back to 1901; and the final phylloxera-related law was promulgated in 1906. Nevertheless, once the epidemic had been scaled back, budget support for the rehabilitation of vineyards surged massively for a while after 1896, although there were also an increasing number of years (1900–1901, 1905–1908, and 1917) when no funds at all were set aside for this purpose.

The efforts to combat phylloxera are extraordinarily well-suited for highlighting the responsiveness of the policy agenda during the time of Dualism. The phenomenon illustrates how an external shock was relayed by the media, how this was swiftly followed by the reactions first of individual members of parliament, and then by the institutions of the legislature and the government on the whole.

At the same time, it also reveals that the loss of media interest in the issue and the waning attention of representatives in parliament did not imply that the government, too, completely lost sight of the problem. Hence, five years after the last interpellation on the phylloxera issue in parliament, the government still drafted and adopted a decree on the subject, and ten years later the cabinet still proposed pertinent legislation which was adopted by the National Assembly. Moreover, even the relevant budgetary outlays reached their highest level after the media's attention had shifted away from the subject. This speaks to the long life-cycle of external shocks from detection to the mitigation of its lasting effects.

Conclusion

The Hungarian policy agenda in the period of the Dual Monarchy can be captured and successfully analyzed with the same tools we researchers use to study twenty-first-century public policy dynamics. One reason is that almost all of the institutions that define modern democracies existed already back then, and their functions were roughly similar to what the respective institutions do today. The other reason is that the various policy venues appear intuitively genuine, that is they appear to be reacting to and are in interaction with the challenges raised by the prevailing socio-economic environment.

This interaction between the socio-economic environment and the policy agenda was made possible by the instruments that allowed for feeding back into the policymaking process the changes in the wider environment (electoral competition, party manifestos, petitions, the press, and interpellations). The issue of national defense is a good illustration of how well our data work: The presence of national defense on the policy agenda was most pronounced when the Balkan wars were raging nearby, as well as during World War I, in which Hungary was directly involved. Our quantitative data also support what previous academic research posited about the role of the prevailing institutional setting; since the military was mostly funded through the joint budget of the Dual Monarchy, the share of military spending in the dedicated Hungarian budget barely changed during the period investigated.

Not only do our data appear valid and relevant, but they also exhibit characteristics that are similar to the trends we found in previous surveys of policy agendas (Baumgartner et al., 2009). We have found that the hypotheses of punctuated equilibrium and institutional friction both apply. The policy agenda of the period was open to change in response to certain influences, which was manifest in the diversity of issues on the agenda and the mutability of the latter. The responsiveness of the policy agenda is also reflected in the changing impact of the various issues over time. We were able to capture the seminal rise in the importance of industrial and education policy throughout the period in question, along with the growing importance of the social welfare safety net.

The generally democratic nature of the regime also becomes apparent in the deeper analysis of the decision-making process. Although the executive was a key player in decision-making, the involvement of a broad range of stakeholders allowed for grassroots initiatives to make their way through the policy cycle all the way to implementation, and even some opposition initiatives ended up being adopted by the governing party. The number of relevant policy players was extraordinarily high. Still, this responsiveness did not extend to all possible issues: When it came to the challenges national minorities faced, the Hungarian elite remained insensitive to social pressure to the very end.

The responsiveness of the regime was also apparent in the connection between the different agendas. The various policy arenas tended to react similarly to the same issue, and the changes we observed in one arena tended to correlate heavily with the changes in other arenas concerning the same topic. All of the above demonstrates that the agenda could react to and evolve in response to changes in the wider socio-economic environment; allowed for the implementation of major reforms pursued by the political elite (e.g., industrialization and education reform); and to cater to external shocks (e.g., in the case of the phylloxera epidemic). The appearance of new issue advocates or policy entrepreneurs (e.g., the People's Party with respect to the issue of anti-secularization) was also a prevalent feature of the political system.

The limits of Dualism-era policymaking were most conspicuous in those situations when an individual demand was aimed at challenging one of the cornerstones of the regime—regardless if that effort concerned the relations with Austria, the right to vote, or the issue of national minorities. The inflexibility of the regime when it came to these fundamental issues ultimately led to its descent into crisis, and as a result, it could no longer hope to survive following the defeat that the Dual Monarchy suffered in World War I.

Acknowledgment The author is thankful to Petra Ruff for the help regarding preparation of datasets.

References

Baumgartner, F. R., Breunig, C., Green-Pedersen, C., Jones, B. D., Mortensen, P. B., Nuytmeans, M., & Walgrave, S. (2009). Punctuated equilibrium in comparative perspective. *American Journal of Political Science, 53*(3), 603–620.

Beck, T. (2005). *A filoxéravész Magyarországon. A kártevő elleni küzdelem az első központi intézkedésektől az államilag támogatott szőlőrekonstrukciós hitelek lejártáig (1872–1910).* Magyar Mezőgazdasági Múzeum.

Bölöny, J., & Hubai, L. (2004). *Magyarország kormányai 1848–2004.* Akadémiai Kiadó.

Buzinkay, G. (2016). *A magyar sajtó és újságírás története a kezdetektől a rendszerváltásig.* Wolters Kluwer.

Gale, G. (2003). Saving the vine from Phylloxera: A never-ending battle. In M. P. R. Sandler (Ed.), *Wine: A scientific exploration* (pp. 70–91). Taylor and Francis.

Good, D. F. (1978). The great depression and Austrian growth after 1873. *The Economic History Review, 31*(2), 290–294.

Hartman, Z. (2000). A Jewish minority in a multiethnic society. During a change of governments: The Jews of Transylvania in the interwar period. *SHVUT* (9), 162–182.

Henn, M. (2018). *Opinion polls and volatile electorates: Problems and issues in polling European societies. First published 1998 by Ashgate Publishing.* Routledge.

Iudean, O. E., & Popovici, V. (2011). The elective representation of the Romanians in the Hungarian Parliament. *Studia Universitatis Petru Maior. Historia* (1), 121–146.

Janos, A. C. (2000). *East Central Europe in the modern world: The politics of the borderlands from pre- to postcommunism.* Stanford University Press.

Kozári, M. (2005). *A dualista rendszer.* Pannonica Kiadó.

Köpf, E. M. (2001). Electoral law in Hungary under the Dual Monarchy. *Hungarologische Beiträge* (13), 53–69.

Lénár, A. (2011). A szakszervezeti mozgalom gyökerei és fejlődési tendenciái a második világháborúig. In M. Dobák (Ed.), *A gazdasági és társadalmi érdekérvényesítés starégiai és szervezeti modelljei a 20. században* (pp. 33–63). L'Harmattan.

Marácz, L. (2012). Multilingualism in the Transleithanian part of the Austro-Hungarian Empire (1867–1918): Policy and practice. *Jezikoslovlje, 12*(2), 269–298.

Mérei, Gy., & Pölöskei, F. (2003). *Magyarországi pártprogramok 1867–1919.* ELTE Eötvös Kiadó.

Müller, W. C., & Ulrich, S. (2014). Procedure and rules in legsilatures. In S. Martin, T. Saalfeld, & K. Strøm (Eds.), *The oxford handbook of legislative studies* (pp. 311–331). Oxford University Press.

Pál, J. (2014). Electoral corruption in Austro-Hungarian Transylvania at the beginning of the dualist period (1867–1872). In A. Colin (Ed.), *Patronage et corruption politiques dans l'Europe contemporaine* (pp. 105–126). Recherches.

Pesti, S. (2002). *Az újkori magyar parlament.* Osiris Kiadó.

Péter, L. (2006). The Army Question in Hungarian Politics 1867–1918. *Central Europe, 4*(2), 83–110.

Péter, L. (2012a). The aristocracy, the gentry and their parliamentary tradition in nineteenth-century Hungary. In M. Lojkó (Ed.), *Hungary's long nineteenth century: Constitutional and democratic traditions in European perspective. Collected studies by László Péter* (pp. 305–342). Brill.

Péter, L. (2012b). Ius Resistendi in Hungary. In M. Lojkó (Ed.), *Hungary's Long nineteenth century: Constitutional and democratic traditions in European perspective. Collected Studies by László Péter* (pp. 113–133). Brill.

Przeworski, A. (2008). Conquered or granted? A history of suffrage extensions. *British Journal of Political Science, 39*(2), 291–321.

Saxonberg, S., & Sirovátka, T. (2019). Central and East Europe. In B. Greve (Ed.), *Routledge handbook of welfare state* (pp. 148–161). Second Edition. Routledge.

Sebők, M., Kubik, B. G., & Molnár, Cs. (2017). A törvények formális minősége: empirikus vázlat. Trendek a magyar politikában – 2. In Zs. Boda & A. Szabó (Eds.), *A Fidesz és a többiek: pártok, mozgalmak, politikák* (pp. 285–310). MTA TK PTI – Napvilág Kiadó.

Stone, N. (1967). Constitutional crises in Hungary, 1903–1906. *The Slavonic and East European Review, 45*(104), 163–182.

Strausz, P. (2011). Gazdaságirányítás, szakmai közigazgatás és érdekképviselet – Kamarák 1945-ig. In M. Dobák (Ed.), *A gazdasági és társadalmi érdekérvényesítés stratégiái és szervezeti modelljei a 20. században* (pp. 19–35). L'Harmattan Kiadó.

Szabó, D. (2008). A magyar parlamentarizmus az Osztrák-Magyar Monarchiában (1867–1918). In Zs. Boros & D. Szabó (Eds.), *Parlamentarizmus Magyarországon* (pp. 11–160). ELTE Eötvös Kiadó.

Vida, I. (Ed.) (2011). *Magyarországi politikai pártok lexikona 1846–2010*. Budapest: Gondolat Kiadó – MTA – ELTE Pártok, Pártrendszerek, Parlamentarizmus Kutatócsoport.

Yavuz, M. H., & Sluglett, P. (2011). *War and diplomacy: The Russo-Turkish war of 1877–1878 and the treaty of Berlin*. University of Utah Press.

CHAPTER 6

The Traditional Authoritarianism of the Interwar Period (1920–1944)

Ágnes M. Balázs

As we explained in the previous chapter, the Dual Monarchy fell apart in the aftermath of World War I, and in the process of the disintegration of the Austro-Hungarian Monarchy, numerous regions with Hungarians populations became incorporated into the territories of neighboring countries. From 1918 to 1919, the political system was extremely volatile, with a quick succession of three different regimes within the span of a year. Initially, left-wing politicians rose to power; the revolutionary Károlyi cabinet proved unstable, however, and was quickly ousted by a communist coup in May 1919. The communist takeover also marked the adoption of Hungary's first written constitution (Bodó, 2011; Siklós, 1988; Szabó, 2019: 160–163).

The ensuing period of the short-lived Hungarian Soviet Republic was highly volatile and political terror was widely used as instrument of power during this time. Finally, Romanian occupation and an anti-communist

Á. M. Balázs (✉)
National University of Public Service, Budapest, Hungary
e-mail: molnarne.balazs.agnes@uni-nke.hu

© The Author(s), under exclusive license to Springer Nature
Switzerland AG 2021
M. Sebők and Z. Boda (eds.), *Policy Agendas in Autocracy, and Hybrid Regimes*, Comparative Studies of Political Agendas,
https://doi.org/10.1007/978-3-030-73223-3_6

119

counterrevolution put an end to ongoing instability. The subsequent period is typically referred to as that of the White Terror (Bodó, 2011). It was followed by another transitional period from 1920 to 1925, which was marked by the gradual consolidation of the new regime and the efforts to lay the foundations for its long-term rule (Lorman, 2007).

The issue of legal continuity was an important one at the time, and a key question within the broader issue was whether the monarchy could be restored and, if so, whether the Habsburgs should be returned to the throne (Pócza, 2019: 143–145; Szabó, 2019: 163–164). In the meantime, Miklós Horthy, an admiral and leader of the anti-communist counterrevolution served as the de facto head of state (or regent) in the "Kingdom without a King." His rule was stable for the most part of the Regency between 1920 and 1946, but with the advent of World War II he gradually was forced by violence to ceded control to Nazi Germany and their domestic allies in the form of the Arrow Cross Party.

The Horthy Era from a Public Policy Perspective

The period between the two World Wars was—as Ilonszki (2000: 242) also emphasizes—one of continuous crisis. Ilonszki stresses three crises in particular. The first was the disintegration of the Austro-Hungarian Monarchy in the aftermath of World War I; the second was the Great Depression; and the third was the rise of the far-right toward the end of the interwar period. From a research perspective, these crises—practically wedged between two other crises (namely, the World Wars)—provide a fertile ground for exploring which policy areas were of preeminent importance during this period.

The disintegration of the Austro-Hungarian Monarchy and the concomitant emergence of a substantial cross-border Hungarian minority was a key turning in the nation's history. We assume that in the nation thus dismembered after World War I, deprived of a significant portion of its former territory and economic clout (Macartney, 1937; Pastor, 2003) as Hungary was, foreign policy issues would move into the foreground of the policy agenda around this time. Another area where the underlying problems would be likely to manifest themselves is foreign trade and defense (in the context of potentially reclaiming lost territories via military means).

In a country that was broken up and became Budapest-centered as a result, infrastructure and macroeconomic issues, too, would become more central (Tomka, 2020). We also need to keep in mind that this was the time when the League of Nations emerged, and hence a new type of international system was beginning to take roots (Amstrong, 1982); we would expect this to leave an imprint on foreign policy and foreign trade. In this context, revisionism and the issue of Hungary's integration into the incipient international system may also come up.

Another consequence of the way World War I ended, and specifically of the Trianon Treaty, is that Kunó Klebelsberg—in his position as the minister for religious affairs and education—and the political leadership at the time, particularly Klebelsberg's successor at the helm of the ministry, Bálint Hóman, saw education as one of the potential avenues for Hungary's resurgence following the harsh terms of Trianon (T. Molnár, 2019; Ujváry, 2016, 2018). We expect, therefore, that during Klebelsberg's term as minister (1922–1931) the share of education on the public policy agenda increased. It is also important to keep in mind that on account of the Great Depression, an external shock also struck in the 1930s (Clavin, 2000; Macher, 2017). This shock—just like the problem of the post-World War I restoration—was liable to influence the presence of macroeconomic issues on the agenda.

Reviewing the academic literature on the subject, we find that during the Horthy era—just as during the period of the Dual Monarchy- see the previous chapter—certain constitutional law issues were front and center. As for its form of government, the country was officially designated as a constitutional monarchy without a monarch, which is why public law literature has argued that the form of government and the monarchy were vital issues at this time (Takács, 2019). In later periods, this strand of research also reflected on other issues, such as what was commonly referred to as the Jewish Question or the appearance of the so-called "new directions of public law" (the increasing authoritarianism of the regime—Schweitzer, 2014, 2017b).

Three major constitutional reforms were discussed preeminently in the contemporary public law literature. The first two focused on the expansion of the respective powers of the upper house of parliament and of the regent (Horthy, who served as the head of state in lieu of a king in the, still, Kingdom of Hungary). The third was the introduction of secret suffrage, which was at the same time accompanied by measures aimed at preempting the anticipated impact of expanding the electorate—which was something that the elite at the time took a dim view of—, namely, the rise of anti-system parties (the far-right parties and the social demo and communists). This was meant to be forestalled by the introduction of covert plural (in practice: a weighted) voting scheme in which some citizens could cast more ballots than others (Balázs, 2016; Molnár, 1938; Püski, 2009: 13–14).

This leads us to assume that the issues of suffrage and constitutional reform would be prominently represented in the various policy agendas. The aforementioned constitutional reform package provides an excellent basis for a case study. This issue pertains to the third crisis mentioned by Ilonszki, while it also reflects on the Jewish Question which ultimately culminated in the Holocaust—our analysis tracked the presence of the Jewish issue on the agenda as well (Braham & Kovács, 2016; Gyurgyák, 2001: 110–196).

Based on our review of the relevant literature, we can also posit that the issues of agriculture and land reform were likely to be important during this time (Thompson, 1993). It is especially vital to examine the presence of the 1920 land reform and the issue of estate reform in general on the policy agenda, and to see how much the presence of agrarian issues was influenced by the emergence and entry into parliament in 1930 of a new agrarian party, the Independent Smallholders' Party. Since we examine the period between the two World Wars the presence of national defense on the policy agenda will also be examined.

THE LEGAL AND POLITICAL ENVIRONMENT OF POLICYMAKING IN THE HORTHY ERA

The form of state and government at this time was peculiar. Hungary was a constitutional kingdom without a king, and as of March 1, 1920, the country was led by Miklós Horthy, who held the position of regent (or governor) between 1920 and 1944 (see Takács, 2019, 2020). To a certain extent, the regent was meant to fill in as the monarch, but the two positions were not fully identical (thus, for example, the regent was not given the so-called supreme right of patronage, which means a right to influence the internal organization of the Catholic Church, e.g., by appointing bishops). Takács (2019: 139) further points out that the official form of state of Hungary is often characterized as a "regency" in the English-language literature.

In terms of mutual relationship between the head of state and the government, it was important for the prime minister to enjoy the confidence of the regent (Boros, 2008: 313). And, as we shall discuss in more detail below, the regent's powers were expanded in 1937 at the same time as the upper house of parliament was also vested with broader powers; the goal was to scale back the rising influence of extremist forces, but the effort ultimately proved unsuccessful. Despite the changes, the regent was not the primary actor in day-to-day policymaking in the period as Horthy was mainly responsible for setting the broader strategy centered around maintaining Christian/right-wing dominance in public life, reclaiming lost territories and retaining independence from world powers highly active in the region (notably the rising Nazi Germany).

Within this somewhat peculiar institutional and constitutional structure, the classic framework of policy agendas research (focusing on input, decision-making, and output phases of the policy cycle) is very much applicable to the period. Starting with the input phase, as the previous chapter presented, Hungarian politics was developed by the standards of the era with the occasional missing pieces. One such piece is the lack of public opinion polls, as such surveys were only conducted in Hungary after 1945 (Henn, 2018: 151). However, the institution of written petitions continued to persist, and it allowed for individual citizens, counties, the capital city and certain other municipalities, or organizations to ask the National Assembly to debate the issues they wanted to raise.

As for political and interest groups, during the first few years of the post-White Terror period, the various armed radical right-wing organizations, along with a variety of social organizations on the far-right, continued to operate, wielded substantial influence and functioned as rivals of sorts to the official governmental institutions. The process of repressing these groups on the whole even while coopting some of them into the regime took place from 1921 to 1922. The impact of these groups on decision-making was readily apparent in the fact that numerous policy decisions—including the so-called Numerus Clausus law to be discussed below—were largely introduced in response to pressure emanating from them (Paksa, 2012: 53–55).

Trade unions were also important players in policy creation and in providing actionable information to the government. As Lénár (2011: 59) highlights, by the end of the interwar period, trade unions had emerged as integral parts of Hungary's economic and social life. They were allowed to operate within the framework of the pact concluded between the government and the Social Democrats, with the provision that they could not engage in politics (Sipos, 1997a: 59–60). Nevertheless, on account of the strong personal ties between their respective leaderships and frequent cross-memberships between the trade unions and the Social Democratic Party, in actuality the trade unions were represented in both municipal committees and in parliament (Lénár, 2011: 59).

Another set of important actors during this period were the professional and commercial chambers, which cooperated with the government in order to realize their objectives (Strausz, 2011: 167) and were even represented in the upper house along with scientific and social organizations, as well as local governments (Püski, 2015: 86–91). In this, the upper house served as another policy venue for influencing policy decision-making. The Budapest Chamber of Commerce and Industry also exercised an important role in the reintegration of territories that Hungary regained, with the help of Nazi Germany, from its neighbors between 1938 and 1941 (Strausz, 2011: 173).

Moreover, it was also generally true that the Hungarian economic chambers assisted the government in it its management of the economic crisis (Strausz, 2011: 177), for example by offering their expertise to the government and the respective agencies of public administration (Strausz, 2011: 175). The issue of corporatism became increasingly relevant in Hungarian public discourse, not merely as a theoretical concept but also in the practical implementation of some corporativist features, which shall be discussed in further detail below as part of our review of how parliament worked during this time (Strausz, 2011: 178–179).

As P. Sipos (1997b) points out, there were organizations that operated in a clandestine manner. *Act III of 1921 on the More Effective Protection of the State and of Social Order* declared the Communist Party unlawful, and—although they were not explicitly named in the act—it also forced the Freemasons into illegality. Despite these restrictions, the period overall was—especially initially—marked by a large number of civil society organizations and a broadly based social discourse. By the end of the Horthy era, this rich organizational life and the concomitantly diverse public discourse had become substantially diminished, just like parliament, as the persecution of dissent was now extended beyond the usual targets of Jews and communists.

We also need to highlight the role of the Alliance of Etelköz[1] as a preeminent internal and non-official policymaking actor of the period; it was one of the most important secret societies at the time (Serfőző, 1976: 3). This organization identified with the Christian-national ideas propounded by the government, but its own ideological objectives were even more radical (P. Sipos, 1997b). The Alliance controlled both the legal and illegal irredentist organizations of the period (P. Sipos & Ravasz, 1997). Its ranks featured a host of prime ministers and ministers, members of parliament, senior civil servants, and it also included opposition representatives in parliament. In addition to prominent politicians, the Alliance also included the prominent leaders of social and business organizations, churches, as well as leading figures of cultural life and academia (Kántás, 2020: 7). Hence, they were pivotal players in the policymaking of the period.

Press freedom did not prevail during this era (Schweitzer, 2017a: 682–683). A large number of newspapers were shut down during the period of the Soviet Republic, and by June 1919 only five nationally distributed newspapers remained (Buzinkay, 2016: 323). On August 8, 1919, the first counterrevolutionary government issued a decree temporarily banning the publication of any newspaper excepting the government's own official paper, the Budapest Official Gazette based on the subterfuge of paper shortage. It was not until September 28 of the same year that the newspapers which had weathered the previous storm were allowed to be distributed again (Buzinkay, 2016: 327).

Buzinkay (2016: 331–332) also points out that all the governments after 1919 were wary of the press, and even though pre-publication censorship ended in December 1921, the press freedom and diversity that had characterized the period leading up to World War I did not end up returning. Legal instruments implemented by way of government decrees, such as the licensing of newspapers by the prime minister and the authority of the minister of the interior to ban newspapers, were used to exercise control over the press (Buzinkay, 2016: 332).

Fifty newspapers were banned between 1921 and 1931, while between 1931 and 1938 the publication of 52 newspapers was suspended, or their right to disseminate news was rescinded (Buzinkay, 2016: 332; Merziger et al., 2019; B. Sipos, 2011b: 120–127). Other methods used

---

[1] Etelköz is the name of the territory where Hungarians lived in the ninth century before conquering the Carpathian Basin.

in this period included media lawsuits and penalties (Buzinkay, 2016: 332–333). The end of the interwar period was once again marked by widespread newspaper bans. Nevertheless, as sources of information newspapers continued to play a pivotal role for decision-makers; this will be highlighted further below in the context of the discussion of the Jewish Question.

For a better understanding of the public policy decision-making process of the era, a brief introduction to the party system of the period is also in order. After the counterrevolution of 1919, the National Smallholders and Agricultural Workers' Party won power with 105 of 208 seats in parliament. They formed a governing coalition with the Christian National Union Party, which emerged out of a fusion of various Christian parties. Already in his inaugural speech, Prime Minister István Bethlen, the other defining politician of the era besides Horthy, announced his desire to merge the two governing parties.

The National Democratic Civic Party, a weak liberal force (with six seats) and the Christian Social and Economic Party were in opposition in the Parliament. The various Christian parties altogether held 85 seats in parliament at the time. Seven seats were held by independent members of parliament, while five seats went to other parties. The first parliament of the interwar period functioned as an interim legislature, its term lasting from 1920 to 1922. Furthermore, because of the ongoing White Terror, the Social Democratic Party of Hungary boycotted the election (Püski, 2006: 44–54). At the time, the public support of the Social Democrats in the Hungarian capital, Budapest, stood at around 15–20% (Hubai, 2001).[2]

István Bethlen was originally active in the Christian National Union Party, but the party was already on the verge of disintegration,[3] and as a result he left and joined the National Smallholders and Agricultural Workers' Party, which was divided between a left and a conservative wing at the time. Bethlen and his team took control of the party and thereby created the formation that became the predominant party of the period, the Unity Party. Although the party's leadership was conservative, it was

---

[2] Approximately 11,6% of Hungary's population (almost 1 million people) lived in Budapest at that time.

[3] The party presented two manifestos for the 1922 election: The respective manifestos of the Christian National Union Party's majority and minority (Püski, 2006: 48).

home to many ideological streams (Püski, 2006: 45–54).[4] The Unity Party and its various subsequent iterations in the position of the predominant party continued to govern Hungary from 1922 until the end of the interwar period, with a minor coalition partner. Their opposition was highly fragmented (Püski, 2006: 54–96).

In 1921 the Social Democratic Party of Hungary concluded a compromise with the government (the so-called Bethlen-Peyer pact, named after the respective leaders of the two parties), which allowed the Social Democrats to operate freely in exchange for abjuring anti-system activities (Lorman, 2003). There was also a Christian opposition that included legitimist (meaning they supported the Habsburgs' claim to the Hungarian throne), Catholic, and staunchly conservative parties. A sliver of liberal opposition was also present in parliament throughout the entire period (Püski, 2006: 65–66).

In 1924, seven representatives who split off the Unity Party established the Hungarian National Independence Party (Party of Racial Defense), a right-wing authoritarian opposition formation which also called for a stronger social safety net; it failed to gain popular traction. However, its leader, and a future prime minister, Gyula Gömbös, rejoined the Unity Party in 1928 and was given the defense portfolio in the cabinet in exchange (Püski, 2006: 59–61). In the 1930s, a new agrarian opposition party, the Independent Smallholders' Party emerged, and between 1931 and 1939 they were represented in parliament with 10–25 seats. By the end of the 1930s, the national socialist opposition was on the rise (Püski, 2006: 71–96).

Twice during the period, the predominant governing party underwent a total makeover. The first occurred when Gyula Gömbös assumed the prime minister's office in 1932 and the Unity Party (officially the Christian Agricultural Workers, Smallholders, and Civic Party) was renamed the Party of National Unity. Subsequently, in 1939, the National Unity Party changed its name to become the Party of Hungarian Life after the breakthrough of the far-right radical wing within the party (Püski, 2006: 77–79; B. Sipos, 2011a: 143).

With respect to the input phase of the policymaking process, it is also important to stress that universal and equal suffrage was not something that was seen as self-evident at this time. After the fall of the Soviet

---

[4] In addition to conservatives, the party also featured agrarian democrats, smallholders, and even politicians who were liberal through and through.

Republic, voting rights were still not regulated by law but by the Prime Ministerial Decree No. 5985/1919. This reflects the undemocratic character of the underlying regulation. From 1920 to 1921, three elections were held on the basis of this decree. Those who were denied the right to vote based on this regulation were only the category of individuals who had already been excluded from suffrage based on the People's Act I of 1918 (Ács, 2013: 25–27).

Two further decrees, however, also deprived those who had been previously convicted of criminal acts as well as monks of the right to vote. As a result of the aforementioned decrees, the share of the population who had the right to vote stood at 40%. Count Bethlen viewed this as too liberal, however, and he sought to reduce the electoral influence of the urban and rural middle classes. This desire gave rise to Prime Ministerial Decree No. 2200/1922 and to Act XXVI of 1925, which were used to restrict suffrage; their implementation resulted in a drop in the share of those who were entitled to vote, down to 30% of the adult population (Ács, 2013: 25–27; Hollósi, 2016: 57–58). It is also important to stress that secret ballot voting was not introduced until 1939, which is why even in the case of the limited segment of the population who actually could vote it was dubious whether the electoral choices reflected their free opinion.

With regard to the decision-making stage of the policy process, we need to briefly reflect on the way parliament worked at the time. Püski (2015: 429–490) breaks the history of the National Assembly between 1922 and 1945 down into three stages: the period marked by the rule of Prime Minister István Bethlen (1922–1928), the period of pre-war transition in the 1930s, and then the German occupation in 1944–45, the time of the puppet parliament (this latter falls outside the scope of our study as it did not allow for autonomous decision-making on behalf of domestic actors).

The short-lived Soviet Republic was followed by a transition period, and as a result the second chamber of parliament was restored only by Act XXII of 1926 (A. Szalai, 2013: 69). From that point on, the Hungarian parliament was once again bicameral, but an asymmetrical bicameralism prevailed (Püski, 2015: 296–307). The upper house was no longer mainly constituted based on the aristocratic principle: it now accommodated the representatives of a wide variety of institutions, such as academic and social organizations; the chambers of business and commerce; local governments; senior church representatives; and even the top brass of the military (Püski, 2015: 86–91). In this, the restoration of the upper house resulted in the increased influence on policy formation of numerous new actors in the political arena. The regent also had the right to appoint new members to the upper house. The authoritarian character of the regime is also apparent in the fact that some military officers were present in the upper house throughout the entire period (Püski, 2006: 239).

As a sign of the commitment to legal continuity with the foregoing period of the Dual Monarchy, the statutory framework governing the powers of parliament was not changed during the Horthy era (Pesti, 2002: 42). Constitutionally, sovereignty was vested in parliament, and in principle every representative had the right to sponsor a bill in the National Assembly. In practice, however, individual members of the National Assembly rarely exercised this right. The prevailing practice was for the representatives to call on the government to adopt a law on a given issue. While in the case of bills proposed by the government a debate in committee was mandatory, individually sponsored bills were generally just scheduled for debate but actually were never adopted or even debated (Püski, 2015: 160). Not all bills proposed by the government were necessarily adopted, however (Püski, 2015: 163).

Bills were drafted in a meticulous and intense process, and they were subject to multilateral consultations also involving experts and interest group organizations (Püski, 2015: 161–162) With an eye toward speeding up legislation, parliament's Standing Orders were amended several times during this period, first in the 1920s and then again during World War II (Püski, 2015: 169–174). Initially, and similarly to the Dualism period, the desire to rein in obstruction in parliament was part of the overarching objective that inspired the reforms of the Standing Orders (Pesti, 2002: 148–161).

Although in the 1920s the actual influence of parliament did not decline—since the legal framework governing its operations remained the same as in the period of the Dual Monarchy—in the 1930s the situation began to change (Pesti, 2002: 42). After 1930, enabling acts were adopted which gave the government the authority to enact decrees in the legislative areas provided for in the given acts. At first, these legislative authorities transferred to the executive concerned the management of the economic crisis, then the goal was to balance the budget; and still later, in 1939, they pertained to national defense (Pesti, 2002: 42–43; Püski, 2015: 180–185).

Of the aforementioned, the latter authorization was never debated in a plenary session (Pesti, 2002: 42–43; Püski, 2015: 180–185). The prime minister at the time, Béla Imrédy, had initially sought a general legislative authority for the government without any safeguards attached, which would neither be limited in time nor in term of its scope (that is to military matters, as it ultimately was—Pesti, 2002: 43). By that point, therefore, the role of parliament in policy decision-making had been substantially reduced, which was clearly indicative of the regime's increasing authoritarianism.

As for external influences on domestic policymaking, at the start of the Horthy period the peace treaty concluding World War I was an obvious factor, as well as Hungary's integration into the newly emerging international order. Yet at the same time, the dissolution of the Austro-Hungarian Monarchy freed budgets of their extant constraints when it comes to foreign affairs and the military build-up of the ensuing years. Finally, by the end of the period in question Nazi Germany had appeared as an unofficial actor with an influence over policy decision-making (a position that was subsequently formalized in the wake of the German occupation of Hungary in 1944); as the occupying power, Germany wielded a discernible influence over a number of policy decisions at the time.

DATABASES

In compiling our case studies on what was referred to at the time as the "Jewish Question," we treated the contents of the contemporary major dailies and weeklies as input factors. To identify the relevant items, we used a keyword search in the digital online archive Arcanum, which comprises copies of the major print media outlets published in that period. We used the terms "zsidó" (Jew, Jewish), "izraelita" (Israelite) and "héber" (Hebrew), and we examined how often these terms were mentioned in the various newspapers between 1920 and March 19, 1944.[5] Since—as we shall discuss in more detail below—many new newspapers were created during this period while others ceased publication, we did not aggregate the mentions by year but used average values instead.

In selecting the relevant newspapers, we strove to consider every print outlet that qualified as a major nationally distributed political newspaper at the time. In the process, we drew on Buzinkay's (2016: 319–390)

---

[5] For the year 1944, we considered data up until March 19, the day of German occupation, which is why our data for that year are incomplete.

comprehensive history of the Hungarian press as well as Arcanum's database of newspapers.[6] We looked at the contents of the newspapers that had weathered previous storms, which included several titles that had been banned earlier and were then distributed under a different name.

On the government side, we looked at both official bulletins and newspapers with semi-official links to the government, as well as newspapers affiliated with governmental figures. The outlets in the pro-government segment included the title called *Függetlenség* (Independence), which was published with some minor interruptions starting in 1933 and professed anti-capitalist, fascist, and Nazi views. Among the newspapers affiliated with right-wing parties and groups (Buzinkay, 2016: 361–363), we also included such papers as *Magyarság* (Hungarians), which was originally a legitimist outlet, was then affiliated with the Small holders' movement, and ultimately aligned itself with the national socialist Arrow Cross movement—and the Nazi-friendly *Új Magyarság* (New Hungarians). We further reviewed several anti-Nazi newspapers, as well as papers attached to the Freemasons and radical, anti-Christian, and liberal newspapers. On the whole, we reviewed 22 newspapers (while we counted those that were reestablished under a different name as one).

Among the parties that were active in the Horthy era, we selected the governing party and the relevant opposition parties, and we coded their manifestos sentence by sentence, assigning a major topic code to each sentence. Our source for the party manifestos was the book entitled *Hungarian Party Manifestos, 1919–1944* (Magyarországi pártprogramok 1919–1944) by Gergely et al. (2003). An important consideration in selecting the manifestos was to ensure that the party that had entered parliament with the largest share of seats would be included in our research, along with the most important opposition party.

It is important to add that the individual parties did not draft new manifestos before each election, nor were the party manifestos necessarily drawn up in election years. Indeed, toward the end of the period in question it would often happen that the party manifesto was drafted in the year following the election. In the interest of comprehensibility, the relevant figures depict the manifestos drawn up for the 1920 elections at the 1920-mark of the timeline, even though they were technically drafted in

---

[6]Arcanum Digitális Tudománytár [Arcanum Digitheca] https://adtplus.arcanum. hu/hu/ (Retrieved: April 21, 2020).

1919. The database comprising the manifestos of 18 parties, broken down sentence by sentence, features a total of 1670 observations.

To capture the election results, we created a database showing the distribution of seats in parliament, and in the process, we subsumed some minor parties in a larger group. In this context, our dataset features the number and percentage of seats won by the respective parties. In addition to the results of the predominant party of the period,[7] the table also includes the number and share of seats won, respectively, by the agrarian,[8] Christian, liberal, and social democratic parties; as well as various national socialist organizations.[9]

We also selected five of the inaugural speeches given by prime ministers when they assumed office based on our assessment of their relevance for our project. Each of the speeches was then coded line-by-line and assigned to major topics. The first such speech was that of Károly Huszár of the National Unification Party in 1920. This was the first inaugural speech of this period delivered to parliament. We selected Count Bethlen's 1921 speech for several reasons: his long time in office as prime minister (slightly in excess of 10 years), the consolidation of the regime that was realized during his term in office, and, finally, because he had a lasting impact on the entire era since the structures he created persisted even after he departed the prime minister's office.

We also examined the speech by Gyula Gömbös, who entered into office in 1932. This intervention is especially interesting because for a long time during the period in question, Gyula Gömbös was acting as an internal rival of sorts to Bethlen, representing a more radical and authoritarian alternative to Bethlen's relatively moderate parliamentarianism. Gömbös had briefly served in the Horthy-affiliated National Army in the 1920s, in fact he initiated the creation of the organization by submitting a proposal to this end to the state secretary for national defense at the time. He went on to serve as a government party representative in the ranks of the National Smallholders' Party. In the 1920s, after Bethlen's parliamentary approach prevailed within the party, Gömbös split and joined the opposition, founding the Party of Racial Defence. Towards the

---

[7] Unity Party, Party of National Unity, and then Party of Hungarian Life.

[8] National Smallholders' Party, Christian Smallholders' Party, and then Independent Smallholders' Party.

[9] In the 1939, election national socialist representatives made it into parliament in the ranks of no fewer than eight different parties.

end of the 1920s, however, he accepted Bethlen's proposal to assume the position of minister of defense, even though he continued to act as an internal opposition to the prime minister.

When the Great Depression struck in Hungary and the Bethlen cabinet fell, the former prime minister continued to pull the strings through his confidantes who stayed on in the cabinet. Finally, Gyula Gömbös assumed leadership of the government in 1932, and he arrived on the scene armed with a major reform program (the National Labor Plan). He realized almost none of it, however, as he died of cancer after merely four years as prime minister (Püski, 2006: 59–61, 71–75, 82–87).

We also examined the opening speech of Kálmán Darányi, who took office in 1936. He was the first prime minister whose tenure was marked by the presence of a major national socialist opposition. His approach toward the Nazi movement was to switch back and forth between a punitive and a conciliatory stance; at times he would adopt some of their policies—yet pruned of their core elements—at other times he lashed out vigorously against them, even using the instrument of bans (Püski, 2006: 91). He is also important because the constitutional reform that was implemented to stem the rise of far-right forces was adopted during his term in office.

Last, but not least, we analyzed the speech of Béla Imrédy, who became prime minister in 1938. Imrédy envisioned changing the political system along corporativist lines, following the Austrian and Portuguese models (Pesti, 2002: 44). Although he struck a moderate tone in his inaugural speech, his first term as prime minister saw the adoption of the first Jewish Law. Seeing the success of Mussolini and Hitler at the time, he became committed to the idea of a dictatorial regime following an official visit to Nazi Germany. However, shortly thereafter he was suddenly ousted by Bethlen and his clique.

The interpellations database of the Hungarian Comparative Agendas Project includes interpellations for the entire period examined, coded for major topics. The database comprises 4024 observations. The project's database of laws includes the policy area of each document, in addition to descriptive information. The individual laws were assigned to major topics and subtopics pursuant to the CAP codebook. Every law was assigned one—and only one—major topic and one subtopic. For the period examined in this chapter, the database of laws incudes 739 observations.

We also drew on a comprehensive CAP database of the entire period in question for Central Budgets and Final Accounts data. That segment of the database includes 25,758 observations, all coded for major topics and subtopics according to the CAP. However, for one year, 1942, we did not have separate budget data. As for decrees, we did not have a database of observations coded according to the CAP Codebook, but some of the pertinent data are nevertheless available. As we were curious to find out how prominently the Jewish Question featured in the decrees, we used the database called Archive of Hungarian Decrees, 1867–1945,[10] to perform a keyword search using the terms "zsidó" (Jew, Jewish) izraelita" (Israelite), "héber" (Hebrew), and "keresztény" (Christian).

For the most part, our analysis of the policy agenda of the underlying period relied on a pairing of issues to CAP major topics, but for some issues we cannot limit the analysis to a single such topic. One such issue is the Jewish Question, where it is not enough to focus on the CAP's civil rights major topic or its subtopic, "Minority rights, ethnic discrimination and racism"—since many anti-Jewish measures were enacted in other policy areas, such as, for example, education or industrial policy. That is why in examining the Jewish Question, we also performed keyword searches in the texts of party manifestos, interpellations, and the laws.

There, we looked for occurrences of the abovementioned markers, such as the term "zsidó" (Jew, Jewish), in the full-text database of the coded party manifestos, as well as in the titles of laws and interpellations. We also introduced a dummy variable called Jewish Question, which assumed a value of 1 when the given item had a bearing on the Jewish issue and a value of 0 when that was not the case. Furthermore, when we were uncertain how to code a given item, we took a more detailed look at the text of the respective law or interpellation. A keyword search was also used in analyzing the issue of suffrage.

---

[10] Archive of Hungarian Decrees (Magyarországi Rendeletek Tára), 1867–1945 https://library.hungaricana.hu/hu/collection/ogyk_rendeletek_tara/ (Retrieved on April 26, 2020).

EMPIRICAL DESCRIPTION OF THE AGENDA

Party Manifestos

We coded the party manifestos of the period based on the sample described above. We found that the ratio of sentences without policy relevance was lower during this period than in the Dual Monarchy. In the ten-year-period of the Dual Monarchy we analyzed, there were four years in which the share of sentences without policy relevance ranged between 50 and 80%; there were three years when it ranged between 42 and 48%; while there were three individual elections when the relevant figure stood at 11%, 9%, and 4.6%, respectively (see Chapter 5).

During the Horthy Era, by contrast, we only found a standout value in the year 1926, when 76.7% of the sentences in the manifesto of the minor coalition partner, the Christian Economic and Social Party, had no policy content. The next highest figure was in 1922, when 25% of all the party manifesto texts were devoid of policy content. By 1924, the share of sentences in the manifestos without policy content had dropped to a remarkably low level (6%). In 1931 and 1932 the relevant ratios were 10.6% and 6%, respectively, while in 1936 and 1939 the share of sentences in the manifestos without policy relevance increased once again (18.5% and 16%, respectively). Figure 6.1 illustrates these trends.

In the next step of our analysis, we discuss the policy areas that appeared in those segments of the party manifestos which featured policy contents, and what the frequency and share of each such area was. The topics of macroeconomics, government operations, agriculture, and labor came up most frequently in party manifestos in the period.

Government operations is a topic that tends to crop up often in other periods as well, in democracies especially so; in the case at hand, it featured most prominently in the manifestos drafted in the early years of the examined period. During the consolidation of the regime, there were several elections in which as much as 20% of the party manifestos would revolve around this issue. But throughout most of the 30s, too, its share of the policy agenda continued to hover around 10%. It is interesting to note that by the election of 1939, this ratio had dropped substantially, to 2.6%. That was because the Party of Hungarian Life and the far-right Arrow Cross Party had next to nothing to say about government operations in the context of the 1939 election. The two parties devoted a mere three sentences in total to the issue, two of which concerned the remuneration of officials while the third said they wanted to "rid parliament of

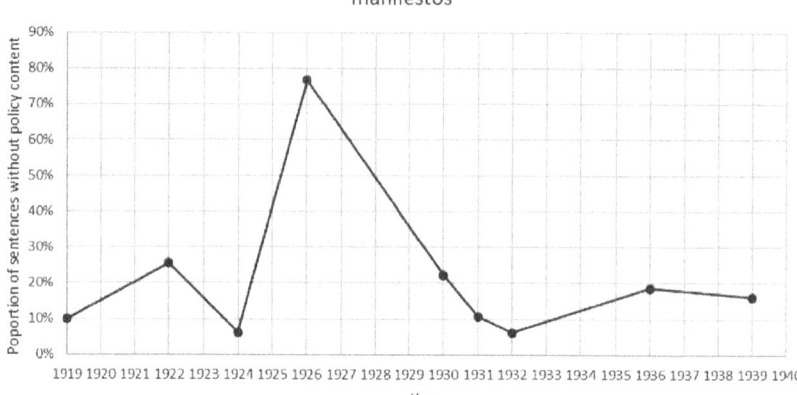

Proportion of sentences without policy content within party manifestos

Fig. 6.1 The share of sentences without policy content in party manifestos by year

personal strife," along with the promise to swiftly implement the pledged reforms.

The drastic decline in the number and share of promises concerning the issue of government operations is an illustrative example that highlights the growing authoritarian trend of the regime. Put simply, in an autocratic regime, leaders are not concerned with sharing or discussing the minutiae of how they government with the public or other political forces. This observation is somewhat nuanced by the fact that at the time the predecessor of the Arrow Cross Party had been recently banned because they had openly proclaimed that their intended goal was to overthrow the regime and to assume power—by violence, if need be (Vida, 2011: 209, 216–217, 237–238). That probably explained why the Arrow Cross Party was more cautious when touching on issues that pertained to the political system as such.

It is further interesting to note that issues falling within the CAP's civil rights major topic was most often mentioned in party manifestos during the early phase of the regime, and then again toward the end of the period we examined. We shall return to this issue in our case studies. We will review the issue of social policy in more detail as well, since the latter also had a tendency to occasionally move to the fore in party manifestos. It is also interesting to take a look at the share of the issue of land owner-ship in the party manifestos, which often experienced a surge.[11] Another interesting observation is that housing, which otherwise moved within the 0–5% range, soared to 8.68% in 1924. It is further clearly apparent that in 1924 and 1931 education policy was much more emphatically present in the party manifestos[12] than in the other years we reviewed.[13]

The party manifestos barely mentioned the environment, energy policy, immigration, and science policy, and the role of transportation was also rather insignificant in terms of its share of the party manifestos—only in 1932 did it capture a share of ca. 4%. Cultural and foreign trade were also relatively underrepresented. The issue of law and crime, too, was rarely addressed.[14] That is worth highlighting because contrary to the hypothesis advanced in the introductory chapter, which posited that less democratic regimes are more likely to focus on law and order issues than democratic regimes, we did not observe this trend in this particular case.

Election Results

The data on the election results in this period show that the Unity Party and its successor[15] held the position of the predominant party throughout the entire period. From 1922 onwards, their share of the seats in parliament oscillated between a low of 57% and a high of 69%. Back in 1922, the Social Democrats held 10% of the seats, but they subsequently dropped to 4–5% and had become a marginal force in parliament by 1939 in the face of systematic persecution by the regime. The Christian parties continuously lost ground as compared to their 40% of the seats (85 seats) at the time when the political systems were first stabilized.[16]

---

[11] In 1919, 14% of party manifestos addressed the issue; in 1922 it was 12.5%; in 1930 it was 22%; in 1936 it was 23.8%; and in 1913 it was 13%. In the other years, the share ranged between 0 and 7%.

[12] 11.5 and 10.4%.

[13] 0–5%.

[14] Generally, this issue made up 0–2% of all promises, and its share only increased between 4 and 5% in 1922 and 1932.

[15] Subsequently the National Unity Party and then the Party of Hungarian Life.

[16] Between 1922 and 1931, they won around 13–14% (32–25) of the seats; in 1935 they won fewer than 6% (14); and by 1939 they had dropped to a mere 1.5% (4 seats).

In the meanwhile, the electoral reform that was introduced to scale back the electoral weight of the far-right, along with the subsequently introduced plural voting, proved incapable of arresting the surge of national socialist forces, and in the 1939 elections various national socialist parties captured almost 19% of the seats in parliament. The share of seats held by classically liberal parties was low throughout the entire period.[17] In sum, the party system of the period was dominated by the right-wing governing elite, yet some degree of expression for other (social or Christian) democratic, or anti-democratic (notably national socialist, since the Communist Party was banned and its leaders moved to exile) forces was tolerated.

Prime Ministers' Speeches

We also looked at the share of sentences without policy content in the inaugural speeches of prime ministers during the interwar period. Well over a third (38.6%) of the 1920 speech by Károly Huszár did not refer to policies. In István Bethlen's 1921 speech the corresponding ratio was 46.7%, while in the case of Gyula Gömbös in 1932 it stood at 42.6%. The proportion of policy-related segments was significantly higher in the case of Kálmán Darányi's 1936 speech, when a mere 19.6% of sentences were devoid of policy content. As Béla Imrédy assumed office in 1938, the ratio rose once again, to 33.61%.

Interpellations

Interpellations are considered a vital instrument in holding the government accountable to parliament. Between 1920 and 1944, 4204 interpellations were presented in the Hungarian parliament. In 1920, 92% of these were presented by representatives who supported the government, and in 1921 this ratio was still as high as 87%. At first glance, one might construe this as an indication of the regime's authoritarian character and the efforts to marginalize the opposition in parliament.

In reality, however, the reason for the high ratio of interpellations by governing party representatives was that a grand coalition was in power

---

[17] In 1922 they held 6.5% of the seats (16); in 1926 they won 4% (10); in each of the two subsequent elections they received 3% of the seats (8); and by 1939 their share of seats had fallen to 1.5% (5).

at that time. Subsequently, the share of government party interpellations continued to decline each year.[18] Interpellations in which governing party representatives interpellated their own government surged once again after 1941,[19] but their proportion did not come close to the ratios observed in the first two years under investigation.

The diversity of the topics raised in interpellations exceeds the diversity of laws and even more so the diversity of thematic areas covered by the budgets.[20] Interestingly, the share of interpellations on the subject of macroeconomic issues was relatively low during this period, it only exceeded 10% in 1932 during the Great Depression and it fluctuated within a rather narrow range of 2–7% otherwise. A high proportion of interpellations concerned government operations, which was an issue that was high on the policy agenda across the board; in the context of interpellations, the annual share of this topic tended to be positioned between 10 and 17%. Its share of the interpellation agenda was highest in the three successive years from 1932 to 1934,[21] while it was distinctly low in 1928 and 1929[22] as well as during World War II.[23] At the same time, we need to keep in mind that during the latter period parliament did not operate normally.

We found a relatively high proportion of interpellations on issues defined as civil rights in the CAP codebook during the various phases of the period in question.[24] That is why the questions related to this broader area deserve a closer look in our case studies. Agriculture and labor were

---

[18] In 1922 it was around 47%; from 1923 to 1925 it ranged between 28 and 31%; and it fluctuated between 17 and 26% between 1928 and 1931. Then until 1936 the share of government party interpellations was mostly around 10–12%, and it increased to a level of 20–22% between 1937 and 1940.

[19] 35–54%.

[20] The value of the Shannon–Weaver index for interpellations was in the 2.5–2.8 range for all years but 1944.

[21] 23, 25, and 20%.

[22] 4 and 6.4%.

[23] Especially in the years from 1942 to 1944, when it stood at 1.6, 4.9, and 0%, respectively.

[24] It was around 10% in 1920 and 1921; between 10 and 13.5% in 1924 and 1925; and around 11–12% in 1931 and 1932. At the end of the era, between 1938 and 1943, the annual share of civil rights-related interpellations was mostly in the 15–20% range. In the other years, their share was mostly in the 5–9% range, and it only fell below the lower figure in 1932 (4.81%) and in 1935 (3.57%).

also relatively important issues. Specifically, the share of these topics on the interpellation agenda was high in 1925, between 1927 and 1930, in 1935, and in 1938. In 1925, a quarter of all interpellations concerned agriculture.

The share of education policy related interpellations, by contrast, was not high.[25] While the issue of law and crime hardly appeared in the party manifestos, there were times when interpellations on this issue became prevalent.[26] That is interesting because the idea that less democratic regimes will tend to focus more intensely on law enforcement bodies aligns with our hypothesis. The environment, energy, immigration, foreign trade, and culture rarely came up as issues in interpellations, and throughout most of the period transportation, social policy, housing, and other economic policies[27] were not significantly represented, either, just as foreign policy rarely took up much ground on the interpellations agenda.[28]

While for the most part the underrepresentation of these topics can be explained by the fact that many of those state responsibilities that are viewed as customary today had not yet become established as such at the time, the trend we observed with regard to foreign policy specifically runs counter to our expectations. We assumed that the consequences of World War I and the widespread demand for revisionism would propel this issue to a higher position on the agenda.

Laws

Only 792 laws were adopted over the period investigated (see Fig. 6.2). This figure is far below the intensity of legislative activity in the twenty-first century. However, part of the story is that only a single law was adopted in 1943, while a mere nine were passed in 1944 due to the war.

---

[25] There were only three years when the share of education policy-related interpellations exceeded 5% (in 1924 it was 6.75%, in 1927 it was 8%, and in 1928 it was 7.3%).

[26] There were several years when the share of law and crime-related interpellations fell in the 8–12% range (1923, 1924, 1931,1933, and 1943), and in 1928 their share even exceeded 18%.

[27] The year 1932, when the share of interpellations concerning other economic policies surged above 10%, marked an exception.

[28] The highest value was 8% in 1927. Furthermore, it was around 6% in 1921 and 1926. During the rest of the period, it was under 5%, indeed, most of the time it was between 1 and 2%.

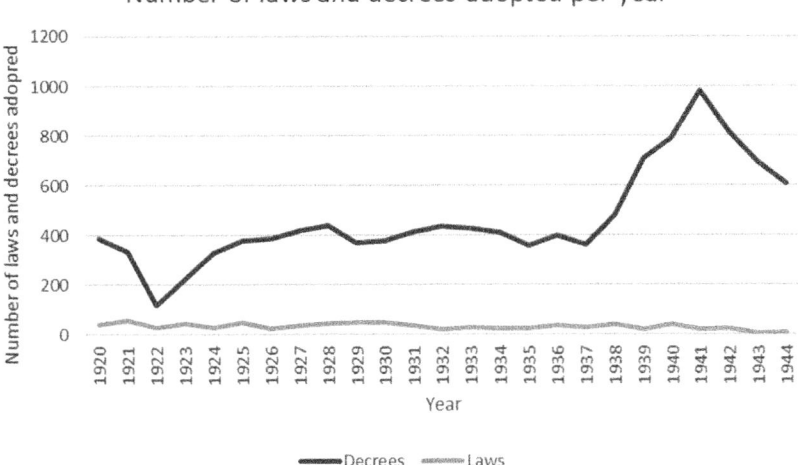

Fig. 6.2   The number of laws and decrees adopted per year

Government operations was the issue that newly adopted laws touched on most frequently,[29] followed by macroeconomics[30] and then law and crime.[31] The category of other economic policies,[32] transportation (until 1939),[33] and the agrarian question were also important.[34] They were followed by labor affairs.[35]

The share of laws concerning government operations was high throughout the entire period, even after 1939, despite the fact that in the elections toward the end of the period investigated we found nothing about this issue in the party manifestos. With respect to legislation, this topic would often take up as much as 20–30% of the legislative agenda

[29] 126 laws.
[30] 106 laws.
[31] 75 laws.
[32] 57 laws.
[33] 46 laws.
[34] 40 laws.
[35] 35 laws.

during the period in question,[36] and in fact in 1939 the share of legislation concerning government operations reached 40%. The consistently high presence of this topic reflects the complete renewal/restructuring of the political system after World War I, often involving the use of solutions that were deemed as transitional already at the time of their adoption, which concomitantly led to continuous changes in the system.

With a share of the agenda ranging between 20 and 30%, the topic of macroeconomics came second when viewed across the entire period, although there were years in which the laws pertaining to the economy only accounted for a relatively low share[37] of all new laws. In 1927 we found intensive legislative activity concerning labor,[38] and between 1935 and 1940 the share of foreign policy-related laws was relatively high,[39] except for two years during this period. In addition to the aforementioned, national defense also made up 20% of the laws in 1922.

Interestingly, contrary to what we found in the party manifestos and interpellations, transportation was relatively well-represented among the laws adopted. Considering that one major party wielded decisive influence over public policy throughout the entire period, we can identify this as a top-down mandated emphasis on the issue of transportation.

A mere 25 of the laws adopted concerned education, and nine of these fell into the period of Kunó Klebelsberg's tenure as minister of education. It is also worthwhile to highlight that almost two-thirds of the laws pertaining to civil rights[40] were adopted between 1938 and 1942. Given the dates in question, one might assume that they were related to the increasing authoritarianism of the regime and the adoption of the Jewish laws. This issue is examined in greater detail.

An interesting tendency regarding foreign trade is that even though it was underrepresented in the other arenas we looked at, in one arena, namely, among the laws, the proportion of foreign trade related issues

---

[36] 1920, 1930, 1932, 1937, 1941, 1942, 1944.

[37] They made up 4–5% of new laws.

[38] 20%, 9 laws.

[39] Ranged between 10 and 17%, except for 1935 and 1937, when their share was 2.8 and 2.6%, respectively.

[40] 9 out of 15 laws.

surged, especially between 1926 and 1932.[41] If we also look at the substance of these laws, we find that most of them served to ratify international treaties. Although the legislature did pass some bills concerning the environment, energy policy, and immigration during the period investigated, the number of such laws was negligible. This is readily explained by the state's different functions and roles as compared to today.

Central Budgets

Examining the data about budgets, we found—unsurprisingly—that the state spent practically nothing on the environment, just as it allocated no funds to energy policy or immigration. Spending was also negligible in the areas of housing, other economic policy, foreign trade, foreign policy, and culture. The examination of budgets also helps us in identifying those policy areas in which regulation was driven from the top and those for which the private sector was primarily responsible. In this context, it is worthwhile to highlight the issue of science policy, which played a minor role in manifestos, laws, and interpellations alike, but nevertheless received a share of the budget ranging between 5 and 7% during most of the period in question.

The spending on education also accounted for about 6–7% of the budget. Social policy was even more prominently featured; its share of budget ranged between 15 and 20% throughout most of the period, and it only fell under 10% between 1920 and 1923.[42] But transportation, too, had a low presence in the other arenas even though this policy area accounted for about 20%—and occasionally even more—of the budget.[43] In addition to the policy topics above, macroeconomic expenditures made up a 15–20% slice of the budget almost throughout the entire period.[44] The share of defense spending was also relatively high throughout, but its role was most pronounced at the beginning and the end of the period analyzed. Throughout most of the period, law enforcement and crime also made up some 9–10% of budget spending. Interestingly, despite its

---

[41] The share of this topic was in the range between 16 and 22% throughout the entire period, except for 1927.

[42] 1.9, 2.7, 3.2, and 6.7%.

[43] 28.6% in 1922 and 26.4% in 1923.

[44] It was even higher in 1920 (29.6%), in 1921 (36.5%), and in 1922 (22.3%).

high share in the other agenda arenas, very little budget spending was allocated to agriculture.

Decrees

An examination of the intensity of decree-making during the period is also highly instructive, especially when juxtaposed with the trends we observed with respect to the adoption of laws (see Fig. 6.2). An increased number of decrees and the greater role of the latter as compared to laws may be an indication of executive dominance and growing authoritarianism. A total of 11,633 decrees were adopted between 1920 and 1944. While in 1922 the number of decrees reached a nadir,[45] we found that the average number of decrees adopted between 1923 and 1937[46] grew and from 1937 on the number of decrees adopted increased even more drastically.[47]

Subsequently, there was a slight decline in the volume of decrees, but a considerable number continued to be adopted.[48] This was clearly also influenced by the state of war that persisted at the time and the adoption by parliament of various enabling acts (transfers of authority). The growing role of decrees, along with the simultaneous decline in the adoption of laws by the legislature, unequivocally suggests a policy agenda dictated by the executive.

CASE STUDIES ON THE POLICY CODES WITH THE HIGHEST VOLATILITY

The Jewish Question

While the above description of the data regarding specific processes and venues of the policy agenda provides a general understanding of the emphases of policy attention, individual cases can highlight the nuances and context of policymaking in the Horthy era. And perhaps no other issue defined this period from a historical perspective than what was commonly referred to as the Jewish Question.

---

[45] 116 decrees were adopted that year.

[46] Generally, between 300 and 400.

[47] In 1938 the number of decrees adopted was still only 481, but in 1939 it surged to 708, in 1940 it was 790, and by 1941 it had risen to 981.

[48] 814 were adopted in 1942, 691 in 1943, and 605 in 1944.

We pointed out above that civil rights as defined in the CAP code-book played a major role in several of the policy arenas we analyzed, although at the same time it needs to be noted that back then this did not involve the emergence of a civil rights regime as we understand it today. In the early phase of the period investigated, the issue was mentioned relatively frequently in the party manifestos.[49] While many of these mentions pertained to legal accountability for crimes committed during the Soviet Republic or similar issues, the manifestos also reflected on equality before the law and the rights of national minorities. Of the various pledges on issues that we classified as human rights issues, 15 revolved around the Jewish Question.

This issue also came up relatively frequently in interpellations,[50] and its share of this type of parliamentary questions was especially high between 1938 and 1943.[51] With respect to legislative activity by parliament, we found the highest values in the years 1938 and 1941.[52] Looking at the data for the years 1938 and 1939, we can already suspect that this may be linked to the so-called Jewish Laws adopted at the time.

A total of 744 interpellations during the period touched on the major topic of civil rights. Of these, over 100 concerned the bans and dissolutions of certain parties and associations—this is already reflective of the authoritarian character of the underlying regime. Furthermore, over 250 interpellations concerned anti-state activities or criminal cases and extraditions. And more than 60 were directly related to the Jewish Question. As for laws with this major topic, three was aimed at limiting the rights of Jews.

Yet, the Jewish Question touches on several major topics in the CAP codebook besides civil rights, and as a result we used a keyword search to identify more material that are relevant for understanding the

[49] In the 1920 and 1921 elections, this issue made up 13% and 20%, respectively, of all the sentences with policy relevance. It was only in 1939 that this ratio rose to 12% again. In 1924, 1931, and 1936, 7% of the promises pertained to this issue, while in 1932 the corresponding figure was 3.4%, in 1930 it was 1.5%, and in 1926 it was 0%.

[50] In 1920 (10%), 1921 (9%), between 1924 and 1926 (around 10–13%), and then in 1933 (11%).

[51] 15–20%.

[52] In 1938 and 1941 this ratio was around 10%, while in 1921 and 1939 it was around 5%. In 1924 and 1936, 3.6% of the laws fell into this category, while in 1940 and 1942 their share was 4.1%. In the remaining years no laws were adopted that pertained to the major topic civil rights.

Jewish question on the agenda

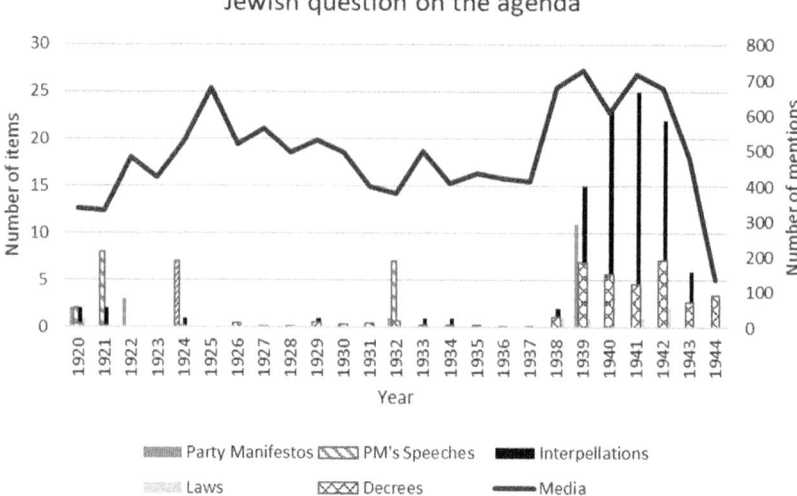

Fig. 6.3   The presence of the Jewish question on various policy agendas (The left axis features the number of sentences in party manifestos and prime ministers' speeches that refer to the given topic, as well as the number of related interpellations and laws. The right axis features the number of decrees on the topic and its average annual mentions in the media.)

case. Figure 6.3 charts the incidence of the Jewish Question in party manifestos, interpellations, laws, prime ministers' speeches, political newspapers, and decrees. With respect to newspapers, we look at the average annual mentions.[53]

We found that although the Jewish Question had been present already at the beginning of the interwar period (a case in point is the so-called Numerus Clausus law of 1920, which put a cap on the number of Jewish students allowed in higher education), it was much more emphatically present on the agenda after 1938. The media was the only agenda arena where it had been covered with similar intensity already as early as 1925.

The Jewish Question had been present in the party manifestos from the very start of the interwar period. In 1920 and 1922, there had been two and three relevant promises, respectively; in 1924 the Party of Racial

---

[53]The data for the year 1944 is calculated up to March 19 of that year, the date of the German occupation.

Defense devoted seven pledges to this issue. In 1932 there was only a single sentence that focused on the Jewish Question, but in 1939 there were 11 that addressed this issue. The Christian National Party's manifesto contained anti-Jewish sentences as early as 1920, and these posited a link between Jews and the Hungarian Soviet Republic and communism. In 1922, the United Party demanded that the constitution and economic life in Hungary be rebuilt on Christian grounds, along with the creation of a Christian commercial and money market and state support for Christian industry.

In 1924, the manifesto of the Hungarian National Independence Party devoted a longer section to attacking Jews, with 14% of their promises (seven in total) centering around the issues of scaling back the role of Jews in economics, society, and industry; the ban on further Jewish immigration; and the expulsion of Jews having foreign citizenship. At the legislative level and in terms of interpellations, however, the issue was not subject to such broad attention until 1938.

The Numerus Clausus law was adopted in 1920, and then it was relaxed again in 1928. Apart from these legislative acts, however, the Jewish Question did not figure in legislative activities until 1938. In the same year, however, a representative of the Christian Smallholders and Agrarian Workers' Party presented an interpellation urging that the adoption of the pending Jewish bill be accelerated. The same party had also presented interpellations about Jews and Freemasons already back in 1921.

Interpellations pointing out failures in compliance with the Numerus Clausus Act were presented by the Christian Social and Economic Party in 1924 and the Unity Party in 1933. In 1925, a representative of the Unity Party interpellated on the subject of the Christian capital city. There was another interpellation on the subject in 1934, by a representative of the National Radical Party. As an outlier, in 1929, there was also an interpellation which spoke out in defense of the Jews, by a Social Democratic representative.

In 1939 the manifestos of the Party of Hungarian Life and of the Arrow Cross Party both emphasized the need for curtailing the rights of Jews, and the relevant demands were no longer limited to scaling back the Jewish influence in economic, social, and cultural life, but there were also mentions of creating a Hungarian state "free of Jews" and the denial of the legal equality of Jews.

The following term of parliament saw a series of anti-Jewish legislation (the so-called Jewish Laws), which increasingly trampled the rights of Jewish citizens; at the same time, there was also a massive surge in the number of decrees concerning the rights of Jews.[54] Between 1938 and 1943, a massive surge in the number of interpellations concerning Jews can also be detected. Almost all of these referred to the implementation of the Jewish Laws, the urging of new anti-Jewish legislation, and the rights of Jews in general.[55]

The first Jewish Law was adopted in 1938, during the tenure of Prime Minister Béla Imrédy. It set a 20% cap on the share of Jewish professionals working in the liberal professions, as well as for any commercial, financial, and industrial corporations that employed more than ten white-collar employees.[56] Interestingly, Imrédy's inaugural speech had been moderate in outlook and had not touched on the Jewish issue at all. In fact, he even subtly criticized the Hungarian national socialist movement. Yet, after the early successes of the Nazi party and his own visit to Germany, he came to support the establishment of a dictatorial system. Subsequently, he was quickly overthrown by Bethlen and his associates. The second Jewish Law[57] was adopted in May 1939, and by that time Pál Teleki was the prime minister. This law was different from the first Jewish Law in that it defined Jewry more in racial than in religious terms, and it went further still in limiting the life of Hungarian Jewry.

The third anti-Jewish law was adopted in 1941, during the premiership of László Bárdossy.[58] This law fully embraced the racial definition of Jewry, and it further banned marriage and sexual relations between Jews and non-Jews. This law clearly reflects the impact of external pressure from Nazi Germany. Another act adopted in 1942,[59] which banned Jews

[54] Before 1938, there were between 0 and 6 decrees a year, while in 1926, 1929, and 1939 their number fluctuated between 10 and 18; in 1928 there were 29. Between 1939 and 1942, by contrast, their number surged to 186–189 each year.

[55] Of the 101 interpellations in this category during the period in question, 99 were presented between 1939 and 1943.

[56] Act XIX of 1938 on Ensuring a More Effective Balance in Social and Economic Life.

[57] Act IV of 1939 on Restricting the Space Occupied by Jews in Public Life and the Economy.

[58] Act XV of 1941 Amending and Modifying Act XXXI of 1894 on the Marriage Law, as well as the Race Protection Measures Relevant in that Context.

[59] Act XV of 1942 on the Agricultural and Forestry Real Estate Owned by Jews.

from buying agricultural real estate, is commonly referred to as the Fourth Jewish Law. At the same time, there was also another law in 1942 that curtailed the rights of Jews, the Act on the Legal Status of the Israelite Denomination,[60] which reversed the previous classification of the Jewish religion as one of the established churches and labelled it a recognized religion instead (which meant a lower status).

The reason for the decline in the presence of the Jewish issue on the media agenda, which is apparent in the figure above, is on the one hand related to the fact that many newspapers were banned. On the other hand, that we only considered newspapers published before the occupation of Hungary by Germany on March 19, 1944. The drop we observe in legislative activity on the subject was caused by the fact that parliament rarely met at the time.

As for the judicial agenda, (Schweitzer, 2005) analyzed the manifestations of the anti-Jewish legislation in the application of the law by the High Court of Administration, which performed public law adjudication and was not part of the ordinary judicial system. He concluded that the issue frequently came up in judgments in which the Court upheld decisions rendered by the public administration authorities[61] in cases in which they had denied to issue certifications to petitioners affirming that they were not Jewish because according to the Jewish Laws they qualified as such, even though they were not affiliated with any Jewish congregation.

In some cases, the Court cited some conflict with the law and called on the authority in question to revise its decision. Indeed, there was a case in which the court filled in a legal loophole left by the legislature, taking an expansive view of the text of the underlying statute with regard to the termination of the mandate of elected members of local governments (construing these terms to also apply to appointed members of local governments in addition to the elected members—Schweitzer, 2005: 177–179). At the same time, some public law scholars spoke out very decisively against the Jewish Laws, while others generally considered the idea of restricting the legal equality of Jews in the interest of the public good acceptable, albeit with certain qualifications, and yet others

---

[60] Act VIII of 1942 on the Legal Status of the Israelite Denomination.

[61] On the role of the Hungarian public administration in the Holocaust, see Gulyás (2016).

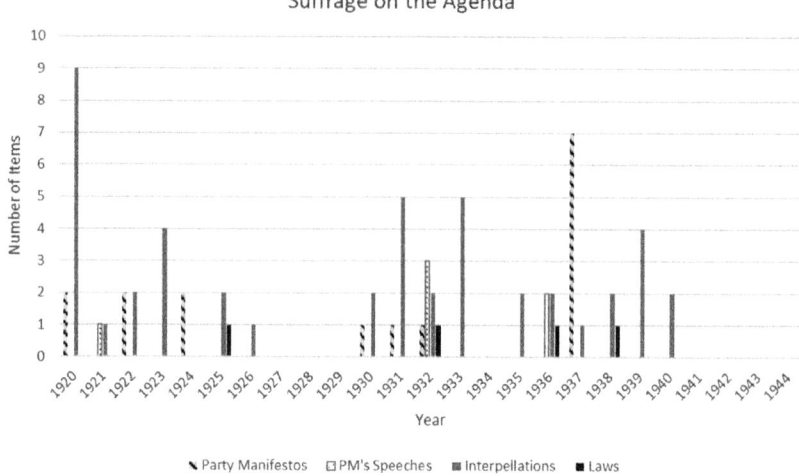

Fig. 6.4 The presence of suffrage on the various policy agendas (The figure depicts the number of sentences in party manifestos and prime ministers' speeches that refer to the given topic, as well as the number of related interpellations and laws)

even though it was downright necessary to do so and sought to publicly legitimate it (Schweitzer, 2014).

Constitutional Reform

Our second case concerns the issue of constitutional reform. From the very outset, demands for universal and equal suffrage with secret ballot voting appeared in the manifestos published during the interwar period, from 1919 up until 1936.[62] Yet almost half of the relevant observations stem from the year 1936. The rights of association and assembly were also regularly raised as issues, also up until 1936. Freedom of conscience and religion (apart from the Jewish Question), by contrast, was only discussed in party manifestos released between 1919 and 1924 (see Fig. 6.4).[63]

---

[62] Sixteen of the 106 promises belonged into this category.

[63] Five mentions overall.

We noted previously that the demand for the introduction of universal and equal suffrage, along with the secret ballot, was continuously on the agenda up until 1938, and at that point it brooked no further delay. It was present in the party manifestos during the entire period, and in 1936 the Independent Smallholders' Party devoted substantial space to this issue. It is also worth pointing to a pledge by the Party of National Unity in 1932 which stated their belief that although a voting rights reform was necessary, it would need to be implemented cautiously, with the "utmost consideration of the national interest."

Demands for a voting rights reform were also voiced in interpellations, with a total of 46 interpellations on the subject. These included calls for the swift implementation of such reforms, as well as issues concerning the electoral register and election fraud. Interestingly, István Bethlen's inaugural speech in 1921 expressed the prime minister's commitment to the introduction of universal and equal suffrage as well as of the secret ballot voting. However, as the head of the predominant party and prime minister for ten years, he had plenty of opportunities to initiate such a reform and yet failed to do so.

Given the intensity of the calls for universal and equal suffrage and the secret ballot, the system of open voting proved untenable; the pressure for a voting rights reform came from too many societal players. However, by 1938 the decision-makers harbored major concerns that far-right forces and the Social Democrats—whose party was labelled an anti-system force—might amass too much electoral clout if the introduction of the secret ballot were to coincide with the expansion of the suffrage. Thus, ultimately the origins of the major constitutional reforms of 1937 and 1938 were driven by these two entirely divergent considerations.

While the introduction of the secret ballot voting had played a major role in Gyula Gömbös' inaugural speech in 1932, it was Kálmán Darányi who discussed this issue consequentially in his own address in 1936.[64] He declared that certain constitutional reforms were necessary. He also emphasized in this context that the government and the opposition would have to cooperate on the issue, that it was in the national interest for them to try to reach a consensus, and that these reforms should not be guided by political considerations.

---

[64] It made up 6% of his speech.

To this end, he held out the prospect of convening an interparty congress, which reflected the desire for a broadly based discourse on the issue and of involving the opposition players in the constitutional reform process. Darányi assumed that the introduction of the secret ballot voting would be necessary, adding that in order to implement it, two other laws would have to be adopted first—the act on expanding the powers of the regent and another on expanding the powers of the upper house.

The promise to include other parties in the process did not turn out to be an empty one. Between December 2 and 4, 1936, an interparty conference was in fact convened to discuss the main issues concerning suffrage (Albrecht, 1937: 17). This reflected the desire for a genuine dialogue with the opposition. As Krivoss (1937: 33–54) points it out, the issues on the conference agenda also included the question of whether the introduction of the secret ballot should be accompanied by a restriction or an expansion of the active right to vote. The leaders of the otherwise highly different parties all agreed that the secret ballot should not be introduced without simultaneously implementing some safeguards.

The arguments raised in support of these reforms were that they served as protection for the 1000-year-old historical constitution; alternatively, those supporting them said that they were in favor of such changes because they wanted to curtail demagogy and the influence of the plutocracy, stressing that the general understanding was that the objective of the "correctives" that were being implemented was to ensure the "rule of the intelligence." Even the Social Democrats considered it important to make sure that certain checks and balances would be deployed to guard against the impact of the electoral reform, i.e., the extension of suffrage. Thus, although they rejected the idea of plural voting, they accepted the need for expanding the powers of the upper house and the regent (Krivoss, 1937: 33–54).

The new voting rights act of 1938,[65] which made the use of the secret ballot a requirement, also implemented a covert plural voting scheme to prevent the breakthrough of extremists. What this meant in practice was that voters were not explicitly assigned to different classes which each had a different number of votes. The gist of the covert plural voting scheme was that the right to vote was contingent on different conditions in the single-member constituencies and in the party list-based ones,

---

[65] Act XIX of 1938 on the Election of the Members of the National Assembly.

respectively. Thus, voters that the legislator regarded as "more mature," or more thoughtful, were allowed to vote in both types of constituencies while the rest could only vote in party list-based ones.

Although the reform ultimately failed to stop the Hungarian far-right from taking power, the electoral data from the era show that the calculations of those who drafted the law were not unfounded. Ultimately, the national socialist parties and their candidates, as well as the Social Democrats, which were also regarded as an anti-system party, received six points less in the single-member districts where the right to vote was restricted than in the districts where seats were distributed on the basis of party lists (Balázs, 2016: 39–40; Hubai, 2001). Both other proposals aimed at controlling the emerging Nazi dominance—the expansion of the powers of the regent[66] and of the upper house of parliament[67]—were approved, but proved, eventually, wanting (Molnár, 1938; Püski, 2009: 13–14).

Land Reform and the Agrarian Issue

Agriculture and land ownership were a further divisive issue of the era. Our analysis of agenda data clearly reflects the impact of *Act XXXVI of 1920 On the More Appropriate Allotment of Landed Estates*, which owed to the efforts of István Szabó de Nagyatád, a prominent rural politician who served as minister of agriculture in three different cabinets. Subsequently, the issue of agricultural and land ownership policy played a prominent role in the inaugural speech of Prime Minister Count István Bethlen as well as several of the major party manifestos drawn up in 1922 (see Fig. 6.5).

Between 1920 and 1924, the number of interpellations on the subject was continuously high, but then it gradually declined until 1927. However, land reform was not the sole issue in the interpellations relating to the broader policy area. From 1930 on, several of the interpellations were not focused on land reform but pertained instead to various subsegments of agriculture (e.g., viticulture; or the shutting down of a local steam mill). Around this time, the issue gained massive traction in party

---

[66] Act XIX of 1937 on the Expansion of the Powers of the Regent and the Election of the Regent.

[67] Act XXVII of 1937 on the New Determination of the Powers of the National Assembly's Upper House.

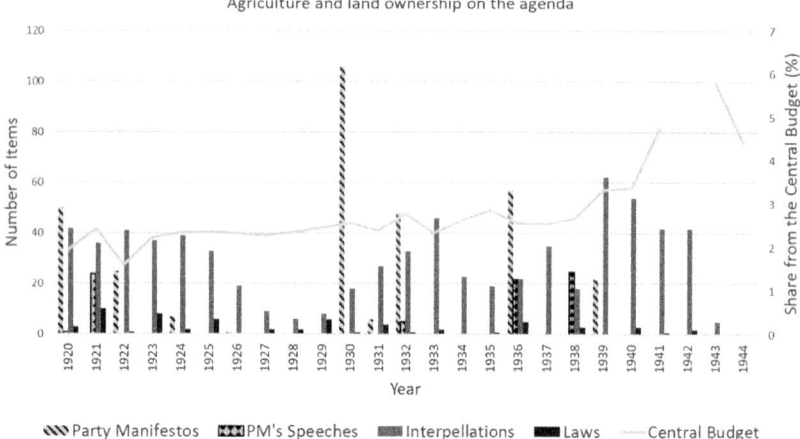

Fig. 6.5 The presence of agriculture and land ownership on policy agendas (The left-hand axis features the number of sentences in party manifestos and prime ministers' speeches that refer to the given topic, as well as the number of related interpellations and laws. The right-hand axis features the share of annual budget spending on the policy areas we analyzed)

manifestos, and not only in that of the Independent Smallholders who had just managed to win some seats in parliament. It is a testament to the importance of the agrarian issue at the time that the Social Democrats adopted a distinct agrarian manifesto dealing exclusively with agrarian issues.

The issue continued to figure heavily in the 1932 party manifestos, and its share among interpellations peaked in 1933. It moved even further to the fore in 1939, and at the time it was not only the number of relevant interpellations that surged, but so did the share of budget spending on agriculture. However, at that point it was no longer the agrarian parties that interpellated heavily on this issue, but the governing party, the Party of Hungarian Life, as well as the Arrow Cross Party and other national socialist parties—often in the context of calling for the expropriation of lands from their Jewish owners.

Education on the Agenda

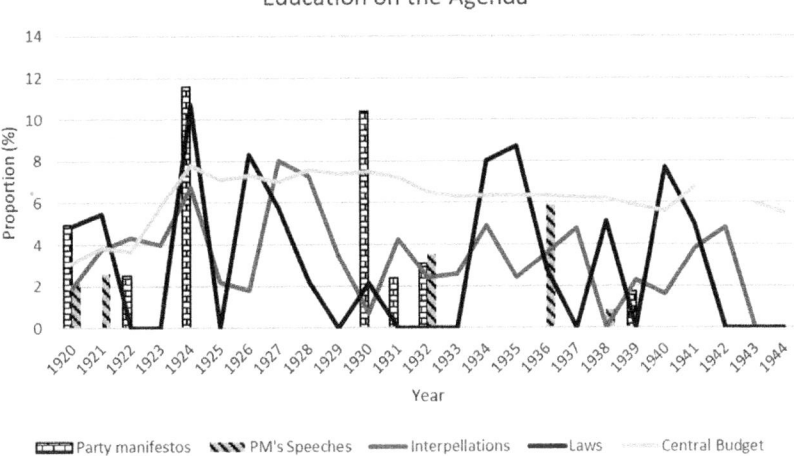

Fig. 6.6 The share of education on the policy agendas

Kunó Klebelsberg's Education Reforms

An examination of the presence of education policy issues on the agenda is instructive because it reveals highly distinctive patterns. Education policy moved visibly to the foreground during the time when Kunó Klebelsberg was at the helm of the Ministry of Religion and Education between 1922 and 1931 (see Fig. 6.6). Almost 5% of the pledges in the party manifestos drafted for the 1920 elections focused on this issue. By 1922, however, the share of this policy area had dropped to half of the previous value. But in 1924 the references to education surged once again,[68] and it continued to feature prominently in manifestos in 1930,[69] only to decline substantially starting in 1931.[70]

As a trend, these figures correlate significantly with Kunó Klebelsberg's tenure as minister. We observed a similar trend with respect to interpellations and laws.[71] Education policy-related interpellations peaked

[68] At the time, 11.6% of sentences with a policy relevance belonged to this category.

[69] 10.4%.

[70] At the time, its share ranged between 0 and 3%.

[71] In 1924, over 10% of the laws pertained to education, while in 1926 the share of education-related laws was 8.3% and in 1927 it was 5.7%. In 1936, 1937, and 1940 their

in 1927.[72] A sizeable portion of the relevant interpellations reacted to the education reform. Issues involving education financing, infrastructure (school construction), textbook accreditation, and teachers' pay made up a substantial proportion of the interpellations on education. Thus, interpellations were typically not used to introduce new initiatives but to reflect on policy decisions that had already been taken.

The impact of Kunó Klebelsberg's tenure as minister is most clearly apparent when we look at the evolution of budgetary expenditures on education. The share of education expenditures as a proportion of total budget spending stood out especially between 1927 and 1931, but it never dropped back to the previous low level observed between 1920 and 1922.[73]

The Birth of the Welfare State

While nation-wide social welfare programs were only implemented during the era of socialism (see next chapter), many important developments took place in the interwar period as well. We found that in terms of its share of interpellations, the issue was especially popular between 1920 and 1925, and then again between 1929 and 1933, and finally once more between 1939 and 1942. With respect to the legislation on the subject, the peak periods were 1928 and 1934–1937. Budget outlays on social issues began to massively increase in 1922, the year when the Social Democrats first entered parliament, and continued to grow in most years—including the period of the economic crisis—until 1938 (Fig. 6.7).

We also observed that the issue often came up in party manifestos, and the manifestos in the 1930s stand out especially in this regard. We found that social spending increased almost continuously starting in 1925 all the

share was around 8%, and in 1920, 1921, and 1941 it was around 5%. In the remaining years, it fluctuated between 0 and 4%.

[72] In 1927 it was 8%, in 1928 it was 7.2%, and in 1924 it was 6.8%. In the other years it mostly ranged between 0 and 4%.

[73] While the share of education spending in the budget was between 3 and 4% between 1920 and 1922, it had risen to 5.8% in 1923, and then surged to over 7% between 1924 and 1931. Its share of the budget dropped to 6.5% in the next year, and then continued to oscillate in the narrow range between 6.2 and 6.4% until 1938. From then on, its share continued to stay below 6% in all years but 1941, but even in that year only 6.7% of the budget were spent on education, although given that it was wartime this figure was not necessarily low.

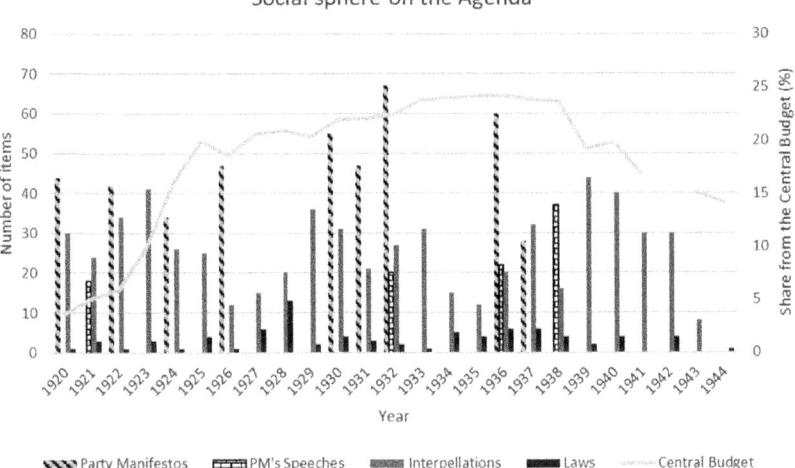

Fig. 6.7 The share of social sector-related issues (health, labor and social welfare) on the policy agendas

way to the beginning of World War II, although it did stagnate somewhat during the time of the Great Depression. Between 1922 and 1936, the Social Democrats presented the highest number of interpellations on the subject. Before that time, the agrarian parties and the Christian National Union Party had brought it up most often, while starting in 1938 the various far-right parties and the Party of Hungarian Life began taking the initiative when it came to interpellations on social issues.

Getting Ready for War and Territorial Revision

After 1920 there was a major decline in the number of laws and inter-pellations concerning national defense matters, and the same trend was manifest with respect to the manifestos and the prime ministers' speeches we reviewed. One reason was that World War I had ended and the terms set out in the peace treaty had been fulfilled. Interestingly, with regard to interpellations we found another standout value in 1936. In 1938 there was a slight uptick in the budget allocations for national defense (see Fig. 6.8). It is important to add in this context that at the Bled Conference in 1938, the Powers of the Little Entente (Slovakia, Romania and

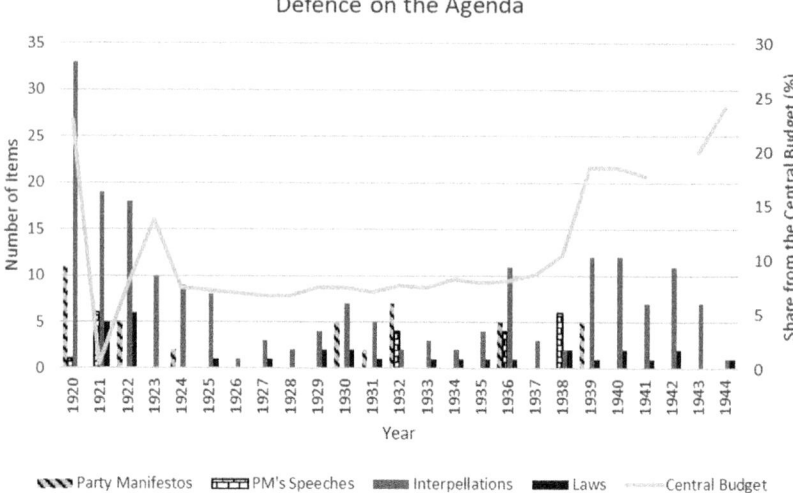

Fig. 6.8   The issue of national defense on the policy agenda

Yugoslavia) recognized Hungary's equal right to arm itself (Winchester, 1973: 746–747). This set a rearmament program in motion. The number of interpellations on the issue began to rise constantly starting in 1939, the year when World War II broke out.

With regard to foreign policy we found that—contrary to what we expected—it did not feature prominently in the party manifestos, in interpellations, or in the budget. The rise in the number of foreign policy-related laws was also not related to the defense of the Hungarian minorities across the border but was instead intended to further Hungary's integration into the emerging international system. Hence, the relevant laws served to promulgate various international agreements and their transposition into national law. The issue of the Trianon Treaty and of transborder ethnic Hungarian communities featured much more prominently in the inaugural speeches of prime ministers.

On the whole, the picture that emerges is one in which until the late 1930s—when several of the formerly lost Hungarian regions were reattached to Hungary—the fate of the transborder Hungarian communities and ex-Hungarian territories was primarily present at the level of rhetoric and ambition. To appreciate the broader context, it is also important to add that on account of the peace treaty concluding World War I, the

Hungarian parliament and government had a limited room of maneuver on this issue—which does not explain the low share of interpellations on the subject, however.

CONCLUSION

We conclude our chapter on the Horthy era by revisiting the hypotheses set out in Chapter 2 related to policy agendas in authoritarian and semi-authoritarian regimes. One of the things we expected to find was that as compared to fully fledged democracies, the regency would feature fewer policy players involved in drafting policies and policy decisions. In the early phase of this period, when it was still unclear whether a military dictatorship or a parliamentary system would ultimately emerge, only a few actors were involved in policymaking.

At the same time, however, throughout most of the period there was an ongoing, broadly based social dialogue that involved business, scientific, and social organizations in the policymaking process. As we saw it in the context of the Jewish Question, even the media exerted some impact. The citizens and the various organizations, as well as municipalities, also had the right to petition any of the two chambers of the legislature. At the same time, it is important to stress that, in and of itself, the involvement of certain actors in the decision-making process is not necessarily a step toward more democracy. Furthermore, toward the end of the Horthy era, civil society organizations as well as social and business organizations had lost most of their influence over the policy process, and in fact, to a significant extent even parliament lost its previous role in shaping policies (despite last-ditch efforts to shore up the upper house in the face of emerging national socialism).

The complexities and dynamics of the regime are clearly present in how military officials sat in the upper house or paramilitary and terror organizations exerted a large influence in the early phase of the examined period. While some of these actors worked with opposition parties to dilute the lure of Nazism, others in the governing elite would adopt Nazi-style policies and ruthlessly clamped down on dissent. Numerous organizations were classified as illegal at the time, the rights of association and assembly were subject to restrictions yet at the same time elections were heavily contested and also had major consequences for policy as in the case of multiparty constitutional reforms.

When it comes to rule by decree, we found evidence in support of this hypothesis during the period in question, since as time progressed and the war approached, executive orders came to play a far more prominent role. Enabling acts were adopted and in the last two years of the period examined parliament hardly even convened. With regard to the hypothesis that legislation is more deliberate under democracy, we found that early during the period in question there were several amendments of the parliament's Standing Orders that were aimed at accelerating legislation and the unified governing party was not shy to solve political problems through unilateral procedural changes.

Furthermore, when it comes to the democratic rights of the opposition, even though they had many formal rights, they were informally severely restricted, both in terms of their capacity to introduce legislation and to participate in parliamentary proceedings in general. As Püski (2015: 161) points out, even though in theory any representative could sponsor a bill, in practice it was rare for them to do so. Instead, the established practice was for representatives to call on the government to draft a law on a given issue. While in the case of government-sponsored bills a debate in the committee was mandatory, the submissions of individual representatives were generally merely assigned to a debate but actually never even discussed. Interpellations, a primary means of control for the opposition in advanced democracies, were extensively used by government-affiliated MPs in the two most authoritarian phases of the era, namely its beginning and its end.

Nevertheless, there is some evidence of the ruling party's desire to involve the opposition, and the interparty conference held in 1936 to discuss the planned constitutional reforms highlights this. We also found evidence in the data that the presence of the Social Democrats in parliament played a role in making social welfare issues more prominent on the agenda, while the emergence of the Smallholders as a parliamentary party in 1931 led to a surge of agrarian issues debated in parliament. We should also not forget about the presence of the agrarian chamber in the upper house.

Finally, we assumed that less democratic regimes will be less inclined to pay attention to public services. In this particular context, the evidence about this period is limited since as compared to today, the state's functions were very different back then. We saw that the issue of healthcare hardly ever made it onto the agenda. The role of education, by contrast, surged substantially—mostly during the time of Kunó Klebelsberg as the minister in charge of education—and we found a significant emphasis on this issue in the party manifestos, interpellations, and legislative acts, as well as in the budgets of the period.

Acknowledgment The author is thankful to Tamara Egri for the help regarding processing prime ministerial speeches and other databases.

REFERENCES

Ács, N. (2013). A magyar választási rendszer főbb változásai 1848-tól 1989-ig. In Á. Cserny (Ed.), *Ünnepi tanulmányok Rácz Attila 75. születésnapja tiszteletére* (pp. 19–40). Nemzeti Közszolgálati és Tankönyvkiadó Zrt.

Albrecht, F. (1937). A kormányzói jogkör kiterjesztése. *Az Ország Útja, 1*(2), 17–22.

Amstrong, D. (1982). *The rise of the international organisation: A short history.* Macmillan.

Balázs, Á. (2016). Plural voting and representation of minorities in Central Europe. *Central European Papers, 4*(1), 32–49.

Bodó, B. (2011, April). The white terror in Hungary, 1919–1921: The social worlds of paramilitary groups. *Austrian History Yearbook, 42*(2011), 133–163.

Boros, Z. (2008). Parlamentarizmus a Horthy-korban (1919–1944). In B. Zsuzsanna, & S. Dániel (Eds.), *Parlamentarizmus Magyarországon (1867–1944)* (pp. 161–386). ELTE Eötvös Kiadó.

Braham, R. R., & Kovács, A. (Eds.). (2016). *The Holocaust in Hungary: seventy years later.* Central European University Jewish Studies Program–Central European University Press.

Buzinkay, G. (2016). *A magyar sajtó és újságírás története a kezdetektől a rendszerváltásig.* Wolters Kluwer.

Clavin, P. (2000). *The Great Depression in Europe, 1929–1939.* St. Martin's Press.

Gergely, J., Glatz, Ferenc, & Pölöskei, F. (Eds.). (2003). *Magyarországi Pártprogramok II. Magyarországi Pártprogramok 1919–1944.* ELTE – Eötvös Kiadó.

Gulyás, É. (2016). The role of public administration in the Hungarian holocaust. General assessment and case study in historical social psychology. *Central European Papers, 4*(2), 80–99. https://doi.org/10.25142/cep.2016.016.

Gyurgyák, J. (2001). *A zsidókérdés Magyarországon. Politikai eszmetörténet.* Osiris Kiadó.

Henn, M. (2018). *Opinion polls and volatile electorates: Problems and issues in polling European Societies.* First published 1998 by Ashgate Publishing. Routledge.

Hollósi, G. (2016). The comparison of the Czechoslovak and Hungarian electoral law in the light of the Hungarian interwar literature. *Central European Papers*, 4(2), 53–67.

Hubai, L. (2001). *Magyarország XX. századi választási atlasza 1920–2000*. CD-ROM. Napvilág Kiadó.

Ilonszki, G. (2000). Crisis and pseudo-democratic compromise. In D. Berg, & J. Mitchell (Eds.), *Conditions of democracy in Europe, 1919–39. Systematic case studies* (pp. 242–262). Palgrave Macmillan.

Kántás, B. (2020). *Árnyékhadsereg? Válogatott dokumentumok a Kettőskereszt Vérszövetség katonai titkos társaság 1920-as évekbeli működéséről*. Hungarovox.

Krivoss, Á. (1937). *Választójog, népesség, adóteher. Gazdaságpolitikai alapon készült választójogi tervezet*. Budapesti I. Ker. Iparoskör.

Lénár, A. (2011). A szakszervezeti mozgalom gyökerei és fejlődési tendenciái a második világháborúig. In M. Dobák (Ed.), *A gazdasági és társadalmi érdekérvényesítés starégiai és szervezeti modelljei a 20. században* (pp. 33–63). L'Harmattan.

Lorman, T. (2003). The Bethlen-Peyer Pact: A reassessment. *Central Europe*, 1(2), 147–162.

Lorman, T. (2007). *Hungary, 1920–1925 Istvan Bethlen and the politics of consolidation*. Columbia University Press.

Macartney, C. A. (1937). *Hungary and her successors: The treaty of Trianon and its consequences, 1919–1937*. Oxford University Press.

Macher, F. (2017). *The 1931 financial Crisis in Austria and Hungary: A critical reassesment* (PhD). London School of Economics and Political Science, London.

Merziger, P., Balbi, G., Barrera, C., & Sipos, B. (2019). Crises, rise of fascism and the establishment of authoritarian media systems. In K. Arnold, P. Preston, & S. Kinnebrock (Eds.), *The handbook of European communication history* (pp. 135–152). Chichester: John Wiley & Sons, Inc.

Molnár, K. (1938). *Alkotmányjogi reformjaink az 1937 és 1938 években*. Danubia.

Paksa, R. (2012). *A magyar szélsőjobboldal története*. Jaffa.

Pastor, P. (2003). Major trends in Hungarian foreign policy from the collapse of the monarchy to the Peace Treaty of Trianon. *Hungarian Studies*, 17(1), 3–11.

Pesti, S. (2002). *Az újkori magyar parlament*. Osiris Kiadó.

Pócza, K. (2019). Closing the expectation gap? Crisis of Hungarian Parliamentarism in the inter-war period. In R. Aerts, van C. Baalen, H. te Velde, M. van der Steen, & M.-L. Recker (Eds.), *The ideal of parliament in Europe since 1800*. Palgrave Macmillan.

Püski, L. (2006). *A Horthy-rendszer*. Pannonica Kiadó.

Püski, L. (2009). Választási rendszer és parlamentarizmus a Horthy-korszakban. In I. Romsics (Ed.), *A magyar jobboldali hagyomány* (pp. 73–101). Osiris Kiadó.

Püski, L. (2015). *A Horthy-korszak parlamentje*. Országgyűlés Hivatala.

Schweitzer, G. (2005). Anti-Jewish laws in judicature practice of the administrative court. In J. Molnár (Ed.), *The Holocaust in Hungary a European perspective* (pp. 167–179). Balassi Kiadó.

Schweitzer, G. (2014). Responses in Hungarian constitutional theory to the so-called anti-Jewish laws (1938–1943). *Journal on European History of Law, 5*(2), 67–72.

Schweitzer, G. (2017a). Die Freiheitsrechte. In G. Máthé (Ed.), *Die Entwicklung der Verfassung und des Rechts in Ungarn* (pp. 669–696). Dialóg Campus.

Schweitzer, G. (2017b). Közjogi provizórium, jogfolytonosság, új közjogi irány. A két világháború közötti magyarországi alkotmányjog-tudomány vázlata. In G. Schweitzer (Ed.), *A magyar királyi köztársaságtól a Magyar Köztársaságig – Közjog- és tudománytörténeti tanulmányok* (pp. 7–45). Publikon Kiadó.

Serfőző, L. (1976). A titkos társaságok és a konszolidáció 1922–1926-ban. *Acta Historica (szeged), 57*(1), 3–60.

Siklós, A. (1988). *Revolution in Hungary and the dissolution of the Multinational State, 1918*. Akadémiai Kiadó.

Sipos, B. (2011a). A Horthy-korszak politikai rendszere (1919–1944). In I. Vida (Ed.), *Magyarországi politikai pártok lexikona 1846–2010* (pp. 137–147). Gondolat Kiadó – MTA – ELTE Pártok, Pártrendszerek, Parlamentarizmus Kutatócsoport.

Sipos, B. (2011b). *Sajtó és hatalom a Horthy-korszakban*. Argumentum.

Sipos, P. (1997a). *A szociáldemokrata szakszervezetek története Magyarországon*. MTA Történettudományi Intézete.

Sipos, P. (1997b). A konspiráció mítosza. Titkos szervezkedések Magyarországon 1919–1944 "Együttlélegzők" – Kis magyar konspirációtörténet. *Beszélő Online, 7*(30). http://beszelo.c3.hu/cikkek/a-konspiracio-mitosza.

Sipos, P., & Ravasz, I. (1997). Etelközi Szövetség. In P. Sipos & I. Ravasz (Eds.), *Magyarország a második világháborúban Lexikon A-ZS*. Retrieved from https://www.arcanum.hu/hu/online-kiadvanyok/Lexikonok-magyar orszag-a-masodik-vilaghaboruban-lexikon-a-zs-F062E/e-F08DD/etelkozi-szovetseg-F091E/.

Strausz, P. (2011). Szociális érdekegyeztetés és gazdaságirányítás – Útkeresés a két világháború közötti Magyarországon. In M. Dobák (Ed.), *A gazdasági és társadalmi érdekérvényesítés statégiai és szervezeti modelljei a 20. században* (pp. 165–215). L' Harmattan.

Szabó, I. (2019). Law I of 1920 and the historical constitution. In F. Hörcher & T. Lorman (Eds.), *A history of the Hungarian constitution: Law, government and political culture in Central Europe* (pp. 159–182). I. B. Tauris.

Szalai, A. (2013). Ami az Alaptörvényből kimaradt. A második kamara mint intézményes megoldás. *Pro Publico Bono. Magyar Közigazgatás, 1,* 71–90.

T. Molnár, G. (2019). The European and local aspects of Klebelsberg's education and cultural policy. In E. Újvári (Ed.), *Európai, nemzeti, lokális kulturális örökség és identitás: European, national, local cultural heritage and identity* (pp. 135–148). Szegedi Egyetemi Kiadó, Juhász Gyula Felsőoktatási Kiadó.

Takács, P. (2019). On Stateform of Hungary between 1920 and 1944: Applicability of the term "Monarchy without a King." *Journal on European History of Law, 10*(2), 139–148.

Takács, P. (2020). Renaming states—A case study: Changing the name of the Hungarian state in 2011. Its background, reasons, and aftermath. *International Journal for the Semiotics of Law - Revue internationale de Sémiotique juridiqu.* https://doi.org/10.1007/s11196-020-09692-y.

Thompson, S. (1993). Agrarian reform in Eastern Europe following World War I: Motives and outcomes. *American Journal of Agricultural Economics, 75*(3), 840–844.

Tomka, B. (2020). The economic consequences of World War I and the Treaty of Trianon for Hungary. Online first. *Regional Statistics, 10,* 19 p. Retrieved from https://www.ksh.hu/docs/hun/xftp/terstat/2020/rs100101.pdf.

Ujváry, G. (2016). Pozitív válaszok Trianonra: Klebelsberg Kuno és Hóman Bálint kulturális politikája. *Korunk, 27*(2), 129–131.

Ujváry, G. (2018). Klebelsberg Kuno és a Trianon utáni magyar felsőoktatáspolitika. In G. Ujváry (Ed.), *Trianon és a magyar felsőoktatás I* (pp. 237–262). VERITAS Történetkutató Intézet.

Vida, I. (Ed.) (2011). *Magyarországi politikai pártok lexikona 1846–2010.* Gondolat Kiadó – MTA – ELTE Pártok, Pártrendszerek, Parlamentarizmus Kutatócsoport.

Winchester, B. J. (1973). Hungary and the "Third Europe" in 1938. *Slavic Review, 32*(4), 741–756.

CHAPTER 7

Agenda Dynamics in Socialist Autocracy (1957–1989)

Orsolya Ring and László Kiss

As one of the losing powers in World War II, Hungary ended up under Soviet military occupation at the end of the war. In its sphere of influence, the Soviet Union strove to create "democracies" that were formally in compliance with the democratic principles that had been previously laid down in Yalta. In reality, however, Soviet imperial interests prevailed over the principles of genuine political competition, political liberties, and democratic representation.

The composition of the cabinets that were installed following the parliamentary elections in 1945 and 1947 did not reflect the preferences of the voters as those had been manifested in the outcome of the respective elections. Despite their absolute majority in parliament, right-wing forces found themselves compelled to enter into a coalition with the

O. Ring (✉) · L. Kiss
Centre for Social Sciences, MTA Centre of Excellence, Eötvös Loránd Research Network, Budapest, Hungary
e-mail: ring.orsolya@tk.hu

L. Kiss
e-mail: kiss.laszlo@tk.hu

M. Sebők and Z. Boda (eds.), *Policy Agendas in Autocracy, and Hybrid Regimes*, Comparative Studies of Political Agendas,
https://doi.org/10.1007/978-3-030-73223-3_7

165

communists and had to cede key cabinet portfolios to them. Ultimately, within the span of a few years, all the other parties outside the communists were either banned, merged into the communist party, or forced to operate as satellite parties. As a result of these developments, by the end of the 1940s a Soviet-type system emerged in Hungary, which was integrated into the international totalitarian empire; and the pivotal political player in this empire was the Communist Party of the Soviet Union (Romsics, 2001: 285–295). While its totalitarian character had given way to a milder form of socialist authoritarianism from the 1960s on, liberal (or any sort of real) democracy only returned with the regime change of 1989–1990.

Hungary became completely bereft of both, external and internal sovereignty alike. The limited multiparty system and limited parliamentary democracy of Dualism, or even the traditional authoritarianism of the pre-World War II era was supplanted by an all-encompassing communist single-party regime. Its totalitarian character was linked to the despotic exercise of personal power by the Stalinist party leader (1945–1956) and prime minister (1952–1953, 1955–1956) Mátyás Rákosi (Bihari, 2005: 98). All vestiges of economic, social, and political autonomy and pluralism were eliminated: the vast majority of productive assets were nationalized, and private property and private enterprise were reduced to a minimum. Any notion of autonomy in the plan/command-based economic system was eliminated, along with democratic liberties and an independent justice system. The secret policy morphed into an apparatus designed to exact terror on behalf of the state (Bihari, 2005: 94–102; Romsics, 2001: 338–346).

CONSTITUTIONAL AND POLITICAL SYSTEM

The new regime, which was based on the 1949 Constitution of the now "People's Republic of Hungary," led to a complete break with historical traditions, and it was essentially a servile emulation of the Soviet constitutional model from 1936. It established the principle of the unity of state power. The functions of the head of state were assumed by a body elected from the ranks of parliament, the so-called Presidential Council of the Hungarian People's Republic; save for the adoption of constitutional amendments, this body was also authorized to exercise the powers of the National Assembly when the latter was not in session (and it was seldom in session—see below). The highest organ of the executive branch was the Council of Ministers (the cabinet), which was accountable to the National Assembly (Bihari, 2005: 96; Romsics, 2001: 338–346). The totalitarian Rákosi regime was ultimately—and tragically briefly—overthrown by the 1956 Revolution (Feitl, 1994; Litván et al., 1996; Romsics, 2001: 387–397). Its success owed to the fact that the Soviet Union was playing for time as the Hungarian uprising coincided with the diplomatic clash between the United States and the Soviet Union over the crisis of the Suez Canal in Egypt. Finally, as part of a deal between the two superpowers, the Soviets were given free rein to execute the military occupation of Hungary (Dunbabin, 2014: 395; Romsics, 2001).

In the meanwhile, János Kádár, who was a minister of state at the time and simultaneously also served as the top leader of the newly reconstituted state party, the Hungarian Socialist Workers' Party (hereinafter also referred to as the MSZMP based on the commonly used Hungarian abbreviation), was taken to Moscow. His stay there was followed by an announcement—timed to coincide with the start of the military intervention—that he would lead a counter-revolutionary government (Rainer, 2013: 9–10; Romsics, 2001: 387–397). The party leader who hallmarked the post-1956 regime—the Kádár regime—served as Hungary's top leader for 32 years in the position of the first secretary of the MSZMP (the same position as secretary general in many other socialist parties), while he also served as the president of the Council of Ministers between 1956 and 1958 and again between 1961 and 1965.

The Kádár regime can be broken down into four distinct phases. The first was the period of harsh dictatorship, which lasted until 1963 and was marked by violent reprisals in the aftermath of the 1956 Revolution. The second major phase was that of the soft dictatorship (from 1963 until 1988), when the single-party regime based on socialist principles continued to rule, but Kádár's previously unlimited powers were reined in along with the state terror, and, in contrast to the foregoing Rákosi era, the regime no longer interfered with the private life of its citizens as long as they stayed loyal to the system. From the regime's perspective, it was enough for the public to acquiesce to the party's rule. The economy continued to be governed based on the tenets of a planned economy, but a little margin was extended for the limited application of market considerations. Although subject to major constraints, intellectual and cultural life also became freer (Romsics, 2001: 425–511; Standeisky, 2005: 235–334; Valuch, 2000: 249–348).

János Kádár's basic political objective was the restoration of the pre-revolution Soviet-type regime, but even as the state took reprisals and implemented restrictions, it also made concessions in the interest of calming the passions in society. As part of this policy of consolidation, a greater emphasis than previously was placed on increasing consumption; the system of the mandatory forfeiture of all agricultural output was not restored; there was a substantial wage increase in the industrial sector; profit-sharing was introduced, and owing to foreign aid (primarily Soviet and Chinese, until the 1970s when Hungary made an opening toward international capital markets), there were major improvements in the food and consumer goods supply of the major urban areas. As part of the process of forced industrialization, investments in heavy industry continued apace, but at the same time the state intensified its efforts at moving modernization forward. Hungary's export capacities were expanded. By 1962, the forced collectivization in agriculture had ended (Varga, 2009).

As a result of the violent clampdown on internal resistance, the number of politically active individuals and of groups with the ability to shape public opinion declined substantially. Throughout the entire period, the leading MSZMP bodies were largely made up of Kádár loyalists. The other fundamental operating principle of the regime was that a modest but constant increase in living standards had to be guaranteed. It was also a priority that the public should not be continuously provoked by having the leadership cult shoved in their faces. Kádár assumed that the people would not be interested in discussing politics as long as these basic principles were respected. At the same time, he found it vital to carve out a role for himself within the leadership and to hold on to the absolute authority vested in his person. The manifestation of any kind of open dissent was completely inconceivable (Rainer, 2013: 16–22; Romsics, 2001: 402–405; Varga, 2009: 201–217).

ECONOMIC CONDITIONS

Since one of the fundamental ideological tenets of communism was that the power of the regime rested on economic pillars, a brief discussion of the economic conditions of the era and their impact on policymaking is in order. These economic pillars were constantly adjusted with the aim of improving the efficiency of the centralized and bureaucratic planned economy and of raising standards of living. It was apparent already in the early 1960s that because of the expenditures related to the Cold War (cf. Cuban Missile Crisis), the cost of servicing the existing loans, and the lack of reserves, the economy would not be able to simultaneously meet the needs of both goals (better economic conditions and a rapid pace of industrialization).

By the mid-1960s the previously taken measures had become untenable, which is why the regime paved the way for the implementation of the economic reform package of 1968. The central idea behind the reforms was that rather than using strict plans and commands, state control over the economy ought to avail itself of the means of economic stimuli. As part of the so-called "New Economic Mechanism," individual corporations were given greater independence, while the role of what was known as the "second economy"—the informal and limited private sector— and that of the traditional private sector increased (Földes, 2019: 4–27; Romsics, 2007: 69–79; Varga, 2002: 201–217).

The artificially controlled price system was replaced by a new framework, in which some prices were determined by trends in supply and demand. Moreover, wages were made subject to individual and corporate performance. On the whole, the reform was a course correction aimed at optimizing the operation of an economy that remained anchored in central planning. Thus, for example, central control over major investments continued to persist. Changes in prices and wages were also strictly regulated. The state continued to extract the profits generated by companies which operated successfully in the global markets, even as the idea of shutting down economically inefficient companies was not even entertained. One consequence of the way the regime worked was that lobbying groups emerged, in which the top executives of the various economic sectors intermingled and bargained with political leaders.

By 1972, however, the opponents of these changes had managed to halt the reform processes. Central control over the industry increased once again, and exports, too, were also centrally regulated again. After the "second oil price explosion" in 1979, some previously abandoned elements of the reform package of 1968 were reintroduced. The role of central control declined and there was tacit support for public engagement in the "second economy."[1] But even as the international economy

---

[1] The more or less private sector of the economy, which operated based on market principles alongside the socialist economy; it first appeared in agriculture, and then it successfully spread to the industrial sector and the service sector, too.

underwent a fundamental transformation, no sweeping changes were implemented in Hungary, and as a result the domestic economy failed to adapt to the global trends.

The goal of the reforms introduced in the late 1970s was primarily to preserve the previously attained standards of living; especially the massive centrally-mandated wage hike of 1973. One decision at the time that had monumental implications for the economy was that the fifty largest industrial corporations were all placed under central control, and the role of central planning increased in all realms of the economy, although the command economy was not restored. As a result of the depoliticization mechanisms deployed by the regime, the debates about the reforms were limited to the political leadership and the elite intelligentsia (Rainer, 2013: 39–44; Romsics, 2007; Varga, 2009: 69–79).

The loyalty of the citizenry played a preeminent role in the stable operation of the regime. The Kádár regime's rejection of the previous era, and the concomitant proclamation of a new politics and ideology, were among the foundational tenets of the regime. From the 1960s on, those in power sought to secure the loyalty of the public by granting people a relatively greater level of freedom in their private sphere, along with a greater "freedom of choice" in private consumption, boosted by a modest "abundance of goods." This *consumer socialism* (or "Goulash communism," in the jargon of the day) provided the basis for the accord between the masses and the regime.

The second level of the regime's base of legitimacy was the creation of a restricted public sphere, which was based on a compromise between the regime and the various sections of the intelligentsia. At the same time, however, the international changes induced by the events in Paris and Prague in 1968, the economic and political regression, increasingly burdened the relationship between the regime and white-collar factions, which led some of the latter to question the foundations of the compromise (Heller et al., 1992: 111–115).

Since the early 1980s, the pressure stemming from Hungary's sovereign debt had been rising steadily, and by the mid-80s the country had drifted into an ever-deepening crisis. The leadership had underestimated the significance of international growth trends. The global economic crisis triggered by the second oil crisis in 1979 left Hungary with a massive deficit that forced the state to assume ever new debts, most of which were used to service previous loans. Furthermore, only a limited and tight-knit circle within the political leadership was aware of the debt problem and the actual data. In 1982, Hungary joined the World Bank and the International Monetary Fund, which meant that it had to make its economic indicators transparent (although the international organizations were also misled) and had to adopt international economic policy prescriptions.

The goal of the reforms introduced in the early 1980s was the creation of a mixed market economy; however, the reforms implemented were only designed to manage the crisis without venturing outside the boundaries delineated by the existing regime, which meant that they were not—and indeed could not be—effective. Hungary's sovereign debt continued to increase while economic productivity continued to shrink (Rainer, 2013: 70–73; Romsics, 2007: 75–79).

To take the edge off growing political tensions, a constitutional amendment in 1983 made it mandatory to nominate at least two candidates per single-member district in the elections for the National Assembly. Although the theoretical possibility had existed already since the end of the 1960s, in practice it had hardly ever happened. In the aftermath of the constitutional amendment, however, some eighty non-official candidates appeared on the ballots across the nation. Meanwhile, restlessness arose within the party leadership as well, pitting those who refused to acknowledge the crisis against those who were concerned about its impact. Ultimately, the economic difficulties and the social tensions they gave rise to, in combination with the internal divisions within the ruling party and the international political changes, led to the crisis and eventual downfall of the regime (Barany, 1999: 113–124; Bozóki, 2010: 7–45; Csizmadia, 2015: 129–136; Rainer, 2013).

We cannot speak of a national foreign policy in the traditional sense in this period, since the measures taken by the national leadership during this time were fundamentally determined by Hungary's allegiance to the Soviet Union. The key foreign policy objective was to make sure that the international conditions were in place for the realization of the domestic and economic policy goals that served to ensure the stability of the regime (Békés, 2011: 111; Borhi, 2004: 269–334). However, Hungary's room for maneuver in foreign policy was not only shaped by its dependence on the Soviet Union, since at the same time it was also dependent on Western credit and technology. Nevertheless, it was also compelled to actively engage in the various international lobbying efforts of the Eastern bloc states.

Starting in the late 1970s, Hungarian foreign policy began to enjoy a peculiar sort of autonomy despite the fact that the relations between the two superpowers were exceedingly fraught at the time. This independence owed to Kádár's success in persuading the Soviets that the stability of the Hungarian regime depended on intense economic and political ties to Western states. Hungarian foreign policy experienced a major change in 1988, when the idea that Hungary could act as a bridge of sorts between East and West began to gain ground (Békés, 2011: 116).

THE POLITICAL ENVIRONMENT OF POLICYMAKING IN THE KÁDÁR ERA

As Csanádi (1991: 15; 1997) argues in her analysis, the following three characteristics capture the modus operandi of the single-party regime: (1) politically monopolized dependent relations and power structure; (2) the mechanisms put in place by the regime in the interest of reproducing the underlying power structure; and (3) the absence of economic rationality. The administrative structure during this time was fundamentally characterized by the side-by-side operation of the respective party and state organs which performed the same functions of control, with the result that at each level of power the relevant institutions were duplicated (see Fig. 7.1).

At the level of formal hierarchies, we find two distinct and parallel systems, as both the party administration and the state/public administration were structured in hierarchically arranged layers. At the top of the two formal hierarchies were the party's first secretary and the prime minister (the president of the Council of Ministers), respectively. In practice, the two hierarchies were not fully separated from one another, they were connected by many threads.

These threads of dependence connecting the relevant party and state institutions also connected the decisions rendered in the respective hierarchies, and even though the decision-makers in the state hierarchy also had some threads of dependency to pull on vis-à-vis the party, those threads of dependence that connected all other hierarchies could only emanate from the party hierarchy, which led to the political monopolization of the dependencies in this system by the party. Finally, since the only way whereby the various players in this system could assert their respective interests was to pull on the threads of dependency, interest assertion was also something that was politically monopolized (Csanádi, 1990–1991: 5–15).

Another key feature of the system was the pivotal role of personal influence and personal relations. The informal relations between the players interwove the respective fabrics of the political, economic, and cultural spheres. The transmission of vital information, the expert consultations that undergirded decision-making, as well as ad hoc problem management all predominantly played out through a system of informal backchannels. This made the underlying system incapable of learning the appropriate lessons from various events and, in the long run, its inability to adapt resulted in a systemic crisis (Heller et al., 1992: 116–117).

The regime was capable of managing all the tensions generated by its operation as long as it had the necessary resources at its disposal; the protracted shortage of said resources, however, led to its disintegration. With the weakening of the forces that held it together, the underlying web of interests became increasingly complex, which undermined the power

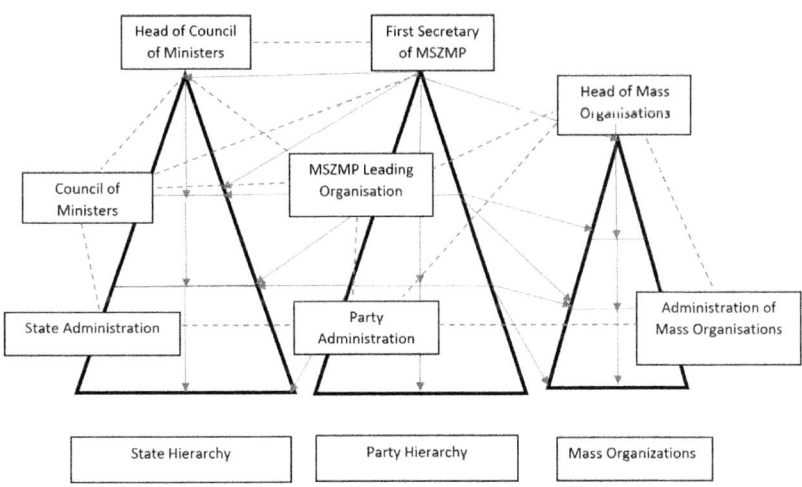

Fig. 7.1   The parallel structures of party and state[2]

[2] Channels of control (dependence) between the state, party hierarchies, and mass organizations.

Personal connections between the various hierarchies. The figure is based on the studies by Mária Csanádi and János Kornai (Csanádi, 1991; Kornai, 1992).

structure. Since the dependencies that connected the state and party hierarchies emanated from a high level and there was only limited room for direct influence, for a long while the regime proved resilient. At the same time, however, decision-makers were massively isolated from society, they found it increasingly hard to find allies, and thus when a shortage of resources emerged, it led to collapse (Csanádi, 1990–1991: 6; 2007).

DATABASES

The main criterion underlying the selection of the databases we used in our analysis was that they had to allow us to explore the particularistic and vital features of the duplicated institutional structures that characterized the period in question. Thus, we coded the archived agendas of the meetings of the Council of Ministers (the government) and of the MSZMP Politburo, as well as eight prime ministers' speeches in the National Assembly (1957, 1958, 1962, 1965, 1967, 1975, 1987, and 1988), along with seven speeches by the party's first secretary at party congresses (1959, 1962, 1966, 1970, 1975, 1980, and 1985). Each of the speeches was coded sentence by sentence. The database of prime ministers' speeches contains 2450 coded sentences, while the database of speeches by the first secretary contains 5011 coded sentences.

We relied on several sources in creating our databases. The source of the prime ministers' speeches was the National Assembly's Protocol and Document Archive, where the full texts of inaugural speeches are available. The speeches by the MSZMP's first secretary were reprinted in full by the daily newspaper Népszabadság, which is digitally available in the Arcanum Digitheca. In examining the legislation of the period, we relied on the materials published in the Hungarian Official Gazette.

For the period between 1957 and 1967, we also used a coded database of the secret decisions adopted by the Council of Ministers. (The list of secret decisions is incomplete because these are only gradually becoming declassified, yet a failure to consider these decisions would render our analysis of the public policy processes deficient.) The database used here includes 5228 coded records. The number of analyzed laws was 243; we also coded 1093 decree-laws and 8651 other decrees. The database of the latter was compiled based on the Optijus database, while the database of the Council of Minister's secret decisions was compiled by drawing on the data in the Hungaricana Public Collection Portal.

We also used the coded databases of the interpellations presented in the National Assembly featuring 357 items. We analyzed the budget with the help of the 5999 coded records in the CAP budget database. With respect to the records of the respective agendas of the Council of Ministers and of the MSZMP Politburo, we relied on the agenda database of the Hungarian National Archive; this served as the basis for the database on the Council of Ministers, which comprises 20,480 coded agenda items, as well as the MSZMP Politburo database, which boasts 19,843 coded items.

The analysis of public opinion surveys is based in part on a data table containing the summaries of public opinion surveys stored in the collection of the Vera and Donald Blinken Open Society Archive's Public Opinion and Media Research collection, and in part on the issues published during this period of the academic quarterly Jel-Kép, which featured public opinion analyzes by the staff of the Hungarian Institute of Public Opinion Research.

Descriptive Statistics and the Trends of Policy Agendas

Public Opinion Surveys

The primary means for the elite to learn about popular opinions was the so-called public sentiment report. The objective of these reports drafted for the ruling party was to inform the institutions of the single-party state about the mood of the population. Since those who drafted the reports were instructed to do so and were typically not in the possession of the requisite analytical skills, they generally just wrote what they imagined the party leaders reading the reports would want to see as the public sentiment.

In December 1986 the MSZMP Politburo decided to conduct regular public opinion surveys to assess the public reception of the political and economic measures that were either being planned or had been implemented already. Throughout the entire period in question, the oversight of this research was entrusted to the Division of Agitation and Propaganda. The Mass Communication Research Center was established in 1969, and it was tasked with drawing up a scheme for administering such public opinion surveys and with implementing them. The main profile of the research center (which was renamed the Hungarian Institute of Public

Opinion Research in 1988) was media research. It also performed public opinion surveys, however, and the most important type of such research were values surveys, along with political and economic public opinion surveys (Vásárhelyi, 2012).

Although there were some smaller outfits in the Eastern bloc that performed projects along the same lines, none of the other countries in the Soviet sphere ever created an institution that performed empirical research on par with the scope or the professionalism of this Hungarian organization. The communist/socialist regimes took different approaches toward the genre of public opinion research. They would often only use them to legitimize their measures, thereby creating the appearance that their policies enjoyed widespread public support. At the same time, surveys showing signs of dissatisfaction would often lead the regime to intensify its efforts at manipulating public opinion (Connor & Gitelman, 1977; Slider, 1985; Welsh, 2013).

The public opinion surveys performed under the Kádár regime differed from those conducted in democratic countries in many respects. For one, in reality the ruling party was not curious to find out what the public thought about a given issue, they only wanted to know what people would be willing to acknowledge publicly. In the period at hand, it is therefore crucial to distinguish between privately held opinions and opinions that individuals would be willing to voice publicly. For the most part, the public opinion surveys during this time could only capture the latter, although as we have learned from the research of (Vásárhelyi, 2016), the difference between privately held and publicly professed views differed from issue to issue, depending on how risky it was to express one's private opinion on the given question. Second, the results of the public opinion surveys were distributed only in a small, select circle, they were not publicly disseminated. Indeed, there were also some "confidential" surveys, which were printed in individually numbered copies and distributed only to a few top politicians.

Data available to us from the surveys performed during the period from 1970 to 1988 show that the central questions of the public opinion surveys touched on various economic policy measures. Starting in the 1980s, political public opinion surveys became more diverse in their outlook, and as a result the topics they surveyed also changed substantially. Public opinion surveys began focusing on issues that were known to preoccupy the public, such as for example Chernobyl, AIDS, Soviet-American summits, or political changes in communist/socialist countries (Vásárhelyi, 2012).

An analysis of the published research reveals that up until the mid-1980s, surveys of East-West relations dominated alongside research on living standards and the economic situation. While there were ten widely circulated analyzes published on the former issue between 1980 and 1985, only four were published between 1986 and 1989. In the second half of the 1980s, by contrast, the main objective of public opinion research was to discern the public's view of domestic policy issues, such as for example their assessments of the government's activities, the activities of the opposition, and the laws on assembly. While between 1980 and 1985 only four research projects focused on these issues, between 1986 and 1989 their number rose to eight.

Looking at the relationship between public opinion surveys and policy agendas, it is readily apparent that a substantial portion of the research concerning the economic situation and current political issues examined the public reception of measures taken by the government. The analysis does not suggest that those in charge had relied on the results of these surveys in deciding upon the policy measures they ended up implementing. The results of public opinion surveys first began to be published in newspapers starting in 1988, up to that point survey results were only been published when they referred to Western countries, and even those came up only sporadically in the press. Since the results of analyzes focusing on domestic policy issues were previously not published, or were only published with substantial delay in low-circulation specialized publications, the result was that they had practically no impact whatsoever on political processes outside potentially top-level decision-making.

Speeches by Prime Ministers and Kádár as First Secretary

International academic literature regards inaugural speeches by prime ministers as orations that lay out central foci of the government's work and of the issues that affect society at large (Jennings et al., 2011). The areas that these speeches touch upon are an indication of the importance of the given political issue. As was discussed above, due to the structure of the single-party state and the party's overall position of control, the prime minister was in a far weaker position than the first secretary, which is why in addition to analyzing the prime ministers' speeches during this period, we also reviewed the speeches delivered by the first secretary at the party congresses. We analyzed the two types of speeches both separately and in a comparative fashion.

Our guiding question in the process was whether by coding these speeches sentence by sentence we would be able to identify characteristic differences between the two types of speeches, and what type of relationship can be discerned between the thematic breakdown of the speeches on the one hand, and the distribution of issues covered by the legislation adopted during this time on the other. We tracked the changes in the policy issues covered by the speeches based on the number of their mentions in each speech.

The period under investigation began on November 7, 1956, as the first Kádár government took office at the time of the suppression of the 1956 Revolution. There were some terms of government during this period when the position of prime minister and party first secretary was held by the same person (this was the case twice with János Kádár, and once with Károly Grósz). All the other prime minister—although they naturally also held high-level positions in the party—could not be regarded as the top leaders of the country because of the way the single-party state-operated.

Analyzing the prime ministers' speeches in the National Assembly by breaking them down into policy topics reveals that three major themes, macroeconomic policy, foreign policy, and government operations, dominated (see Fig. 7.2). Partial exceptions to this overall trend were the speeches of 1957 and 1958, which included a high number of references to the reprisals in the aftermath of the 1956 Revolution; the 1962 speech, which focused on the arms race during the Cold War; and the speech by Prime Minister Miklós Németh in 1988, which laid the groundwork for regime transition. In the latter speech, there was a substantial shift in the ratio of the three traditionally dominant topics, with 86.5% of the sentences in the speech focusing on government operations.

Similarly, to the speeches of the prime ministers during this period, the speeches of the party's first secretary were also dominated by macroeconomic policy, foreign policy, and government operations (see Fig. 7.3). In addition to these, there was also a substantial emphasis on issues that served to buttress the regime's legitimacy at the symbolic level, which tended to revolve around freedom of speech and religion, anti-state activities, and labor policies.

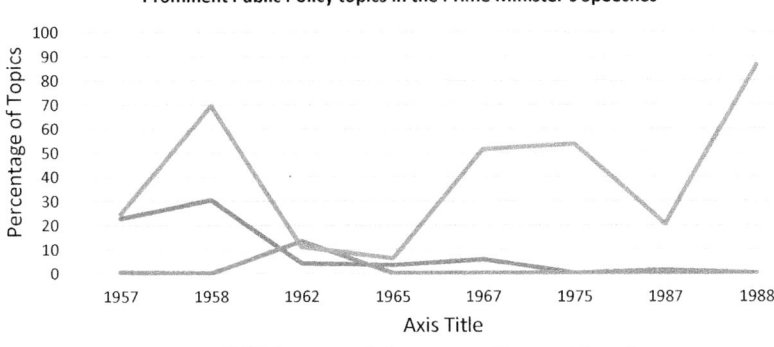

Fig. 7.2 Prominent public policy topics in the Prime Minister's speeches

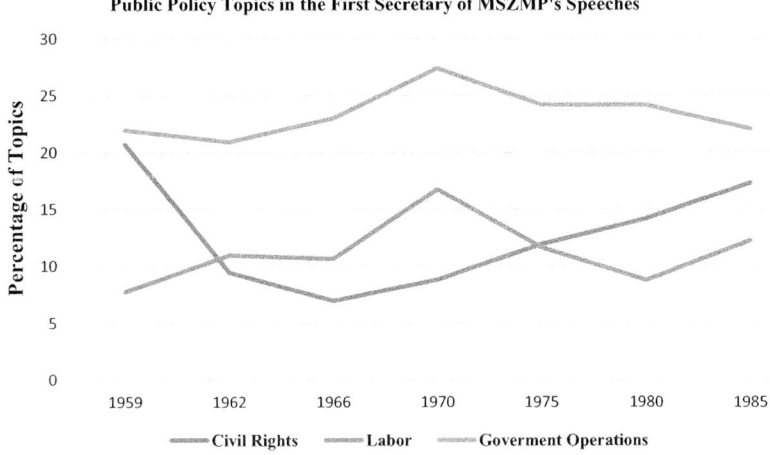

Fig. 7.3 Public policy topics in the first secretary of MSZMP's speeches

The share of individual topics was very stable over time, there were no outliers at any point. If we consider that the speeches by the first secretary were published in a daily newspaper that was read by large swathes of the public, we can assume that the heavy focus on labor, anti-state activities in these speeches was also intended to convey certain messages to wider society.

When it comes to the focus of the legislative activity of individual governments, we found major differences between the speeches given by the prime ministers and the first secretary. The share of foreign policy related legislation as a share of all legislation was continuously low until the terms of the last two governments of the era, and even the share of government operations was not as high in the legislative output as in the speeches.

The government's focus on agricultural policy and employment policy, respectively, shaped up interestingly, however. Up until 1967, the share of agricultural policy legislation was exceedingly high, while between 1967 and 1987 labor (and macroeconomic) legislation became dominant. The share of financial regulations and trade policy-related legislation exceeded 10% of all legislative output during the terms of the last two governments of the period, which were in office toward the end of the 1980s.

Interpellations

One of the characteristic features of the Kádár era was that the formally enshrined central role of the National Assembly in the political regime was in practice reduced to sham parliamentarism (Pesti, 2002: 163). As is typical of unfree political systems, the Kádár regime, too, maintained some institutions prevalent in liberal democracies in order to buttress its own legitimacy, but in practice the existence and operations of these institutions did not realize any genuine popular sovereignty or real separation of powers. The actual decision-making and controlling organs were non-state bodies and—in some cases even—informal players; in the communist/socialist regimes specifically, this meant the party apparatus and the party's top leadership (Brooker, 2014: 150–151).

Thus, the main function of the legislature operated by the regime was to reinforce its own legitimacy (Schuler & Malesky, 2014: 682). The legislature also had some role in the limited inclusion of the public in political affairs, in reaching out to voters, and it also provided the ruling party with an outlet for collecting information. In designing the parliaments of communist/socialist regimes, a key consideration was to ensure that they would constitute no threat whatsoever to the existing order: their election was non-competitive and, in reality, they lacked the power to hold the government accountable even though they were constitutionally vested with the function and authority to do so. They were subordinated to the ruling party in their actions and remained extraordinarily passive. Their involvement in policymaking in the form of plenary debates, legislative amendments, and committee debates was minimal (Molnár, 2018: 228–230; Nelson & White, 1982: 191–193).

Even though the Constitution of 1949 defined the National Assembly as the nation's "supreme body of State power," it was not actually given the freedom to take any genuinely independent actions (Feitl, 2019: 271–278). Parliament rarely convened, and when it did it was devoid of serious debates. In between the sessions of the National Assembly, its responsibilities were exercised by the Presidential Council (the collective head of state elected from the ranks of the members of the National Assembly). Similarly to other state institutions, the Presidential Council, too, was subject to the control of the ruling party (Bihari, 2005: 392–393).

It was also for the purposes of input legitimacy—that is for the sake of keeping up the appearance of democracy—that regular elections were held for the National Assembly. Furthermore, with a nod toward the principle of direct democracy, the members of parliament were in principle subject to the possibility of recall by their electors and, moreover, starting in 1985 it also became mandatory to nominate more than one candidate in each single-member district. Nevertheless, these polls did not functionally serve as genuine elections.

There was only one umbrella organization, the Patriotic People's Front, that was allowed to nominate candidates and it was only in the very final stages in the regime's existence, in 1989, that recalls actually began to occur (except for situations in which the ruling party itself initiated a recall). Even in situations when more than one candidate was allowed to run in a district, they each had to commit themselves to the manifesto of the Patriotic People's Front. Moreover, in such multi-candidate situations, the candidates who were allowed to run against each other possessed the same sociodemographic characteristics and were virtually indistinguishable from one another.

The votes were canvassed without any external oversight, and the high voter turnout was generated by a mix of compulsion and intimidation. Except for the 1985 election, turnout never dropped below 97%, and the share of the votes cast for the candidates of the Patriotic People's Front were typically in excess of 99%. Thus, elections were not only unsuitable for reflecting the political differences and nuances in society, but they were in fact ideal for concealing any type of political pluralism. Further-more, they also gave rise to an appearance of national unity, which was an important instrument of self-legitimation for the regime (Feitl, 1994, 2019).

The elections in this era did not follow a perfectly uniform pattern, although the first long phase without competitive elections, which lasted until 1985, does look homogeneous. The single-member districts were introduced for the term between 1966 and 1970, and this was followed in 1983 by the requirement to nominate more than one candidate in each district. The system of single-member districts helped elect a growing number of local candidates to parliament, and as a result the National Assembly increasingly emerged as an arena in which local communities were represented (Feitl, 1994; 2019: 70–72).

In the first phase of the Kádár era, the National Assembly adopted a few dozen laws per term, and the number of interpellations, the primary form of parliamentary questions, in a term never exceeded fifty. By the 1985–1988 term, parliament became more active (see Fig. 7.4), and the National Assembly passed over 100 laws, with a similar number of inter-pellations (Molnár, 2018: 230). In an effort to nominally hold on to earlier parliamentary traditions, the National Assembly's new Standing

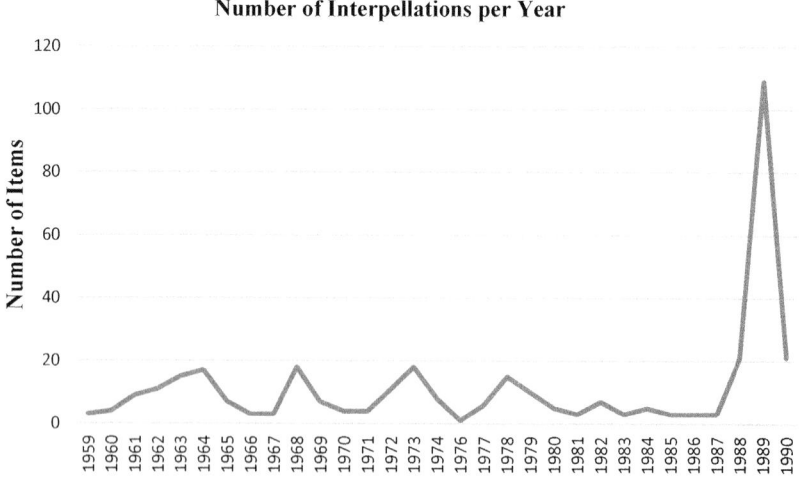

Number of Interpellations per Year

Fig. 7.4   Number of interpellations per year

Orders adopted in 1950 allowed for the possibility of interpellations, although they failed to lay out detailed rules for these. The previous rules that remained in place were the obligation of the interpellated minister to respond; the right of the representative to offer a rejoinder to the minister's response; as well as the vote in the plenary about the minister's response.

The reform of the Standing Orders adopted in 1956 changed these, adding further institutions to the list of those that could be interpellated. Previously, the Council of Ministers had been the sole institution that these questions could be addressed to, but the reform also made the Presidential Council and the chief prosecutor subject to interpellations. The new rules also specified how interpellations could be submitted and presented, and they provided further details concerning the mandatory response.

As of 1967, the rules also opened up the possibility of interpellating state secretaries, while a requirement was adopted that the responses by ministers that had been rejected by parliament would need to be debated in the competent committees of the National Assembly (with which the regulations of interpellations became identical with those of post-1989 democratic rules). In line with the prevailing rejection of the principle of separation of powers at the time, an amendment adopted in 1972 allowed for interpellating the president of the Supreme Court.

Following the 1985 election, the right to interpellate was restricted. As opposed to the previous requirement that interpellations had to be submitted 24 hours in advance, the new rules stipulated that the question and the text of the interpellation had to be submitted three days before the plenary, while at the same time the scope of questions that could be raised was also curtailed (Molnár, 2018: 232). The insignificance of the institution of interpellations is a useful indicator to highlight the limited role played by parliament in the socialist regime—its main function was to legitimate the regime rather than to exercise control over it and holding it accountable (see Sebők et al., 2017 on the functions of interpellations).

When viewed across the entire period, three issues stand out in interpellations in terms of their prominence. Some 10% of interpellations pertained to environmental, transportation, and regional and housing policies, respectively. These three dominant issues in the thematic focus of interpellations are highly illustrative of the broader role of interpellations in the single-party regime—which was also discussed above; in other words it serves to highlight that they were primarily limited to raising local concerns (Molnár, 2018: 233). It is also notable that none of these were among the dominant policy issues in the legislative activity, party decisions, or prime ministers' speeches.

If we zoom in on the thematic distribution of interpellations in the last two years of the regime, we detect a major shift. Although transportation policy still features as the most often-raised topic, interpellations concerning government operations moved into second place, followed by financial regulations and trade policy. We also observed a major increase in the interpellations concerning civil rights, law and crime policy, national defense (an area that was completely absent between 1959 and 1988), and social welfare.

Law-Making

Besides the abovementioned trends vis-á-vis speeches by the prime minister and the first secretary, law-making in the Kádár regime was in generally a dull affair. The most important personnel or policy decisions were sanctioned by the first secretary and the usage of delegated authority (see the role of the Presidential Council) was widespread.

The structure of the source of laws in the period was rather complex on account of the structural arrangement of classic communist/socialist regimes, the duplicated hierarchy featuring parallel state and party organizations, and the position as quasi-authorities of certain societal organizations (e.g., the classic mass organizations). The most important carriers of legal norms in most socialist regimes were laws. And the right to create laws was vested in parliament.

These general rules applied to the Hungarian socialist regime, but with many caveats. According to the Constitution, during the times when the National Assembly was not in session, its powers were exercised by the Presidential Council of the Hungarian People's Republic. The Presidential Council adopted decree-laws, but the Council was obliged to present these at the next session of the National Assembly. The Constitution also authorized the Council of Ministers to adopt decrees.

The relationship between laws and decree-laws, their respective shares of the total legislative output, was the subject of pronounced attention already back then (see Fig. 7.5). It was generally understood that the number and share of decree-laws should be reduced, while that of laws should be increased. Already at the time, reducing the role of governance

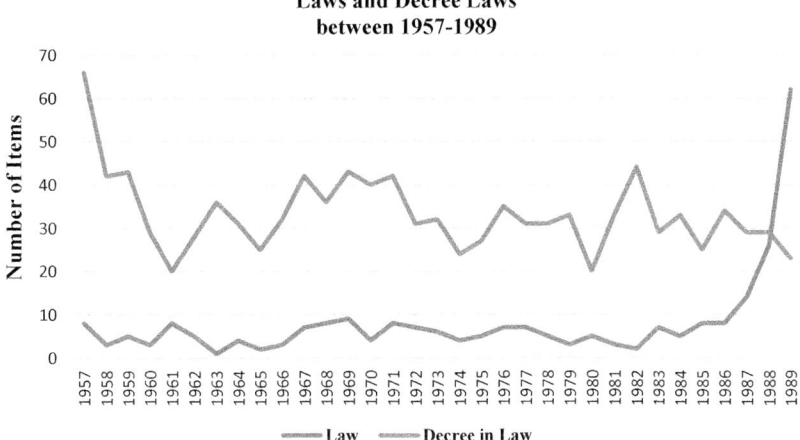

**Laws and Decree Laws
between 1957-1989**

Fig. 7.5   Laws and decree-laws between 1957 and 1989

by decree was perceived as a fundamental precondition of democratic control (Kovács, 1966: 23).

Despite this insight, the number of laws adopted by parliament lagged significantly behind the number of decree-laws adopted by the Presidential Council. Throughout most of the period, the ratio between the two was around 4–5 decree-laws for each law adopted by the National Assembly. The situation only began to change by the late 1980s. By 1987, the ratio had dropped to 3–1 in favor of decrees with the force of law; in 1988, the number of laws and decree-laws were roughly balanced; and, finally, in 1989 the number of laws exceeded that of decree-laws for the first time.

In addition to the time series analysis, it also makes sense to zoom in on the legislative activities under individual governments during this period. While decrees adopted by the Council of Ministers were instruments that were most prodigiously used by governments during the early and the final phases of the regime, between 1958 and 1987 ministerial decrees predominated.

By the end of the Kádár era, there was a shift in the legislative activity of the Presidential Council, and rather than adopting decree-laws, it increasingly limited itself to issuing decisions—if we break the numbers down by terms of government, we find that this shift occurred under the Grósz government that entered into office in 1987. The adoption of laws peaked during the rule of the Németh cabinet, however, which began governing at the end of 1988; 7% of the legislation that entered into effect during this time were laws adopted by the National Assembly, whereas in any other term of government during the period investigated, the share of such laws in the total legislative output never exceeded 2%.

We also observe interesting trends when looking jointly at the various sources of law and the policy issues on the governmental agenda. We find that macroeconomic policy issues were predominantly regulated by high-level legislation that is laws or decrees adopted by the Council of Ministers or by ministries. The areas of law and crime policy were regulated heavily by laws and by decree-laws, decisions adopted by the Presidential Council, and National Assembly resolutions. Foreign trade and foreign policy were predominantly regulated by decree-laws, as well as ministerial decrees and the decisions of the Presidential Council. Finally, government operations were mainly subject to regulation by decision-level legislation, while social policy was predominantly subject to regulation by way of decrees adopted by the Council of Ministers.

The Council of Ministers and the MSZMP Politburo

The operating principles and organizational structure of the ruling party, the Hungarian Socialist Workers' Party, which existed from November 1956 to October 1989, were governed by the party's Rules of Procedure. The first Rules of Procedure were adopted by the party congress held in June 1957. These rules were an amended version of the Rules of Procedure of the pre-1956 Revolution ruling party, the Hungarian Workers' Party.

The next major reform of the Rules of Procedure and of the internal election system within the party occurred only in 1989. The Rules of Procedure provided that in the period between party congresses, the Central Committee would act as the ruling party's highest controlling body. The Central Committee decided on the "most important" social, political, ideological, cultural, and organizational issues, as well as the personnel appointments within the scope of its authority; it represented the party in its relations with the sister parties, the mass organizations, and the state institutions.

The Central Committee convened "as necessary" but at least once every three months. Its members and substitute members were elected by the party congress. The Central Committee elected the members of the Politburo from its ranks, and between sessions of the Central Committee, the Politburo steered the party. The Politburo had the authority to take decisions on both matters of principle as well as practical issues; it drafted the party's stances regarding political business and also managed its day-to-day affairs. Initially, it met weekly, and then shifted to meeting every other week.

The full or edited texts of its decisions were relayed in the form of decisions, position statements, or directives to the parties designated in the respective document and to the "Archive of Decisions," and they could also be published in the confidential internal bulletin or the press. In addition to its regular meetings, the Politburo also held special and closed sessions. Closed sessions were used to debate personnel questions, criminal policy issues, or international party relations. When a special meeting could not be convened, a so-called "vote on the fly" was conducted. In such a situation, written proposals were circulated along with a list of the names of the Politburo members, and the members expressed their consent by signing their names (Németh, 1995: 18–29).

The Council of Ministers continued to operate in line with the spirit of the 1949 Constitution and was subject to the control of the ruling MSZMP. This was also reflected in the fact that there were times when the government was headed by the party's first secretary, János Kádár. In 1957, Kádár had the Constitution amended to remove the enumeration of the various government ministries in the document. This meant that it was no longer necessary to amend the Constitution in order to reorganize the ministries, and hence the two-thirds supermajority to this end was also no longer required. While the number of ministries and thus the number of cabinet members changed several times during this era in 1989 there were 12 ministries, the same number as in early 1949 (Szabó, 2006: 286).

The overlap in the personnel of the party leadership and the government persisted throughout the entire Kádár period. The head of government, for example, was always a member of the Politburo, but other Politburo members were also often members of the cabinet even as they could simultaneously also serve as members of the Central Committee.

An examination of the items on the agendas of the meetings of the Council of Ministers during this period reveals that the most commonly discussed topics were macroeconomics, government operations, foreign policy, foreign trade, and agriculture. The agenda of the Politburo, by contrast, predominantly focused on government operations, along with foreign policy, labor policy, and issues pertaining to science and technology. This division of labor regarding policy areas between formal institutions of a given polity is unusual in democratic parliamentary systems, although in historical perspective (see the joint foreign policy with Austria during Dualism—see Chapter 5), or in contemporary presidential systems it is far from being unheard of.

Two contrasting areas of interest in this era are agriculture and labor. On the one hand, the distribution over time of agriculture's presence on the agenda of the Council of Ministers was massively correlated with the reform measures, mostly handled by the cabinet. However, the Politburo was also active in this field (see below). On the other hand, our data also show that issues involving labor policy tended to be predominantly debated at the meetings of the Politburo. The latter is also reflected in the emphases of the speeches by the first secretary, where we identified labor policy as one of the issues that stood out in terms of importance. This is indicative of the preeminent status of labor-relations in socialist autocracy.

Finally, declassified sources show that the overwhelming majority of secret decisions concerned government operations (an annual average of 12.5%), foreign policy (22.22%), and foreign trade (15.41%). It is worth juxtaposing this data with the legislation published in the Hungarian Official Gazette, where the share of foreign policy and foreign trade topics did not exceed 5%. This serves to highlight that secret decisions cannot be left out of the analyzes of the sources of law in Hungary at the time. Notably, as the regime neared its collapse, in 1988, the share of foreign policy issues among the legislative items published in the Hungarian Official Gazette suddenly surged to 16.5%. The reason is that while previously ambassadorial appointments had been enacted in the secret decisions of the Council of Ministers, starting in 1988 they were published in the Official Gazette.

Party Decisions

As we pointed out previously, a fundamental feature of the administrative structure of socialist regimes in general was the duplication of the various levels of political control in both the party and the state apparatus, and the parallel operation of each such layer in the state and the party, respectively. Although they were not recognized as distinct sources of law, party decisions issued by the ruling party had a major impact on the policy agenda.

Following the principle of "democratic centralism," these decisions had a binding effect on all party organizations and, by virtue of party discipline, they were also binding for the entire membership, including the prime minister and ministers, as well as members of parliament.

Party decisions were taken by the leading organs of the party, the Central Committee, and the Politburo. Between 1957 and 1989, a total of 334 party decisions were adopted. When we analyze these based on the Comparative Agendas policy codes, it emerges that the decision-making activity of those at the helm of the party was rather diverse in its thematic outlook, with their focus spanning all major topics except for energy, immigration, and land policy. Most party decisions fell into the category "government operations," including the decisions on the party's own international governance and regulations. In terms of their share of the decisions, government operations were followed by macroeconomics, labor, and agricultural policy, which shows readily that beyond the political processes, the party leadership was mostly concerned about economic planning and regulation. Moreover, we also found that the same four main major topics stand out in both the party decisions and legal statutes.

CASE STUDIES

Labor and Social Welfare—Instruments of Legitimation

The system of social security operated as a branch of the socialist planned economy. As a system that was capable of exerting an influence over the life circumstances of broad swathes of society, it stood in the direct service of the party-political interests during the period in question. It served as a central element in the process of consolidation that defined the policies of the Kádár regime after 1956, which were meant to neutralize (M. Szabó, 1988: 156) and pacify society, and to steer it away from dabbling in politics toward focusing on consumption instead (Valuch, 2003: 366–368). This required access to massive economic resources. Those who study the history of Hungarian social welfare policy essentially agree that the Kádár era's social welfare policies—which were actually "standards of living policies"—were used to stabilize the position of the regime (Horváth, 2012; Szalai, 1992; Tomka, 2012).

The hard-core communist Rákosi regime of the early 1950s had rejected policy activism in the realm of social welfare. After 1956, Kádár first deployed it as an instrument to facilitate collectivization in agriculture, expanding the scope of the social security system to the peasantry which was being consolidated into agricultural cooperatives. By the mid-1960s, social welfare policy had increasingly emerged as an instrument to raise standards of living. As an analysis by Szalai (1992: 40) shows, the objectives of economic policy (which continued to benefit from artificially low wages) clashed with the objective of consolidation, which was based on increasing popular consumption. To alleviate this tension, the Kádár regime reorganized and revamped social policy expenditures as "social security benefits" (or rights). It was crucial that the peasantry (now organized in cooperatives) was entitled to pension from 1957 on. In 1967, the childcare allowance was introduced and from 1972 it was extended to be a universal benefit. The compromise proved successful and it allowed for its long-term consolidation.

Similarly, to its social policy approach, the Kádár government also changed the regulations implemented by the foregoing regime in the area of population policies. During the Rákosi era, issues pertaining to demographic processes were primarily regulated by administrative methods and criminal law instruments (such as an abortion ban). Starting in the mid-sixties, these policy elements were supplanted by a family policy based on a system of positive discrimination and subsidies. However, even in combination with all the other pertinent policy instruments (such as the homeownership subsidy for families and the childcare allowance) the government failed to effect a turnaround in the unfavorable demographic trends. What it did contribute to—along with other instruments of social policy support that was being expanded at this time—was the long-term success of Kádár's consolidation policy.

The pivot in the second half of the 1960s is also readily apparent in the legislation adopted during this period. Starting in 1966, we observe a rise in the share of social welfare policy and labor policy (including the regulations of worktime and wages) topics in the regime's legislative output. The peak year in this respect was 1967 when 11% of all the legislation adopted concerned the major topic labor policy.

The social welfare and labor topics are also closely connected. The changing function of the social security system, along with the increased flexibility of the centrally determined wage and work time rules and the family policy incentives, all served to pave the ground for the 1968 economic reform and to alleviate the social tensions anticipated by the leadership. The resurgence after 1971 of legislation concerning labor policy was a reflection of a new trend, namely, the growth in the volume of wage policy measures after this area was reregulated once again in the wake of the decision to axe the 1968 economic reform.

The interconnectedness between labor and social welfare is also apparent in the reactions of the CEOs of state-owned corporations to these reforms. Recognizing a way to skirt the strict wage and labor-management regulations, they increasingly availed themselves of the possibility of sending workers on sick leave because the previously allocated pay of such workers functioned as a "reserve" and could be potentially used to pay premiums to others (J. Szalai, 1992: 32–33). The connection between these two areas was also an inherent feature of the way the regime operated, since all types of social insurance scheme benefits were tied to the individual's status as an employee, no alternative welfare regimes were in place (Tomka, 2012: 29).

The growing role of social welfare is well-tracked in budgetary trends as well. Even though the share of budget allocations for social welfare did not even reach 10% in the early 1960s, such spending had surged to over 20% by the second half of the 1970s and to 35% by the late 1980s. Nevertheless, demographic trends contributed as much to this increase in social spending as the policies pursued by Kádár. Between 1960 and 1975, the share of pensioners in the population increased almost 2.5-fold even as the pensions per pensioners increased 2.7-fold during the same period, with the result that the pension system emerged as an ever-greater burden on the budget (Szalai, 1992: 30).

In turn, large swathes of the population focused on securing the decent income security that came with being a pensioner. In many cases (e.g., for miners or members of law enforcement) the opportunity for early retirement was effectively a form of delayed compensation. As a consequence, according to the Statistical Office's representative surveys on income, payouts from the social security system made up 11% of the average household income in 1967, surged to 20% by 1977, and then climbed further to reach 25% in 1987 (Szalai, 1992: 42–43).

The Cold War and Defense Spending

The Cold War threat explains why the share of sentences in the prime ministers' speeches referencing national defense increased drastically starting in 1962 (from 0 to 13.4%). This change was also reflected in the rising number of items of legislation featured in the Hungarian Official

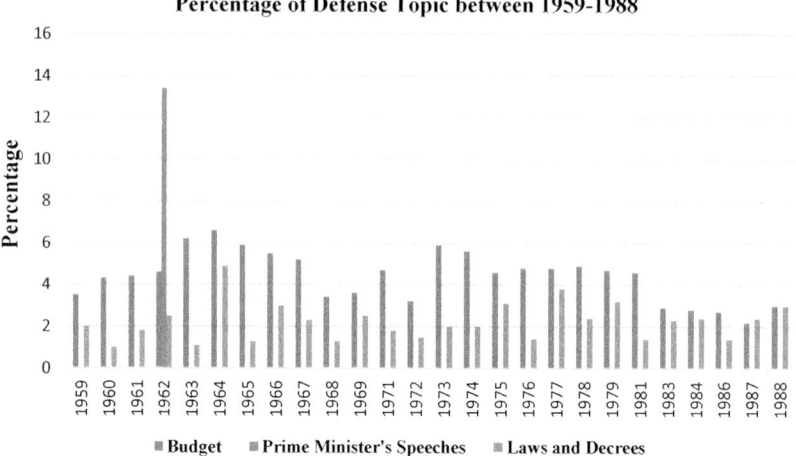

Fig. 7.6   Percentage of defense topic between 1959 and 1988

Gazette in 1964 (from 1–2 to 4.9%) and the share of defense spending in the budget (from 4.4 to 6.6%—see Fig. 7.6).

In July 1961, Cuba, which was led by Fidel Castro at the time, concluded a military pact with the Soviet Union. Pursuant to this agreement, Soviet medium-range nuclear missiles were installed on the island. Faced with a rigorous reaction on the part of the United States, the Soviet leader, Nikita Khrushchev, ultimately backed down and ordered the withdrawal of Soviet missiles from Cuba, and in response, US President John F. Kennedy pledged that the United States would not attack Castro and also promised to withdraw American missiles from Turkey (Naftali et al., 1997; Zubok & Pleshakov, 1997).

Since the Soviets had planned their operation in Cuba in secret, the crisis caught their satellite countries in the Eastern bloc by surprise and found them ill-prepared. The Hungarian leadership was informed about the events by the Supreme Commander of the Unified Forces of the Warsaw Treaty Organization (known as the Warsaw Pact),[3] who recommended that in light of the looming threat of a war, all units attached

---

[3] The Warsaw Treaty was the military and political mutual defense pact of the communist/ socialist countries in Central and Eastern Europe between 1955 and 1991.

to the Unified Forces be put on alert, and he requested a report by the next day about the actions taken. As a clear sign of the limited policy autonomy of the Hungarian party elite, available sources indicate that the Hungarian military was probably mobilized directly from Moscow, while the Hungarian party leadership was unaware of what was happening. The state of alert was only lifted upon the conclusion of the Cuba Crisis on November 22, 1962.

In light of the tense international situation that had emerged in the 1960s, the Ministry of National Defense drew up long-term plans for the modernization of the Hungarian People's Army, which is coordinated with the supreme command of the Warsaw Pact. The main objective was to bring the Hungarian army up to the level of the other militaries of the Warsaw Pact nations. Between 1961 and 1965, the emphasis was on the structural and material/technological modernization of the Hungarian military.

In the aftermath of the Cuban Crisis, the trend that had commenced in the spring of 1961 persisted, and hence defense spending was increased once again (Békés & Kalmár, 2014: 93). In September 1962, the Ministry of National Defense set the number of active-duty military personnel at 85,000; by 1972 the number was set at 92,000–95,000. In reality, however, the actual number of active-duty personnel was 106,400 in August 1963, while the target for 1970 was 120,000–122,000.[4]

The surviving documents on the deliberations of the MSZMP's top leadership organs and of the Council of Ministers on this issue show that neither of these bodies addressed the crisis situation. They apparently acquiesced themselves to the fact that they had no influence on how the crisis was being handled. For the members of the Warsaw Pact, the Missile Crisis clearly highlighted the extraordinary extent of their dependence, and they protested this in several forums. It was also due to these protests that a series of meetings between Warsaw Pact deputy-foreign ministers was launched, which quickly emerged as an important forum for the alliance in coordinating their joint operations and decision-making (Békés & Kalmár, 2014: 96).

In Hungary, the trajectory of defense spending was not only influenced by Hungary's membership in the Warsaw Pact, but also by its membership

---

[4] The August 30, 1963, report of Lajos Fehér to the Politburo. MNL-OL, M-KS-288. f. 5/312.

in the Council for Mutual Economic Assistance (COMECON),[5] which sought to coordinate the member states' military production. In response to a Soviet initiative, a large-scale armament program was launched in the Eastern bloc in the 1960s. During the implementation of the second five-year plan, Hungary increased the originally allocated amount of 34.5 billion forints of direct defense spending by 4.2 billion forints.

As part of the international division of labor between the COMECON countries on military-industrial production, Hungary's responsibility was to produce armored transportation vehicles, air defense artillery, and radio locators. Between 1950 and 1975, Hungary's foreign trade balance with respect to the trade in military industrial goods was continuously in deficit, which exacerbated the country's economic problems (Germuska, 2010: 99–132).

The 1968 Invasion of Czechoslovakia

Another major development in this era regarding national security and military affairs was related to the Warsaw Pact invasion of neighboring Czechoslovakia. The year 1968 was a decisive one for the Kádár regime in many respects, and the changes that occurred in Hungary at the time cannot be properly understood without appreciating the impact of the international context. The elements of this international context ranged the student rebellions in the West all the way to the Soviet-directed intervention in Czechoslovakia.

The countries of the Warsaw Pact launched their invasion of Czechoslovakia on August 20, 1968, in response to the reforms announced by Secretary-General Alexander Dubcek, which were interpreted as an effort on the part of Czechoslovakia to abandon the Warsaw Pact (Bischof et al., 2009; Eidlin & Eidlin, 1980: 1–35; Goodman, 1969; Mitrovits, 2012: 136–140). Once more, government documents are void of details of Hungary's involvement in occupying forces.

In this, the case is reminiscent of that of Cold War mobilization. The decisions on the substance of the military intervention were not rendered by domestic bodies but at the international meetings of the Warsaw Pact countries. A detailed analysis of the data also reveals that the events of 1968 were only raised in the deliberations of the party's leading bodies.

---

[5] COMECON was the organization for coordinating economic cooperation between the communist/ socialist countries of Central and Eastern Europe between 1949 and 1991.

The issue did not figure at all on the agenda of the open sessions of the Council of Ministers. Analyzing the documents related to the leading organs of the ruling party MSZMP, we did detect a quantitative change, even if not at the level of agenda, but at least in terms of growth in the number of sessions. The preeminent significance of the international events of 1968 was also reflected in the intense attention devoted to the issue at the sessions of the Central Committee, which managed the MSZMP between party congresses.

The MSZMP's Central Committee met five times a year on average, but in 1968 it met a total of eight times, with three of those meetings being held in August. The latter three meetings were also different from the standard-setting in that the representatives of the cabinet were also present, and the agenda of the meetings was devoted exclusively to international issues, to ponder the invasion of Czechoslovakia and the situation in the Middle East and in Vietnam. The Politburo, which managed the everyday affairs of the MSZMP, met 42 times in 1968, as opposed to its annual average of 37 sessions a year. It met most often in July (6) and August (6), and of these 12 sessions, the agenda of seven were entirely devoted to the situation in Czechoslovakia.

The digitized versions of several daily newspapers published at the time also tell an interesting tale of the role of the media in socialist autocracy. During this period the press was not a forum for the publication of diverse opinions but a means whereby the political leadership informed public opinion and conveyed official propaganda. The press system was so tightly and directly controlled at the time, that the newsrooms had a direct telephone line connecting them to the major party organs (Bussemer, 2008; Feitl, 2008: 128–131; Pap, 2019: 27–29). Notably, in 1968, Czechoslovakia appeared in the Hungarian dailies far more often than usual. In fact, from the start of the year until the summer, a series of positive items were published which endorsed the reform attempts in Czechoslovakia.

However, by August the number of articles increased further, and this time several major dailies published a full-page notice in support of Hungary's participation in the military intervention in Czechoslovakia. As is apparent based on the word frequency cloud in Fig. 7.7 based on these texts, the articles mainly reflected what was being said in the various meetings of official bodies, and they were strongly propagandistic in nature, stressing the "helping" nature of the manoeuvers and the defense of the "socialist order" as a justification for the intervention.

Fig. 7.7   Word frequency cloud based on front-page journal articles of August 1968

The Endgame of the Regime from 1985 on

Starting in the 1980s, Hungary's public debt began to exert a growing negative impact and by the mid-80s, the national economy was descending into a deepening crisis, the details of which were for a long time known only to a small and restricted circle within the political leadership. The reforms introduced in response to the crisis—such as the replacement of the previous single term, nationalized banking system, which had prevailed since 1947 and was well-suited for the needs of the planned economy, with a dual banking system in 1987—were aimed at creating a mixed market economy. Despite these efforts, sovereign debt soared continuously while economic productivity kept declining. In the meanwhile, conflicts emerged within the party leadership between those who refused to acknowledge that a crisis was afoot and those who were concerned about its impact (Barany, 1999: 113–124; Ripp, 2006: 19–46).

The electoral reform in 1983 not only made it mandatory to nominate at least two candidates in each single-member district in the elections for the National Assembly, but it also set up the so-called Constitutional Law Council, a parliamentary committee which marked a step toward the emergence of constitutional jurisprudence. Despite the multiple nominations in the single-member districts, not a single opposition candidate was elected to the National Assembly in 1985. But the reforms aimed at creating a competitive parliamentary election system that would allow for genuine ideological choices continued. In 1987, the MSZMP Politburo issued a guideline to continue the modernization of the political institutional framework (Feitl, 2019: 166–180).

Some of those in the party who called for such changes believed that these steps would be necessary to ameliorate the economic situation. The surging reform communist wing of the party represented the youngest generation within the MSZMP. Kádár's position waned steadily, and he began losing his grip on party leadership. The changes in the party's outlook were also reflected in a series of measures taken in 1987/1988, whereby the regime sought to boost economic efficiency.

This included for example the aforementioned dual banking system and the process of privatization launched in these years, which was still spontaneous and was being implemented without a comprehensive plan. In essence, privatization meant that the state was withdrawing from certain segments of the economy; they turned companies that the state could no longer operate profitably over into private ownership. The year 1988 also saw change at the top of the party leadership, with Kádár being ousted as the MSZMP's first secretary and replaced by Károly Grósz. The absence of fundamental and deep reforms continued to boost the ranks of the reform communists, who called for a "peaceful transition" (Romsics, 2013).

In the meanwhile, the number of active opposition groups in Hungary increased steadily, and the party did not take violent action to keep them in check because they feared that such measures would hurt Hungary's international standing and impair its ability to secure foreign loans. The various opposition groups that had previously worked separately from one another held their first joint meeting in 1985 in Monor. One of the foundational events in the history of the Hungarian opposition, the Lakitelek conference, was held in 1987. The reform communists were also represented there, along with two of the biggest parties of post-regime change democracy: the right-wing MDF, and liberal SZDSZ. In addition to giving shape to an emerging political pluralism, the new party formations were also an indicator of the disintegration of the single-party dictatorship (Romsics, 2001: 537–584; 2013).

The changes that occurred during this time are also easy to track with the help of our databases. Public opinion surveys were administered more frequently and the topics that they explored grew increasingly diverse, as survey questions concerning current issues that were at the forefront of public interest increasingly moved to the center of public opinion research as well. As compared to previous speeches by prime ministers, we also found a major thematic shift in Prime Minister Miklós Németh's inaugural speech in 1988, as well as in the topics raised in interpellations in parliament, with an especially pronounced growth in the issues involving the major topic government operations.

A growing proportion of both interpellations and the promulgated legislation touched on financial regulations and trade policy, in addition to government operations. There was also a fundamental change with respect to legislative activity. By the end of the period in question, the Presidential Council's legislative activities had undergone a transformation, and rather than adopting decree-laws, the Council increasingly limited itself to issuing decisions, while the place that decree-laws had previously occupied in the overall legislative output was increasingly taken over by laws.

Important changes occurred also with respect to the relationship between secretly and publicly adopted legislation, with a very distinct shift toward a higher share of public legislation. In a decision of November 22, 1988, the MSZMP Politburo stated that it respects the National Assembly's absolute authority to legislate, as well as the autonomy and governmental responsibility of the Council of Ministers; thus, from this point on the party abdicated direct control over governmental activities.

CONCLUSION

Non-democratic regimes need legitimacy just as much as democratic ones do, and the analysis of policymaking in the socialist autocracy of the Kádár era supports this claim. This is reached in part through input legitimacy—in other words: through the appearance of democracy—, and in part through increased efforts aimed at output legitimacy (Scharpf, 1999), that is governance aimed at meeting popular needs such as the one for security or a decent standard of living. Furthermore, these regimes frequently avail themselves of leader-centric legitimacy as well as the legitimacy that symbolically charged policy issues provide. All this can work as long as the economic environment is suitable, in other words as long there is enough financial support for the system.

Our data—thus for example the exceedingly high share of budget allocations on social policy starting in the 1970s—are illustrative of the constant effort directed at increasing output legitimacy. At the same time, the peculiarly designed electoral system—which harbored no risk for those in power—, the way the National Assembly continued to operate, and the publication of a designated set of legislative items all served to keep up the appearance of democracy.

While democratic legitimacy improves the effectiveness of governance since it helps ensure that citizens abide by the rules and cooperate with the authorities in the implementation of public policy (Murphy, 2006; Tyler, 2011), the non-democratic regimes investigated in this book largely boosted the public's willingness to cooperate through concessions granted in the framework of compacts that the regime entered into with society, all the while they also drew on the armed forces—as needed—to enforce compliance.

A reliance on law enforcement and the military did not necessarily require them to take real action, it was enough to evoke a sense of menace in the collective memory of society. Although the violent practices of the state's security apparatus that had characterized the Rákosi era—which included both open and hidden forms of physical violence, both of which were clearly apparent and known throughout all of society regardless of the specific form they happened to take—was supplanted in the 1960s by a cleverer, in a sense invisible, presence of the state's security apparatus. Yet this reformed secret police approach was equally effective in permeating all of society and all areas of everyday life, thereby supporting the implementation of the policies designated by the party leadership.

The leadership cult surrounding János Kádár was constructed using distinctly less conspicuous methods than had been the case with the cult of Rákosi previously. In fact, the goal was to visibly distance the Kádár regime from its predecessor in this realm, too. There were fewer images of Kádár on display in public institutions and in the press, and no institutions were named after him while he was alive. In building the personality cult surrounding Kádár, the legends disseminated about him through informal channels proved more important. Thus, the widely circulated perception was that he was a modest and puritanical person who used to be a hard-working manual laborer. The goal was to build an image of Kádár as a leader who had come from below and risen to the top, who maneuvered deftly to stand up for Hungarian interests vis-à-vis the Soviet leadership (Horváth, 2013: 71).

Our data shows the prevalence of several symbolic public policy issues on the policy agenda that were designed to promote the integration of society. One such example was the condemnation of the 1956 Revolution, which was an emphatic issue in the prime ministers' speeches of 1957 and 1958, or the sense of menace experienced at the time in connection with the Cold War, which was a central topic in the prime minister's speech of 1962. The use of symbolic issues that were meant to legitimate the regime was also reflected in other data we gathered—such as our data on legislation and budgets—even though these were primarily conveyed to society through articles disseminated on the cover pages of daily newspapers.

The data at our disposal did not end up conforming to our earlier expectation that non-democratic regimes devote more public attention to law enforcement, but in other respects the underlying idea was borne out. The explanation for the dynamic we found was the logic based on which the regime worked. The operation of the armed services was more likely to be regulated by secret legislation—and through covertly operating organizations and committees—than one would expect under a different regime. A portion of these secret legislative provisions remains classified and unavailable to the public to this very day, and even those items of legislation are accessible have only been available in the public realm for a few years.

This has made it either impossible or only partially possible for us to track the funding that the regime allocated to the respective organizations, even though we know that the Hungarian intelligence services enjoyed a special status within the Soviet bloc in the area of technological/scientific intelligence, which was in all likelihood a costly expertise to acquire. Such activities were funded through the offshore-like network of foreign trade corporations, however, which is why they never appeared in the budget (Borvendég, 2018: 14).

During the Kádár era, the decision-making authority with respect to national defense, the military industry, and internal security rested with the National Defense Council (1952–1962) at first, and then with the National Defense Committee (1962–1990). Up until 1976, only the highest echelon of the leadership was aware of these bodies, they were never referenced in any official bulletins or collections of legal texts (Germuska, 2014: 13–18). The National Defense Committee met 8–10 times a year and rendered around 60–90 decisions annually.

To put this data in perspective, we can juxtapose it with the fact that on average, the Council of Ministers and the MSZMP Politburo each discussed issues involving national defense about 20 times a year, while about 10 items of legislation on the issue were published each year in the Hungarian Official Gazette. This leads us to conclude that even though the highest levels of political leadership focused a great deal on the armed services—and the efforts to keep the relevant documents classified could also be an indication of this heightened attention—, a detailed and quantitative analysis of this claim would necessitate compiling further databases. This finding has relevance for all studies of policy dynamics in authoritarian regimes: archival research and the direct investigation of the practices of the elite (such as interviews with top-level office holders) may prove more important than the analysis of publicly available or official data.

Our research also clearly confirms the expectation that the thematic distribution of decisions taken by the post-totalitarian Kádár regime was not primarily reflective of public preferences but of the agenda pursued by a decision-maker with barely limited powers. Information about the issues that were of interest to the public either failed to register with the decision-makers or did do so only to a very limited extent. The political regime was devoid of independent and critical media, and thus media coverage was dominated by issues that the political leadership dictated. The media lacked the ability to influence the political agenda. Similarly, the results of public opinion surveys also did not play a substantial role, the public reception of the measures taken by the government did not feedback into policy decision-making to allow for taking corrective measures. This finding has relevance for our analysis of the government-controlled media of the period of illiberal democracy in Hungary after 2020 (see next chapter).

The decision-makers had very limited awareness of what social problems should have been regarded as priorities in need of urgent solutions. The issues that were put on the agenda ended up there because they aligned with the ruling party's political interests. According to the informational disadvantage hypothesis proposed by (Chan & Zhao, 2016), the free flow of information is limited in autocracies, which makes it harder for policy information to reach the decision-makers. This makes institutional friction and policy punctuations more pronounced.

We also detected evidence of this phenomenon in the Hungarian budget data (Sebők & Berki, 2018), and our analyzes of the database at our disposal yielded a higher kurtosis value than one would expect under a normal distribution (see the Chapter 4 on Data and methods and Chapter 9). With respect to the regime investigated here, we would add another factor to the information-deficit hypothesis. Our analysis has shown that the punctuations in the policy agendas of the Kádár era were partly caused by Soviet decisions that skewed the role of certain policy areas in the Hungarian policy arena. We referenced several examples to illustrate that Hungarian decision-makers were at a major informational disadvantage in this area. In summary, we can conclude that in the absence of other policy players (i.e., politically active citizens, independent civil organizations, competing parties, and a free press), the ruling party had an almost exclusive control over most of the policy agenda in Hungary between 1956 and 1989—and Moscow had control over the rest.

REFERENCES

Barany, Z. (1999). Out with a whimper: The final days of Hungarian socialism. *Communist and Post-Communist Studies, 32*(2), 113–125.

Békés, C. (2011). Hungarian foreign policy in the bipolar world, 1945–1991. *Foreign Policy Review, 1,* 65–97.

Békés, C., & Kalmár, M. (2014). Hruscsov, a kubai rakétaválság és a szovjet blokk. *Acta Scientiarum Socialium, 42,* 85–96.

Bihari, M. (2005). *Magyar politika: 1944–2004: politikai és hatalmi viszonyok.* Osiris Kiadó.

Bischof, G., Karner, S., & Ruggenthaler, P. (2009). *The Prague spring and the Warsaw pact invasion of Czechoslovakia in 1968.* Rowman & Littlefield.

Borhi, L. (2004). *Hungary in the Cold War, 1945–1956: Between the United States and the Soviet Union.* Central European University Press.

Borvendég, Z. (2018). *Az „Impexek" kora. Külkereskedelmi fedéssel folyatott pénzkivonás a „Népgazdaságból" a Kádár-rendszer idején az állambiztonsági iratok tükrében.* Állambiztonsági Szolgálatok Történeti Levéltára-Nemzeti Emlékezet Bizottsága.

Bozóki, A. (2010). A magyar demokratikus ellenzék: önreflexió, identitás és politikai diskurzus. *Politikatudományi Szemle, 19*(2), 7–45.

Brooker, P. (2014). *Non-democratic regimes* (3rd ed.). Palgrave Macmillan.

Bussemer, T. (2008). *Propaganda: Konzepte und Theorien.* Springer-Verlag.

Chan, N. K., & Zhao, S. (2016). Punctuated equilibrium and the information disadvantage of authoritarianism: Evidence from the People's Republic of China. *The Policy Studies Journal, 44*(2), 134–155.

Connor, W. D., & Gitelman, Z. Y. (1977). *Public opinion in European socialist systems.* Praeger Publishers.

Csanádi, M. (1990–1991). Átváltozások. Hogyan bomlott fel a hatalmi rendszer Magyarországon? Hogyan bomlott fel a hatalmi rendszer Magyarországon? *Társadalomtudományi Közlemények, 1–2.*

Csanádi, M. (1991). Structure, cohesion and disintegration of the Hungarian party system. In G. Szoboszlai (Ed.), *Democracy and political transformation* (pp. 325–350). Budapest: Hungarian Political Science Association.

Csanádi, M. (1997). *Party-states and their legacies in post-communist transformation.* Edward Elgar.

Csanádi, M. (2007). Party–state systems and their dynamics as networks. *Physica A: Statistical Mechanics and Its Applications, 378*(1), 83–91.

Csizmadia, E. (2015). The Hungarian democratic opposition in the 1980s. *Intersections: East European Journal of Society and Politics, 1*(4), 119–138.

Dunbabin, J. P. D. (2014). *The Cold War: The great powers and their allies.* Routledge.

Eidlin, F. H., & Eidlin, F. (1980). *The logic of "normalization": The Soviet intervention in Czechoslovakia of 21 August 1968 and the Czechoslovak response.* Fred Eidlin.

Feitl, I. (1994). Pártvezetés és országgyűlési választások 1949–1988. In G. Földes & L. Hubai (Eds.), *Parlament képviselőválasztások 1920–1990.* Politikatörténeti Alapítvány.

Feitl, I. (2008). A nyilvánosság és feltételrendszere – 1968. *Múltunk, 53*(3), 128–156.

Feitl, I. (2019). *Az államszocialista korszak álparlametje.* Országház Könyvkiadó.

Földes, G. (2019). Economic reform, ideology, and opening, 1965–1985 (Special issue). *Múltunk, 4–27.*

Germuska, P. (2010). *Vörös arzenál Magyarország részvétele a nemzetközi hadiipari együttműködésben a KGST keretei között.* 1956-os Intézet, Argumentum Kiadó.

Germuska, P. (2014). *A magyar középgépipar. Hadiipar és haditechnikai termelés Magyarországon 1945 és 1980 között.* Állambiztonsági Szolgálatok Történeti Levéltára-Argumentum Kiadó.

Goodman, R. M. (1969). The invasion of Czechoslovakia: 1968. *The International Lawyer, 4,* 42–79.

Heller, M., Némedi, D., & Rényi, Á. (1992). *A magyar nyilvánosság szerkezetváltozásai a Kádár-rendszerben. Értékrendek és társadalmi-kulturális változások,* 109–118.

Horváth, A. (2013). *A magyar sajtó története a szovjet típusú diktatúra idején.* Médiatudományi Intézet.

Horváth, S. (2012). *Két emelet boldogság - mindennapi szociálpolitika a Kádárkorban.* Napvilág Kiadó.

Jennings, W., Bevan, S., Timmermans, A., Breeman, G., Brouard, S., Chaqués-Bonafont, L., Green-Pedersen, C., John, P., Mortensen, P. B., & Palau, A. M. (2011). Effects of the core functions of government on the diversity of executive agendas. *Comparative Political Studies, 44*(8), 1002–1029.

Kornai, J. (1992). *The socialist system: The political economy of communism.* Oxford University Press.

Kovács, I. (1966). Demokrácia és jogalkotás. *Állam és Igazgatás, 16*(1), 13–24.

Litván, G., Bak, J. M., & Legters, L. H. (1996). *The Hungarian revolution of 1956: Reform, revolt and repression, 1953–1963.* Longman Publishing Group.

Mitrovits, M. (2012). Kádár és Dubček 1968-ban. In G. Földes & M. Mitrovits (Eds.), *Kádár János és a 20. századi magyar történelem* (pp. 125–146). Napvilág Kiadó.

Molnár, C. (2018). A magyar törvényhozás napirendje a XVIII. századtól napjainkig. In Z. Boda & M. Sebők (Eds.), *A magyar közpolitikai napirend. Elméleti alapok, empirikus eredmények* (pp. 204–223). MTA TK PTI.

Murphy, K. (2006). Regulating more effectively: The relationship between procedural justice, legitimacy, and tax non-compliance. *Journal of Law and Society, 32*(4), 562–589.

Naftali, T., Fursenko, A., & Lebow, R. N. (1997). One hell of a gamble: Khrushchev, Castro & Kennedy, 1958–1964. *International Journal, 52*(4), 725.

Nelson, D. N., & White, S. (1982). *Communist legislatures in comparative perspective.* Springer.

Németh, J. (1995). *Az MSZMP központi vezető szervei üléseinek napirendi jegyzékei 1956–1962.* Magyar Országos Levéltár.

Pap, M. (2019). "Jobb, mint remélték, de…" Az 1968-as gazdasági reform és politikai propagandája a Népszabadságban. *Médiakutató, 20*(1), 25–37.

Pesti, S. (2002). *Az újkori magyar parlament.* Osiris Kiadó.

Rainer M., J. (2013). *A Kádár-korszak: 1956–1989.* Kossuth Kiadó.

Ripp, Z. (2006). *Rendszerváltás Magyarországon 1987–1990.* Napvilág Kiadó.

Romsics, I. (2001). *Magyarország története a XX. században.* Osiris Kiadó.

Romsics, I. (2007). Economic reforms in the Kádár era. *The Hungarian Quarterly, 187,* 69–79.

Romsics, I. (2013). *Rendszerváltás Magyarországon.* Akadémiai Kiadó.

Scharpf, F. W. (1999). *Governing in Europe: Effective and democratic?.* Oxford: Oxford University Press.

Schuler, P., & Malesky, E. J. (2014). Authoritarian legislatures. In *The oxford handbook of legislative studies.* Oxford University Press.

Sebők, M., & Berki, T. (2018). Punctuated equilibrium in democracy and autocracy: An analysis of Hungarian budgeting between 1868 and 2013. *European Political Science Review, 10*(4), 589–611.

Sebők, M., Kubik, B. G., & Molnár, C. (2017). A törvények formális minősége: Empirikus vázlat. In Z. Boda & A. Szabó (Eds.), *Trendek a magyar politikában 2. A Fidesz és a többiek: pártok, mozgalmak, politikák* (pp. 285–310). Napvilág Kiadó.

Slider, D. (1985). Party-sponsored public opinion research in the Soviet Union. *The Journal of Politics, 47*(1), 209–227.

Standeisky, É. (2005). *Gúzsba kötve.* 1956-os Intézet.

Szabó, M. (1988). A legitimáció történeti alakváltozásai. *Medvetánc, 1,* 139–170.

Szabó, P. C. (2006). *A magyar állam története.* Bölcsész Konzorcium.

Szalai, J. (1992). A társadalombiztosítás érdekviszonyairól. Történeti vázlat a hazai társadalombiztosítás funkcióinak változásairól. *Szociológiai Szemle, 2,* 27–44.

Tomka, B. (2012). Szociálpolitika Magyarországon a Kádár-rendszer időszakában: intézmények, funkciók és szakaszok. *Múltunk, 2,* 27–49.

Tyler, T. R. (2011). *Why people cooperate: The role of social motivations.* Princeton University Press.

Valuch, T. (2000). A cultural and social history of Hungary 1948–1990. In L. Kósa (Ed.), *A cultural history of Hungary in the nineteenth and twentieth century* (Vol. 277). Corvina-Osiris Kiadó.

Valuch, T. (2003). A "gulyáskommunizmus". In I. Romsics (Ed.), *Mítoszok, legendák, tévhitek a 20. századi magyar történelemről* (pp. 69–76). Osiris Kiadó.

Varga, Z. (2002). Agriculture and the new economic mechanism. *Hungarologische Beiträge, 14,* 201–217.

Varga, Z. (2009). *The Hungarian agriculture and rural society: Changes, problems and possibilities: 1945–2004.* Szaktudás Kiadó.

Vásárhelyi, M. (2012). Report on the research conducted from 01.06.2012 to 31.07.2012 on the topic "Public opinion and media research in Hungary, 1969–1991," supported by the International Visegrad Fund.

Vásárhelyi, M. (2016). Média- és közvélemény-kutatás a Kádár-korszakban. *Médiakutató, XVI*(1), 93–96.

Welsh, W. A. (2013). *Survey research and public attitudes in Eastern Europe and the Soviet Union: Pergamon policy studies on international politics.* Elsevier.

Zubok, V., & Pleshakov, C. (1997). *Inside the Kremlin's Cold War: From Stalin to Krushchev.* Harvard University Press.

CHAPTER 8

The Policy Agendas of Liberal and Illiberal Democracy (1990–2018)

Zsanett Pokornyi and Eszter Sághy

The year 1990 marked the beginning of a new era in Hungarian politics. The socialist autocracy that had reigned for over 30 years was replaced by a liberal democracy. The People's Republic was supplanted by a Republic built on liberal democracy and the institutional structure, along with the policymaking process, was transformed in the image of Western democracies. While under the socialist regime policy decisions had been rendered based on the principles delineated by the ruling party (MSZMP—see previous chapter), under the democratic regime, newly minted institutions, such as the Constitutional Court, the State Audit Office, and the office of the President of the Republic established a veritable separation of powers system. Along with the substantial privileges that were now being afforded to the opposition, these institutional changes also resulted in

Z. Pokornyi (✉)
Centre for Social Sciences, MTA Centre of Excellence, Eötvös Loránd Research Network, Budapest, Hungary
e-mail: pokornyi.zsanett@tk.hu

E. Sághy
University of Bath, Bath, UK

M. Sebők and Z. Boda (eds.), *Policy Agendas in Autocracy, and Hybrid Regimes*, Comparative Studies of Political Agendas,
https://doi.org/10.1007/978-3-030-73223-3_8

the inclusion of several new players in the policy decision-making process (Körösényi, 2015).

As "the frontrunner in post-communist democratization" (Enyedi, 2016: 211), Hungary designed the operations of its own parliament in accordance with the models observed in Western democracies, in which both the government (see Jennings et al., 2011) and the opposition (Bräuninger & Debus, 2009) wield substantial influence on the policy-making process. As a result, there was a massive surge in the amount of information that the government could use as inputs for policy decisions.

In setting the policy priorities that guided their work, Hungarian governments had to act as "master jugglers" to allocate agenda space to the increasingly complex set of issues (Jones & Baumgartner, 2005: 52) coming their way from such a wide variety of newly empowered players. The changes that manifested themselves in post-1990 Hungary in response to the new dynamics in the flow and selection of information align with the relevant insights in the analysis of Jennings et al. (2011), who investigated European democracies and found that government operations, macroeconomics, and international affairs were the areas with the largest impact on the activities of the government.

THE JOURNEY FROM SOCIALISM THROUGH LIBERAL DEMOCRACY TO THE ILLIBERAL STATE

In the interest of making the transition process more effective, the various players involved in the democratic transition sought to forge a broad consensus among stakeholders. The negotiations were not conducted with a specific endpoint in mind (Bozóki, 2015: 2–6), and the issues pertaining to government operations and the work of parliament were treated as key problems by the political players throughout the entire phase of negotiations. Thus, the prevailing trends in the domestic policy arena were determined by the distinct aspirations of the various actors and the political compromises between them.

Democratic parties established in the late 1980s (including MSZP, the legacy party of the former ruling party, and Fidesz, led by Viktor Orbán from its foundation) presented their own distinct policy narratives (which public opinion could use to identify them; see Walgrave et al., 2009: 154–158), and they also used policy proposals to react to the activities of the other parties and realign their strategies in a constantly changing system of party competition (Green-Pedersen & Mortensen, 2010: 2–4; Walgrave et al., 2009: 772–773). Correspondingly, the unshackled flow of information, combined with the policy messaging strategies of various players in Hungarian politics emerged as key elements in shaping the policy agenda.

As a consequence of the intra-party and interparty conflicts, and due to the general difficulties associated with transition, by the early 2000s party pluralism that had defined the early years of the Hungarian transition had given way to a bipolar party system (see Enyedi & Tóka, 2007). In the process, the relationship between the government and the opposition also became increasingly polarized. On the one hand, despite the checks built into the system, the type of parliamentarism adopted favored the government (see Körösényi, 2001: 17) and especially the prime minister which led to a presidentialization that was only exacerbated in the illiberal period. At the same time, the policy reforms implemented by the government often generated intense political debates. In line with findings regarding other cases, in Hungary these debates typically focused on macroeconomics (such as fiscal "consolidations") and international affairs (first the relationship with neighboring countries, and later EU accession).

The first twenty years of liberal democracy was characterized by a modernization consensus between post-communists (MSZP) and neoliberals (SZDSZ—see Sebők, 2019). These forces were in government for 12 years out of 20 in this period (they took over a mismanaged economy from a right-wing coalition, and lost one election in 1998 to Orbán's—then—conservative alliance). The left-liberal status quo produced tangible results in the form of introducing a fully fledged market economy which became deeply embedded in global structures, as well as bringing the country to EU membership. Yet, by the second half of the 2000s, the dual financial and leadership crisis brought the ruling coalition down and paved the way for the second Orbán government.

In 2010, Orbán's Fidesz party gained a two-thirds, constitutional majority in parliament and initiated an overhaul of political systems which was now moving steadily away from liberal democracy. In keeping with his right-wing populist strategy, Orbán replaced extant liberal institutions and the prevailing political culture with what he called an "illiberal" variant of democracy.[1] He did so by weakening the rule of law, neutralizing both the instruments and institutions of the system of checks and balances, marginalizing the political opposition and ramping up polarization (Bartha et al., 2020: 4).

This effort was further helped by the highly fragmented and internally divided opposition (see Chapter 3 on Regimes), and a deep partisan divide in social discourse and public thinking (Patkós, 2019). As the main component of what Enyedi (2016: 16–18) has termed "populist polarization," Fidesz has structured the interparty rivalry around the main ideological cleavages in the population, and it has framed the electoral battle as the struggle between the people of good faith and the corrupt elitist opposition, which is beholden to foreign interests.

Bozóki (2015: 13) argues that Viktor Orbán has structured his policies around five central pillars: (1) power centralization, in which all authority is concentrated in the hands of the leader; (2) a "rhetoric of national unification," in which the main narrative theme of the prime minister's policies is the idea of national unity based on the values of work, home, order, family, and security; (3) a "change of elites," with the new elite being entirely made up of people who are loyal to the prime minister, while any voices that are critical of the government are discredited; (4) the "practice of power politics"; and (5) an "emphasis on revolutionary circumstances." This latter served as a legitimizing factor for far-reaching constitutional and policy changes as Orbán interpreted his election victory as a historic development that allowed him to use his supermajority in parliament to react to the special revolutionary circumstances (also see Bozóki & Hegedűs, 2018).

One of the first decisions of the Fidesz government was the introduction of a new constitution called the Fundamental Law. This move, which reverberated widely, laid down the cornerstone of the new regime. As part of the government's overall strategy, the election system was modified, the membership of the National Assembly was halved, while the powers

---

[1] In his speech at Tusnádfürdő in 2014, Viktor Orbán referred to the new regime as an illiberal democracy. "(…) so in this sense the new state that we are constructing in Hungary is an illiberal state, a non-liberal state. It does not reject the fundamental principles of liberalism such as freedom, and I could list a few more, but it does not make this ideology the central element of state organization, but instead includes a different, special, national approach. (..) [T]he reorganization of the Hungarian state is underway, in contrast to the liberal state organization logic of the previous twenty years" (Viktor Orbán at Tusványos, on 26 July 2014).

of the Constitutional Court were narrowed and those of the President of the Republic were also changed.

Starting in 2010, Orbán governed as a crisis manager and, in that role, he refashioned the relations between the government and its followers (Körösényi, 2017: 18–19). As part of this change, only those were entitled to the benefits doled out by the government who were deemed worthy of such support. One of the central tenets of the government's communication became the claim that the economy was growing robustly under Fidesz's stewardship due to the new workfare regime (extended public works, reduced unemployment insurance, and social benefits) which led to a state in which "Hungary performs better" (the latter continues to feature as one of the party's slogans to 2020).

An important element of the underlying macroeconomic strategy was the "strengthening" of labor policy indicators (e.g., a growth in the number of employees). The government further also introduced the system of national consultations, in which citizens can express their opinions on the issues that the executive deems to be of preeminent importance by responding to specific questions put to them by the government regarding these issues. The consultations have emerged as important instruments in the government's efforts at justifying certain decisions it has taken (and in this are reminiscent of how socialist autocracy used public opinion polls—see the previous chapter).

As the new structure was taking shape, the quality of democracy began to decline (Enyedi, 2016: 211). The measures aimed at weakening the rule of law in Hungary generated intense international attention and reactions. Numerous international organizations spoke out against the decisions by the Fidesz government. In its report on the 2014 election, for example, the Organization for Security and Cooperation in Europe (OSCE) took exception to the campaign regulations which undermined the equal competitive framework for all competing parties, and it also noted the problem of media bias. In 2018, the European Parliament adopted the Sargentini Report on the situation of the rule of law in Hungary. The report argued that the independence of the judiciary, freedom of expression, and the rights of minorities were being threatened in Hungary. In response to the abovementioned report, the European Council launched a so-called Article 7 procedure against Hungary to ascertain whether the EU member state is in violation of the European Union's fundamental values.

The conflict with international organizations which take a critical view of Fidesz's actions in government and with the European Union has boosted the role of international affairs on policy agendas. As typical features of populist politics, the criticism of supranational institutions; the emphasis on the supremacy of nation-states (Bartha et al., 2020: 3); shoring up cooperation with the Visegrad Four countries of Central-Eastern Europe; and issues involving the ethnic Hungarian communities across the borders have emerged as the dominant elements in the government's foreign policy strategy. All in all, and despite internal and international criticism the illiberal sort of democracy was solidified in Hungary in the 2010s.

The Legal and Political Environment of Policymaking in Post-1990 Hungary

On the one hand, democratization after regime transition was helpful in allowing representative democracy to channel the values and interest of the citizens through the decisions of parliament and the cabinet. On the other hand, its emphasis on the liberal part in liberal democracy significantly constrained elected leaders, and especially the executive to perform its functions.

The Constitutional Court, as the watchdog guarding constitutionalism (see Pócza, 2015; Sólyom et al., 2009), and the presidency, as the watchdog of democratic operation (see Szomszéd, 2005), made sure that the executive power would not transgress its authority in a tightly construed separation of powers system. The wide array of policy issues requiring a two-thirds majority in the unicameral parliament also empowered the opposition and proved to be a significant veto point in the decision-making process.

As a consequence of these, and also the precarious legitimacy of a newly established political system, the first two decades of the post-transition policymaking process in Hungary was marked by consultations among parties and between parties and civil society, as well as increased social dialogue (Boda & Patkós, 2018). The involvement of engaged civil society organizations in the decision-making process—and their potential support or rejection of a policy—could also impact the success of given policy reform.

As part of the dialogue that emerged between the government and the opposition during the decision-making process, interpellations and speeches in the plenary during the sessions of parliament provided the opposition with the opportunity to raise issues that were neglected by the government, and to ensure thereby that these issues stayed in the limelight for longer periods. As a result, one corollary of the emerging democratic debate culture was that the pace of legislation was relatively slow and deliberate. Even though in a vast majority of cases there were still unresolved and disputed issues between the parties even once the new law became effective, the protracted debates prior to its adoption did in fact tend to improve the quality of the laws (Sebők et al., 2017; 2020), and this was also manifest in the comparatively low number of subsequent amendments and vetoes.

The media's channels of communication also expanded as a consequence of the prevailing democratic political culture. Owing to the dynamic development of television, radio and the print press (and later the internet), voters, too, could continuously track the various phases of decision-making (by watching the live television broadcasts of the sessions of parliament, for example). The media tended to focus predominantly on the business of the government and the National Assembly. Despite the fact that its own influence on the policy agenda was rather weak after regime transition (Boda & Patkós, 2018), the media did emerge as an important instrument for parties in the dissemination of their messages or in their efforts at attacking their opponents.

The expansion in the range of alternatives offered by the parties and the media's increased role in conveying political messages allowed voters to select and cast their votes for those political forces that offered the best solution in the policy areas that they found important. As compared to the foregoing socialist regime, the preferences of the public had a greater influence on the reform measures proposed concerning the management of the social (Ferge & Juhász, 2004) and economic costs (Bakos, 1994) associated with the transition period. Despite the generally technocratic tendencies of MSZP-SZDSZ coalitions, in some cases popular pressure was able to modify proposed reforms or even halt them (see for example the case of the healthcare reform proposal discussed below; the reform proposal in question was nixed after it was rejected by the public in a referendum).

Starting in 2010, the Fidesz party led by Viktor Orbán won three successive elections in Hungary. The favorable circumstances of a post-crisis, booming global economy, in combination with the measures aimed at bolstering the power of the governing party, allowed Fidesz to set out the long-term consolidation of the illiberal regime. The rules enshrined in the new Fundamental Law (e.g., the narrowing of the powers of the Constitutional Court, the selection of figures with strong ties to the governing party to the position of the President of the Republic and as judges on the Constitutional Court and the chief prosecutor, along with the weakening of the opposition, through gerrymandering, for example), essentially hollowed out the democratic safeguards that were put in place at the time of regime transition.

As is typical for populist parties, the prime minister has risen above the cabinet (see Körösényi, 2019), casting himself as the "leader" of his people and clearly acting as a personalist leader (Bartha et al., 2020). The concentration of power in his hands (see Lengyel & Ilonszki, 2010) had a fundamental impact on the transformation of the debate culture and decision-making processes that had emerged as part of this second regime transition from liberalism to illiberalism.

Even though it ended up changing only little in the ways the formal framework governing policy decision-making was set up during the democratic transition in the 1990s (that is policymaking was still performed in the framework of a unicameral system, with a government that was accountable to parliament, while the rights of assembly, association, speech, and free media were still being extended and the media continued to feature voices that were critical of the government), Fidesz changed the system by adding components that strengthened the position of the executive power within that framework. The policymaking process became more closed and parliament began to operate as a "law factory."

As the function of parliament as the overseer of the executive branch was weakened, the reforms proposed by the government were increasingly introduced in a top-down manner, often accompanied by major protests on the part of the opposition or civil society (Boda & Patkós, 2018; Enyedi, 2015: 10). In drafting reforms, the government proved increasingly unwilling and less inclined to engage in a prior debate about the substance or to involve a broad range of political players in the consultation. And even though interpellations and speeches in parliament continued to provide the opposition with an instrument to hold the government accountable, actual change was seldom exerted as bills were adopted with less amendments and with meaningful debates supplanted with state secretaries reading out from written statements.

Fidesz was also actively involved in creating a slew of pseudo-civic organizations which legitimized government decisions for the general public

(Körösényi, 2017: 20). The details of policies and the public opinion surveys and focus groups undergirding these decisions were increasingly drafted by think tanks and law firms staffed by young Fidesz associates with political or business aspirations; these institutions were lacking in transparency and accountability. Building a strong base of personal power was a key pillar of the prime minister's strategy. In addition to shoring up the role of such political actors, the strategy also involved the creation of a circle of entrepreneurs with close ties to the government (the so-called national bourgeoisie).

In exchange for their loyalty, these entrepreneurs were furnished with major government grants and public procurement commissions for their projects. The influence of external players, such as opposition parties or NGOs without ties to the government, was minimal. The policy capacity of society was weakened, while that of the state was boosted. The government was mostly free in determining policy contents and shaping the policy agenda, as its activities were hardly regulated by institutional or constitutional constraints (Boda & Patkós, 2018), all this in stark contrast to the veto point-laden system of pre-2010 liberal democracy.

Fidesz also saw the transformation of the media as a priority. One component of this strategy was the efforts aimed at thwarting the operations of the opposition press (see the sudden shutdown of the biggest political daily, Népszabadság, which had investigated scandals involving figures in the government) and attempts at discrediting it. At the same time the governing party sought to build a pro-government media empire. As this network was expanded, the process included the absorption of the state-owned public radio and television channels, numerous major commercial television and radio channels, weeklies and dailies, the complete network of county-based local press, as well as the online platforms affiliated with these outlets.

As a result of this process, the media became even less capable than before of independently shaping the policy agenda. Because of the accelerated pace of legislation in the term from 2010 to 2014, the media consistently lagged political processes and had a hard time keeping up with a policy agenda overwhelmed with new proposals across the board of policy topics. Similarly to the first two decades after regime transition, it continued to focus on governmental and parliamentary work (Boda & Patkós, 2018). At the same time, the channels of public communication created by Fidesz focused exclusively on the issues highlighted by the government (e.g., immigration policy or service fees of utilities owned by multinational companies) or on news items that sought to portray the government's various "enemies" of the day (e.g., the opposition, the European Union, migrants, or Hungarian-born liberal billionaire George Soros) in a negative light.

As mentioned above Fidesz's power was built on the propagation of the idea that Hungary is facing off against enemies and the exploitation of symbolic and wedge issues. In these contexts, the government (and especially the prime minister) could cast themselves as the defenders of the homeland. This has led to a change in the relationship between the government and public opinion. The strategy of the executive power was no longer based on putting the issues that society considers vital front and center. The new goal was instead to use the media channels at the governing party's disposal to push issues onto the voters' agenda that serve to reinforce the government's position of power.

Databases

The Hungarian Comparative Agendas Project research group has built 10 databases covering the period from 1990 to 2018. These databases touch on the most important policy venues. We analyzed the media agenda based on articles published on the respective cover pages of the print editions of the most widely read right-wing newspaper, Magyar Nemzet, and the most popular left-wing newspaper, Népszabadság.[2] In the case of Magyar Nemzet, our data series goes back to 2002, while in the case of Népszabadság the first articles in the database date back to 1990. The data series for both publications end in 2014.

The source for the cover pages was the Arcanum Digitheca. The units of observation were individual articles, which we coded by major topic. In the case of Magyar Nemzet, our database featured 18,004 articles that had been double hand-coded, of which 9668 were published before 2010, and 8336 were published after 2010, during the period of the Orbán regime. For Népszabadság, our analysis drew on 37,144 articles, 27,880 of which were published before 2010 while 9264 were published after 2010. We used both hand-coding and machine learning-based coding to assign policy topic codes (see Appendix A2).

---

[2] Magyar Nemzet was reclaimed by the Fidesz media empire in 2018, while Népszabadság was shut down in 2016.

We analyzed the work of the parties[3] based on the manifestos they published and their electoral pledges.[4] The two databases feature the relevant data for all the parties whose lists won sufficient votes to clear the five-percent-threshold for entering parliament. A special case in the database is Fidesz, which stopped publishing a manifesto as of 2014. Our source for the party platforms was the official manifestos published by the parties. The manifestos touch on most policy areas, and thus we coded them sentence by sentence. The database comprises 39,139 observations in total, 26,738 of which date from before 2010 while 12,401 were generated after 2010.

We followed a similar logic with respect to electoral pledges. shows the number of promises made by the parties between 1990 and 2010; the respective shares of rhetorical and policy contents in these promises; and what percentage of them were fulfilled. Similarly, to the manifestos up to 2010, we also examined these in the context of the parties that won representation in parliament. In total we analyzed 11,688 pledges out of which 881 promises were proffered by Fidesz and MSZP, the two parties that were always certain to win seats in parliament.

The database comprising the prime ministers' speeches is made up of two main components, namely, speeches in parliament and those delivered outside the National Assembly. We collected the speeches from the official websites of the National Assembly and the prime minister's office, respectively.[5] We processed all speeches delivered in parliament by the prime ministers before 2010, and then all speeches regardless of the forum after 2010. In the case of the speeches by Viktor Orbán (Fidesz, 1998–2002, 2010–2018), and the parliamentary statements by Ferenc Gyurcsány (MSZP, 2004–2009) we coded the relevant texts sentence by sentence, while in the other periods we broke the speeches down by paragraphs.

The source was the official website of the Hungarian parliament, the National Assembly. The database for parliamentary speeches included

---

[3] Our analysis also drew on the results of the JUDICON project which analyzes the decisions of the Constitutional Court (Pócza, 2019). We wish to express our gratitude to Gábor Dobos for granting access to the relevant databases.

[4] For more information on the database featuring the pledges of the parties and underyling methodology see (Sebők et al., 2013).

[5] The database only includes proactive speeches, it does not include the responses to questions (e.g., answers to questions during sessions of parliament or interviews).

12,553 observations (10,476 of which were sentences; 5754 of the latter were from the pre-2010 period, while 4722 came from the post-2010 period; there were also 2083 paragraphs). As for the speeches delivered outside parliament, the database includes 54,395 observations, which were coded sentence by sentence.

The database of interpellations, one of multiple forms of parliamentary questions, comprises all relevant items between 1990 and 2018. We collected the texts of the interpellations from the official website of the National Assembly. We included interpellations by the representatives of all parties—opposition and governing parties alike—before 2010 and after 2010. Unlike speeches, which cover several areas, interpellations reflect on a single policy area, which meant that the unit of observation in this case was the entire text of the given interpellation. We categorized the documents thus collected by both major and subtopics. The database comprises 5730 observations, of which 3955 date back to the period before 2010, while 1775 items from the post-2010 period.

Our analysis of the agenda of the legislature was performed on a database of the laws adopted between 1990 and 2018. The texts of these laws were collected from the official site of the Hungarian Official Gazette. With respect to laws, the unit of observation was the entire document, coded for major topics and subtopics. The database includes 4162 laws, 2532 of which date back to the pre-2010 period while 1630 entered into effect after 2010. We drew up the data sheets on executive decrees based on similar guidelines that we used with regard to laws.[6] We collected the texts of the decrees from the Hungarian Official Gazette. The unit of observation was the entire document, which we coded for major topic. This process yielded a total of 24,913 observations, 16,023 of which dated from the time before 2010 and 8,891 of which were issued after 2010.

Finally, the budget database includes data from the annual budgets adopted between 1990 and 2013. We collected the texts of the budgets from Új Jogtár (New Legal Archive) database. We included every annual budget published before 2010. We coded the documents in this database by budget lines, assigning each of them to major topics and subtopics. The database comprises 68,445 observations.

---

[6]The database does not include municipal decrees or decrees issued by autonomous regulatory public bodies.

Descriptive Statistics of the Policy Agendas of the Liberal and Illiberal Periods

In the first part of our analysis we focus on the overall trends of the policy agendas between 1990 and 2018. We approached this task from two different angles. For one, we looked at the quantitative features of different policy agendas (e.g., how many pledges or interpellations were made), while we also explored if there were major shifts in the attention focused on given policy areas (e.g., which areas stood out). Furthermore, in the interest of a comprehensive examination of differences between the liberal and illiberal periods, we also performed comparative analyzes.

Media

In a party system that was gradually becoming bipolar, two daily newspapers, Magyar Nemzet and Népszabadság emerged over time as the preeminent channels for the dissemination of messages on their respective sides of the political aisle. The two newspapers played an equal role within their respective peer groups of right-wing and left-wing media outlets, respectively, and their similarities were manifest both in terms of their structure (thus, their cover pages tended to feature an average of 12 articles with a length of one paragraph each), as well as in their contents. And while their cover pages also featured a large number of tabloid news items, on account of the newspapers' intense ties to the political sphere they also covered the most important political events and policy news.

Both Magyar Nemzet and Népszabadság saw some changes between the two regime types separated by the year 2010. Prior to 2010, the covers of both newspapers tended to be dominated by policy issues. In the case of Magyar Nemzet, 78% of the articles on the cover page addressed policy issues, while in the case of Népszabadság this was true of 76% of the items. However, while in the right-wing newspaper macroeconomics and government operations dominated the cover pages, on Népszabadság's cover sports news—which is not a policy topic in the CAP Codebook—were also often in the foreground. There were also major differences between the newspapers with respect to the distribution of issues which enjoyed a medium-level—that is neither outstandingly high nor outstandingly low—presence on the cover pages.

As for dominant topics, while in the case of Magyar Nemzet healthcare was prominently featured, on the left issues concerning political parties and crimes tended to be at the forefront. We did not observe major changes either in Magyar Nemzet or in Népszabadság in this respect after 2010. However, in terms of the distribution of policy vs. other topics, the pronounced politicization of the illiberal period left a massive mark. As a result, 85% of the articles published on the cover of Magyar Nemzet— which has strong ties to Fidesz—concerned policy-related news, while in the case of Népszabadság there was only a slight 2-point increase in the share of such articles, up to 78%.

Party Manifestos and Pledges
In the pre-internet era with the competition between newly formed parties during regime transition, for opposition and governing parties' alike manifestos played an important role in the dissemination of their messages. Before 2010, all parties issued detailed and lengthy manifestos to persuade voters and orient interest groups. And although in some cases they focused on different subareas of the various policy domains, the manifestos in general touched on all thematic areas of policy agendas. Furthermore, they also reflected on each other's promises and strove to come up with the best possible alternatives that would bolster the voters' trust in them.

The areas that figured most prominently in the manifestos tended to be macroeconomics, education, and government operations, while immigration and energy (which did emerge as key issues in the government's communication after 2010) and the issue of state-owned lands tended to be covered less prominently. The pre-2010 manifestos of the left-wing parties tended to focus especially on macroeconomics, education, social policy, and government operations. The manifestos of the right-wing parties tended to be very similar in terms of their thematic focus, highlighting especially issues involving macroeconomics, health, education, domestic commerce, and government operations. Thus, before 2010, party manifestos focused especially on the institutional and economic pillars of the regime, as well as on issues involving public services.

The year 2010 saw a massive shift in the partisan composition of the opposition, with many former major parties disappearing—except for MSZP (which also lost massively in strength, however)—while new parties entered the scene. Among the new opposition parties, the manifesto of the far-right Jobbik focused especially on international affairs and government operations, while the left-wing Green Party LMP emphasized macroeconomics and the environment. The established left-wing party MSZP, by contrast, continued to highlight the areas of education, domestic commerce, and social policy.

The previous emphasis on public services in the party manifestos had decreased substantially by that point, and their previous central place was taken by issues falling into the category of government/parliament operations and the institutional structure of politics. Fidesz's political turn after 2010 also left an imprint on the party manifestos. The subjugation of policymaking to political communication was apparent in the fact that the party did not release a manifesto in 2014. What they offered by way of orientation for the general public was the slogan: "We will continue what we started."

This shows that the party no longer sought to inform the public about its policy decisions and goals. Instead, it ran a personalized campaign which cast the prime minister as the guardian of the Hungarian people and discredited opposition politicians as "clowns." The propagation of the idea that Hungary was facing enemies home and abroad also played a major role in the governing party's communication and was the first instance of adopting the wedge-issue based approach as advocated by Arthur Finkelstein, the Israeli–American negative campaign guru hired by Fidesz.

Our observations concerning manifestos were also reinforced by the changing trends with respect to specific electoral pledges. In addition to their manifestos, the parties can also seek to persuade voters about their fitness for office with their promises made public in the manifestos or other public communication. In our research, we looked at the changes in Fidesz's policies and rhetoric in their pledges before and after 2010. In the term from 1998 to 2002, Fidesz made 462 promises to voters. And although a significant proportion of these were of the rhetorical kind (330), a major portion of those with a policy content were realized (61 were realized and 11 were somewhat realized). Between 2010 and 2014, Fidesz increased the number of its promises to voters. It made 527 statements involving promises, out of which 512 were rhetorical statements. As a result, the policy content was negligible, and a mere five of the relevant promises were realized (six were not). After 2010, therefore, the rhetorical elements completely prevailed overwhelmingly and crowded out policy contents.

Prime Ministers' Speeches

While speeches in the legislature are directly addressed at members of parliament, at the same time they are also aimed at the general public. That is why already at the time of regime transition (and in fact even in previous periods), prime ministers weaved rhetorical and symbolic elements into their speeches. In order to understand the aforementioned shift from policy-driven to rhetoric-driven politics, we looked at Viktor Orbán's speeches while he served as prime minister before 2010 (1998–2002) and after 2010 (2010–2018). We categorized the sentences in the database with the help of a dichotomous variable that either took a value of "policy relevance" or "no policy relevance." Then, we compared how the distribution of the values changed in this category between the first, second, and third Fidesz governments. Our results show that similarly to what we found with respect to pledges, after 2010 the rhetorical elements came to predominate in the prime minister's parliamentary speeches, too.

Homing in on the speeches between 1998 and 2002 specifically, we found that Orbán's speeches in parliament were primarily centered on presenting policy goals and results. These were complemented by relatively slight amounts of rhetorical contents, which were primarily used at the beginning and the end of the speeches. Hence, in terms of their frequency, these two respective types of contents were very unevenly distributed in the speeches delivered during this period (the difference between them was over 1000 mentions in favor of policy contents). Starting in 2010, however, we find a trend that begins to shift in the opposite direction. Even though policy contents continue to dominate in the speeches, the gap between the respective frequency in the mentions of the two types of contents diminished significantly. Correspondingly, at this point the distance between them drops to 100–200 mentions annually, and by 2017 it is as low as 50.

These results indicate that in recent years Fidesz was less likely to use speeches in parliament for presenting policy proposals, which does not mean that it did not communicate its policy accomplishments in other ways. In line with Viktor Orbán's status as a "leader of his people," the prime minister primarily used extra-parliamentary forums for giving speeches even as he spoke rather infrequently in parliament, where he tended to address only the most important issues or some current event. He presented the government's comprehensive goals and results to voters in speeches delivered outside the walls of parliament.

The policy (or ideological) course pursued by the government was laid out in greater detail in his speeches held in Tusnádfürdő, at an annual event for ethnic Hungarian community in Romania, held in the Romanian municipality of Băile Tușnad. At the same time the government's accomplishments and the list of future action items were discussed in his traditional annual State of Hungary address early in the year before a friendly audience of Fidesz allies. These choices show the diminished importance of parliament and formal constitutional institutions in the illiberal period.

Prime Minister's Speeches and the Legislative Agenda
In parallel with the weakening of the democratic safeguards, after 2010 we also observed an increasingly strong connection between the government's communication and legislative activity. We found that ever since regime transition, the policy preferences stressed by the prime ministers in their speeches in parliament had always had a visible impact on the subsequent legislative agenda of the National Assembly. However, while before 2010 these goals were to a greater or lesser extent adjusted by parliament as it performed its legislative work, after 2010 the goals and objectives laid out by the prime minister in his speeches ended up being adopted in the form of bills more or less in the same form as the prime minister had initially proposed them.

In analyzing this phenomenon, we looked at the parliamentary speeches by two prime ministers. We juxtaposed the speeches by Viktor Orbán following 2010 and the left-wing politician Ferenc Gyurcsány (pre-2010). In the 2000s, Gyurcsány emerged as the greatest political rival of Orbán. At that time, the clashes between the leading politicians drew more public attention than ever before. Thus, Gyurcsány's person was just as decisive for the left as Viktor Orbán's was for the right. To test our hypothesis regarding the shift toward unilateral agenda-setting, we analyzed the three areas that cropped up most frequently on the governmental agenda, namely macroeconomics, international affairs, and government operations.

In our comparative analysis we found that after 2010 the contents of the prime minister's speeches were more likely to be reflected in subsequent legislation than during the two Gyurcsány governments. We found with respect to all three policy areas which we tracked that although the frequency with which a given issue was mentioned in speeches fluctuated wildly, the laws did not tend to track these patterns. Policy announcements were not followed by a rise in the number of the laws affecting the given area, their value remained stable after the speeches. After 2010, however, the speeches began to presage a growth in the number of laws. In this period, we found that the rising trajectory of an issue in the speeches was followed by a rising trend in the laws adopted concerning the given area.

Interpellations

The use of the more flexible instruments of oral communication was not limited to the governing parties, they were also available to the opposition. The most important parliamentary instrument of this kind are interpellations. Even though government party representatives can also avail themselves of interpellations—and they in fact do in some cases—this type of parliamentary question—associated with a formal vote on the response of the cabinet's representative—is primarily useful for the opposition. This assumption is reinforced by the trends we found: while the number of interpellations presented by the opposition fluctuated between 400 and 800 in the period investigated, those presented by the government side ranged between 1 and 300 per government cycle.

We also found differences when comparing the period before 2010 and after 2010. The most conspicuous gap was the one we saw in the first term of the transitional period following regime change. Between 1990 and 1994, the number of government party interpellations fluctuated between 50 and 100, while the interpellations presented by the opposition could number as many as 500. After declining toward the end of the 1990s, the massive gap between the number of government parties and opposition interpellations began to increase again in the early 2000s.

In the 2000s, there was another change, with the number of governing party interpellations declining once again and the number of those presented by the opposition rising continuously. While the number of questions from the governing party representatives ranged between 100 and 200, opposition members of parliament interpellated between 500 and 600 times per government cycle.

This gap widened even further under the illiberal regime, in which the number of opposition interpellations exceeded 700. Since the opposition's privileges were considerably weaker in light of the government's two-thirds majority and constitutional reforms, interpellations figured more prominently among the instruments that the opposition could draw on to hold the government accountable and to question its policies.

The policy areas that were most frequently addressed by interpellations also highlight the main objective of this type of parliamentary question. In light of the general efforts to question the credibility of the government's actions, it is hardly surprising that the issue of government operations was exceedingly preponderant among the topics raised in the interpellations during this time, both before 2010 and after 2010. In the liberal era, government operations were followed by health, agriculture, law and crime, while in the illiberal period macroeconomic policy became the second most interpellated issue.

Laws

In post-1990 Hungary, several hundred laws are promulgated in the Official Gazette each year. However, the frequency of laws pertaining to each policy area will be massively influenced by the overall trend in the number of laws adopted in a given year. Thus, in order to understand the changes in the agenda of the legislature, we first need to look at the quantitative changes in the number of laws.

The number of laws adopted per year has been relatively stable over time. Between 1990 and 2010, the annual value ranged between 400 and 600. While we saw a somewhat greater fluctuation between 1990 and 2002 (between 1990 and 1994 the number of laws hovered just above 400 per year, this figure increased to 500 in the next term of parliament, only to drop again between 1998 and 2002), between 2002 and 2010 it was rather stable once again. Then, after 2010, the pace of the legislature picked up again.

At the same time, with the new political situation generated by Fidesz's supermajority, the legislative process accelerated and also became less transparent. The more intense legislative pace was especially apparent in the term between 2010 and 2014, when the number of laws adopted per annum exceeded 850. Furthermore, even though the fact that the pillars of the new regime had been laid during its first term—and as a result the pace of new legislation declined somewhat after the 2014 election—the number of laws adopted each year continued to be extraordinarily high (exceeding 700).

As for the distribution of policy topics, before 2010, issues relating to public services dominated the agenda of the legislature, including especially macroeconomics and government operations, while labor, law and crime, as well as domestic commerce also featured prominently. Our results show that the long-term agenda of the legislature after regime transition was dominated by macroeconomics, law and crime, and domestic commerce. In addition to the aforementioned, issues involving international affairs and government operations also ranked high on the list of the most frequently regulated areas.

After 2010, the dominance of issues involving public services declined somewhat as there was a greater emphasis on areas involving the institutional structure of the regime. In addition to macroeconomics and government operations, law and crime, and domestic commerce dominated. In addition to the latter issues, international affairs stayed at the forefront of legislative activity, primarily due to international treaties. European Union-related matters dominated this area, as their ratio made up between 30% and 44% of all laws passed by parliament (Bíró-Nagy & Galgóczi, 2018: 46).

We have already analyzed the impact of prime minister's speeches on legislative activity. We also looked at three cases related to the impact of opposition parties. In the first step, we examined what share of the laws adopted by parliament had been sponsored by the government and the opposition, respectively, which helped us ascertain the respective impact of the two sides on the legislative output of parliament. To nuance this further, we also looked at the share of legislation sponsored by individual members of parliament as a percentage of all promulgated laws as member introduced bills can circumvent the usual processes of ex ante impact assessment.

Finally, we examined whether there was a surge in the number of Constitutional Court decisions with respect to laws initially proposed by the government, and if so, how large that surge was. The combative steps taken by the newly established illiberal governing majority were certain to generate an increase in the number of legal complaints. Nevertheless, on account of Fidesz-related judges on the Constitutional Court, as well as the narrowing of the Court's competence, it turned out to have no real influence on the growing control of the executive over the other two branches.

Examining the share of bills proposed by the government and opposition, respectively (Fig. 8.1—see Molnár, 2018; Sebők et al., 2020), it is apparent that the government dominated the legislative process both before and after 2010. Nevertheless, prior to 2010 the opposition also had a discernible impact on the overall process of legislation. This impact

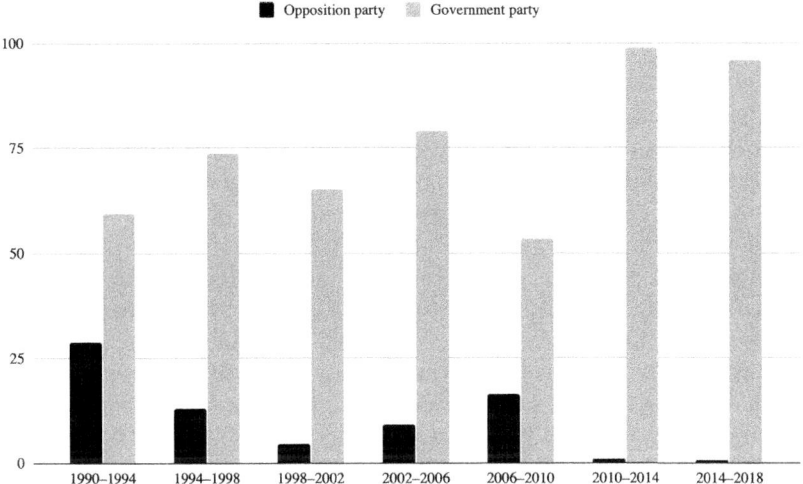

Fig. 8.1 The count of adopted laws by introducer

was most pronounced in the period immediately following the regime transition, when 27% of the laws ultimately adopted had been proposed by the opposition.

Although the influence of the opposition on the total legislative output declined steadily until 2006, it increased again between 2006 and 2010. Then, after 2010, we saw another decline in the opposition's impact on legislation, which was drastic and considerably more extreme than what we observed in the earlier period. Bills that were proposed by the opposition made up fewer than 5% of the laws adopted by parliament in both terms after 2010.

The changes in the number of bills sponsored by individual government party representatives reinforce the overall picture of growing government dominance in the realm of legislative output. Proposals sponsored by government MPs, as opposed to cabinet ministers, had a discernible impact on the legislative output already before 2010, but their number soared thereafter. The bump was especially pronounced between 2010 and 2014, when their annual number was between 15 and 20. Subsequently, when the laws creating the legal framework that undergirds the new regime had been created, the number of such laws began to decline again.

We saw a change not only in the opposition's role as a democratic check on the government's power, but also in the role that the Constitutional Court played as a democratic safeguard before 2010 and after 2010. The Constitutional Court's role weakened substantially after 2010. The question is, therefore, how many complaints were filed with the Court concerning bills that had been proposed by the government and adopted by parliament, and which then had to be adjudicated in decisions rendered by the Constitutional Court.

An analysis of the Court's decisions highlights the lacking effectiveness of complaints filed against the government's policy decisions. Before 2010, the Constitutional Court rendered 601 rulings, 16 of which pertained to decisions proposed by the government. After 2010, however, the body rendered significantly fewer decisions in total, 240, of which 22 concerned bills that had been proposed by the government (the analysis of the outcomes of these decisions requires further research).

On the one hand, this highlights the declining role of the Constitutional Court as an institution in the system of democratic checks and balances. The Court was substantially less active than previously, rendering 350 fewer decisions than before. And although the share of decisions concerning laws proposed by the government increased, their absolute number continued to remain low. Thus, the judicial body had no substantial impact on the government's influence over the work of the legislature.

Decrees
The changes in the agenda of the National Assembly are extremely similar to the trends we observed in the other category of legislation, namely, decrees, which reflect the legislative will of the executive branch of government. This is hardly surprising since decrees and laws have a certain degree of interconnectedness due to delegated legislation (when the legislature delegates its authority to the executive to work out policy details). Thus, for example, in the case of the regulation of the price of pharmaceuticals, the government can use decrees to specify the prices in given subareas.

In addition, decrees can serve as vital tools in implementing the government's goals. Throughout the entire period investigated, the dynamic of change in the number of decrees adopted runs counter to the trend in the number of laws. Drops in the number of laws are associated with increasing numbers of decrees and vice versa. Several hundred decrees are published per annum in the Hungarian Official Gazette, a figure that is similar to the number of laws published each year. However, unlike in the case of promulgated laws, the annual number of which fluctuated between 400 and 600 throughout most of the period, in the case of decrees the low starting value in 1990 (somewhat fewer than 250 promulgated decrees) gave way to a continuous increase.

This process peaked twice, in 2004 and 2008, when the executive branch issued over 1200 decrees a year. Starting with the year 2004, the year of EU accession, and therefore a major regulatory upheaval, the number of decrees were characterized by a high base value and major volatility. This fluctuating tendency continued to prevail after 2010. Our results indicate that even though the changes in the Hungarian political system also had an impact on the number of decrees adopted, it had been a favored instrument for governments all along in shaping their policies. Even changes in government did not affect that broader trend.

We also found policy areas that were especially likely to be regulated by decrees. Before 2010, the areas most commonly subject to decrees were agriculture, macroeconomics, health policy, government operations, and domestic commerce, while with respect to the area of transportation, decrees typically pertained to the public services dimension of the broader thematic area. The post-2010 shift in emphasis manifested itself in the form of a higher share for government operations, macroeconomics, domestic commerce, and law and crime.

Budgets
Budgets establish for each year how much revenue the government plans to collect and under what title, and how it wishes to allocate these revenues across various policy areas. In other words, the budget is one of the fundamental pillars of regulating policy areas. In Hungary, the fiscal year coincides with the calendar year and budgets are adopted every year. Budgets can be analyzed in terms of the line items or the sum of appropriations—money allocations—to each area (Sebők & Végh, 2018: 154).

The diversity of budgets was rather high in the period investigated, yet there were certain policy areas that continuously played a preeminent role in the budget laws after regime transition, just as some policy areas stood out in the agendas of the other policy arenas. Among these areas, that of government operations stands out especially, followed by law and crime, and education. And although the same trend prevailed before and after

2010, too, in the second half of the 2000s social welfare, housing, and international affairs also played a major role in this agenda.

Case Studies

As we have shown with respect to the general trends of policy attention, various policy agendas react to international and domestic developments, and their structure may also be influenced by the policy preferences of major political actors and stakeholders. The government actively selects the information available in a plural-democratic political systems and acts on them according to its own preferences (see Jennings et al., 2011; John & Bevan, 2012). In the second part of our analysis, we looked at four cases which had a major impact on the policy agendas of their time.

We chose five cases covering both the liberal and illiberal period. Privatization moved to the fore in the 1990s as a key issue of economic transition, while the similarly controversial highway construction plan and a botched healthcare reform became closely associated with the socialist-liberal governments of the 2000s. As for the post-2010 issue, we scrutinize two key examples of the polarizing tactics of consecutive Orbán governments: the public utility service fee cuts of the early 2010s and the anti-immigration campaign of the second half of the decade.

The Issue of Privatization in the Mid-1990s

In addition to creating new institutional and legal frameworks, after the regime transition it also became necessary to facilitate the transition from the socialist planned economy to a free-market economy. An important aspect of this metamorphosis was related to the privatization of the assets that had been managed by the state under socialism. Thus, the question of privatization emerged as one of the key issues in the economic policy of the transition period.

The implementation of privatization was among the primary, most divisive issues of the first two government cycles. The expectation for consecutive governments was privatization would boost productivity through its focus on profit-oriented thinking and the possibility to bring in international investors. This would have contributed, in turn, to the adoption of state-of-the-art know-how in many sectors as well as fresh capital to modernize production capacities. The criticisms of the process—which were chiefly aimed at its overly centralized nature; the limited room for autonomous action by corporations, municipal governments, and other related institutions; as well as the risk that a significant portion of the new owners would emerge from the ranks of former leading functionaries in the socialist regime—along with the high level of sovereign debt confronted the first two post-transition governments with major challenges (Mihályi, 2000).

There were several phases of privatization in the 1990s. On the whole, it dominated policy agenda for several years (see Fig. 8.2). Our results show that privatization was following a rising trajectory in the 1990s. It peaked following the adoption of the privatization law in 1995, and then the issue began to decline in importance until the end of the 1990s. And even though it experienced surges again in the first half of the 2000s, toward the end of that decade its role continued to wane as the Hungarian economy had come to be dominated by multinationals (which trajectory was decidedly altered with the formation of the second Orbán cabinet—see below).

The surge in the issue of privatization was most distinct on the agenda of interpellations and the speeches of prime ministers. Starting in the 1990s, interpellations began to focus increasingly on this issue, and, on the whole, it reached its distinct zenith in the 2000s. Between 1990 and

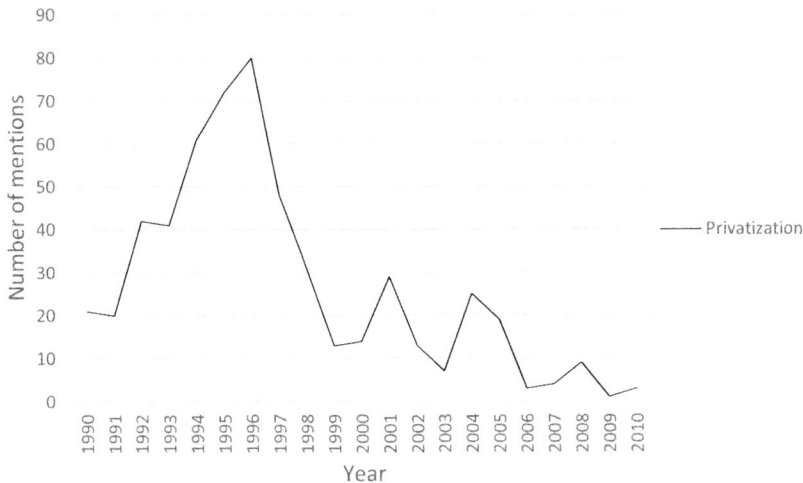

Fig. 8.2   The issue of privatization in prime minister's speeches

1993, Prime Minister József Antall rarely touched on the issue of privatization in his parliamentary speeches despite its paramount importance in transition. His two successors, Péter Boross and Gyula Horn dwelt more heavily on the subject while speaking in parliament. And although we saw a massive surge in the role that this issue played in the prime minister's speeches that year, after 1995 the privatization waned substantially.

At the same time, although it was less conspicuous than in the dimension of speeches and interpellations, the issue did also appear on the media agenda. Népszabadság devoted several covers to this issue, and in a reflection of the intensity of the parties' communication on the issue, the number of cover page articles reached their peak in 1996. As the parties' interest in the topic dispersed, so did the impact of privatization on the media cover pages. We found a similar trend in the realms of budgets and legislation. While in terms of laws and budgets the topic peaked in 1995, with respect to decrees the most intense focus on privatization came a year later, in 1996.

The Issue of Highway Constructions in the 2000s
For the 2000s, still in the liberal period of post-regime change democracy, we selected two issues that led to a surge on a wide range of policy agendas. First, there was the wave of highway constructions between 2002 and 2006, which led to an increased focus on this topic (besides its inherent importance, this was due to the corruption charges associated with the procurements). It also caused a major crack in the cooperation of the socialist and liberal parties which were only temporarily resolved.

Second, we investigate the biggest policy fiasco of the 2000s, a health insurance privatization plan that led to a referendum loss, the disintegration of the political alliance of MSZP, and SZDSZ which lasted for more than two decades and the eventual supermajority of Viktor Orbán in the wake of the 2010 elections.

The issue of highway and public roads constructions had become pressing by the early 2000s as rural communities were increasingly left out of export-led growth built around urban centers. Hence, a consensus emerged for higher budgetary allocations to extend the network. In a period of loose fiscal policy and the impending application—due to EU accession—of the Maastricht criteria prescribing budgetary restraint it also presented one of the few opportunities to initiate major public projects with private contractors.

The minister in charge of the economy and infrastructure at the time, István Csillag had been nominated by SZDSZ, the junior partner in the coalition. He made the controversial decision of using a restricted tender format which contradicted the government's previous commitment to transparency in public procurement. The offers submitted were also significantly higher than what had been estimated initially. Furthermore, in addition to this scandal, several major automobile producers decided to rescind their previous offers and cancelled their plans to build plants in Hungary (e.g., Peugeot), which the government also assessed as a failure on the part of the minister. In short course, Prime Minister Medgyessy, dismissed Csillag, but SZDSZ threatened to break up the coalition so it was Medgyessy who got the sack in the end.

His successor, Ferenc Gyurcsány appointed a new liberal minister, János Kóka to handle matters of transportation. Treating highway construction as a priority, the government approved the opening of 247 km of newly constructed highways and other major roads between 2002 and 2006. Highway construction peaked in 2006. In that year alone, 177 km of new roads were opened up to public use—a major feat for a relatively small European country.

The highway construction spree initiated by the government also had an impact on the policymaking process. Transportation policy had moved up on the policy agendas already in 2002. So much so in fact that in that year its presence on the agenda took on its highest annual share in the twenty-year period following regime change. The most conspicuous change happened in the area of decrees and the cover page articles in Népszabadság. Furthermore, we also saw a change in the emphasis on this issue in interpellations and the articles published in the right-wing press.

This demonstrates that the issue preoccupied both sides of the political divide, if from completely different angles (economic growth vs. government corruption). Although the interest generated by the impetus that the issue received at the time would subsequently dampen over time, it kept the issue near the top of the agenda continuously until 2006. When the program was concluded, however, the attention focused on transportation policy began to diminish as well. And even though it moved to the fore again in 2007 thanks to a final round of decrees and interpellations, there was a persistent decline thereafter until 2010.

The Healthcare Reform of the Second Half of the 2000s

The state-controlled healthcare system of socialist autocracy was retained in the first decade of liberal democracy more or less intact even as liberal reforms challenged the welfare status quo from time to time (Szikra – Tomka, 2009). The path dependency of the evolution of Hungarian healthcare had long been a thorn in the side of neoliberals in SZDSZ and also the modernizational streams of MSZP (see Sebők, 2019). What reform actually had happened in the 1990s, the autonomy granted to social security (including healthcare) state funds and the decision to entrust them to civilian oversight was equally unacceptable to market fundamentalists and was quickly ended by the—then conservative—Fidesz government when it first took power in 1998. Besides the partial privatization of state pension funds at the behest of the World Bank in the late 1990s, no other comprehensive social security or healthcare reform was enacted until the mid-2000s.

The hesitancy of consecutive governments in addressing this area was typically caused by the differences in the opinions and the clashing interests of the government and the various professional organizations in the healthcare sector, respectively, as well as the resistance of the medical chamber, which has an ambivalent relationship with the government to this day. Forced into action by a radicalized SZDSZ, in 2006 and 2007, the left-liberal prime minister at the time, Ferenc Gyurcsány, sought to reform the Hungarian healthcare system with a comprehensive plan.

The plan included proposals for the introduction of a mandatory fee for visits to general practitioners and outpatients visits to other state-owned healthcare institutions, as well as a daily hospital inpatient fee, along with a plan to transition to a health insurance scheme in which for-profit private insurers competed for customers and secured the services of providers.[7] However, the government dove into the drafting of its reform package without trying first to secure the support of strong allies, i.e., the healthcare organizations. The reform proposals elicited intense reactions in the public and the opposition, led by Viktor Orbán, sensed opportunity.

The outrage over certain aspects of the reform package was amplified by the political infighting between coalition partners, as well as the crisis of confidence which had been sparked by what became known as the

---

[7] The essence of the envisioned health insurance system was the creation of health funds, in which private investors would have been allowed to acquire minority stakes.

"Öszöd Speech" by Prime Minister Gyurcsány.[8] These political debates peaked in 2008, when the Fidesz-KDNP party alliance, which was the leading opposition force at the time, successfully initiated what became known as the "three-yes-referendum," in which the party proposed to scrap the recently introduced outpatient and inpatient fees in healthcare, as well as the tuition fees in state-owned institutions of higher education. Since over 80% of the votes cast were against the fees in question, the healthcare reform effectively failed and was abandoned by the government. This led SZDSZ to leave the coalition and the subsequent political turmoil paved the way for Orbán's landslide victory in 2010.

Healthcare reform not only influenced the agenda of the executive branch and governing party groups in parliament, but it also had an impact on the opposition's activities, the media, and interest groups, direct democracy even. In the coverage of the left-wing Népszabadság and in decrees health policy had been emphatically present ever since regime transition, and throughout the entire period its role never declined substantially (see Fig. 8.3).

The most spectacular shift occurred in the prime minister's communication. An analysis of his speeches in parliament reveals that the 65 mentions of healthcare in 2007 was the highest value in any prime minister's speech on health policy since the regime transition. During these years, health policy also moved into the foreground in both the opposition press and the activities of the other parties. The right-wing Magyar Nemzet, for example, devoted more cover page articles to the issue—64 in total—in 2007 than at any other time before. A total of 48 interpellations were presented on the issue in the same year, which marked a standout value as compared to previous years.

Thus, in terms of the policy agenda, the year 2007 revolved to a substantial extent around health policy. Subsequently, further conflicts between MSZP and SZDSZ, which led to a minority, and then a caretaker government, the Global Financial Crisis, and the resignation of Prime Minister Gyurcsány in 2009 combined to shift the public attention away

[8] In May 2006, Prime Minister Gyurcsány held a speech before a closed meeting of MSZP's parliamentary caucus in the resort town of Balatonőszöd. This speech was subsequently leaked and became notorious since in it the prime minister acknowledged that they had governed based on lies ever since 2004. The speech marked massive outrage in society when it was subsequently made public in September. Gyurcsány, who is still active in politics today, continues to be widely associated by other political players as well as large segments of the public with the speech he gave in Balatonőszöd.

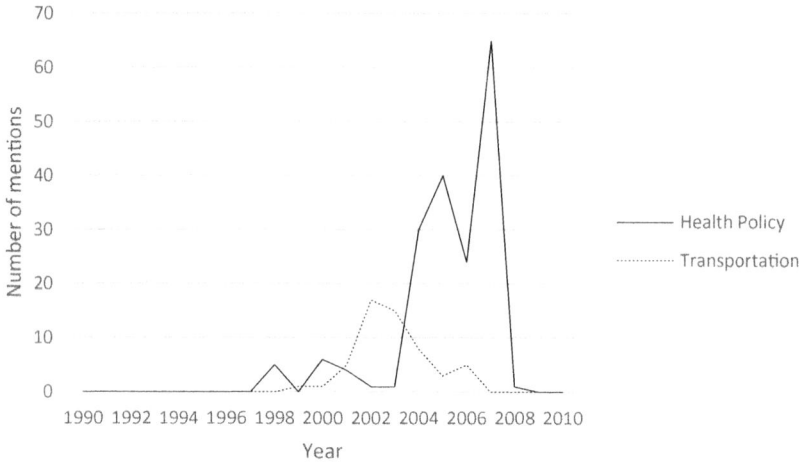

Fig. 8.3   Transportation and healthcare in prime minister's speeches

from health policy. And while this area continues to be very important in Hungarian politics, after this peak it failed once again to dominate the policy agenda the same way it did in the mid-2000s.

Utility Service Fee Cuts—the First Flagship Issue of the Illiberal Era
As mentioned above illiberal democracy was built in Hungary by Viktor Orbán with wedge issues which helped burnish his credentials as a populist, "man of the people" leader. These issues were carefully selected with focus groups and surveys, and were consequently push it into the center of public discourse via a centrally organized media machine. These issues, thus elevated to the rank of "flagship issues," and which were imbued with symbolic relevance in government communication, resulted in a more pronounced focus of the government's agenda.

In turn, this resulted in a substantial decline in the share taken up of the policy agenda by other previously preeminent areas and, in general, a concentration of the agenda. At the same time, these changes also affected the strategy of all other actors. Thus, in addition to promoting the government's political goals, these issues were also liable to detract the attention of the political players, the media, and ultimately the electorate from the policy decisions rendered in other areas and their impact. In the political space as it shaped up after 2010, we find only a handful of such issues. We analyze two of these in this chapter. The first one is the public utility service fee cuts announced in 2012 and the other was immigration, which burst onto the top of the agenda suddenly in 2015 (Fig. 8.4).

After gaining power in 2010, Viktor Orbán set out policies to support families and the construction of a 'work-based society' (basically, a work-fare regime) as two of his main goals. As one of the first steps in the realization of these larger goals, he launched what became known as the "rezsicsökkentés" in Hungarian, a package of measures that the prime minister referred to as the "public utility cost fight" (similarly to the "financial war of independence" of the early 2010s, which referred to the repayment of IMF loans).

The government announced its public utility cost reduction program in 2012 and began its practical implementation in 2013, in several phases. The gist of the program is that in the interest of easing the financial burdens of households, the consumer prices for public utilities would be reduced by the providers at the instruction of the government with no compensation. As part of the program, the household prices of natural gas, electricity, and district heating, as well as chimney cleaning and wastewater management were reduced (Böcskei, 2015: 103). In a parallel

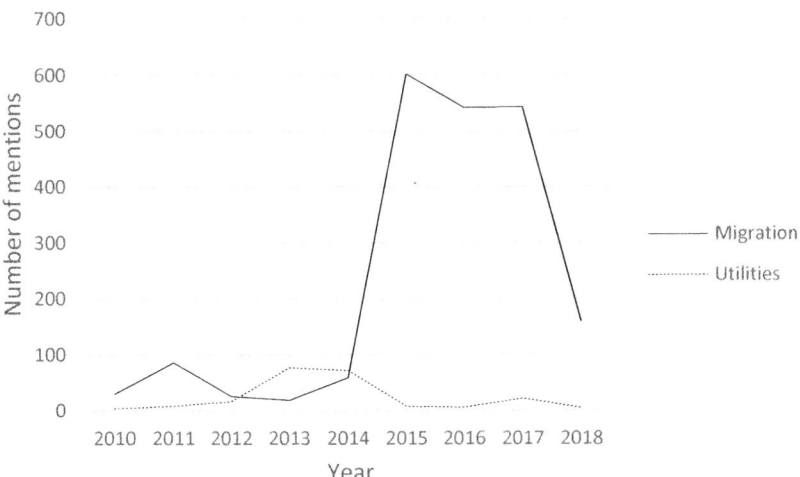

Fig. 8.4   Utilities and migration in prime minister's speeches

process, the government offered to buy out multiple multinational energy companies (such as E.On and GDP Suez) of their local branches therefore creating a double incentive to leave the Hungarian market which led to the government reclaim full authority in terms of pricing and the communication of these fee reductions.

The issue suddenly exploded into public discourse at the end of 2012 and in early 2013, in preparation for the 2014 parliamentary elections, and it quickly transformed the structure of the governmental agenda. The issue peaked in 2013. Since the surge in its role had been manufactured by Orbán's media strategists, the government's communication at this time was also tightly tied to this issue. Hence, there was a massive surge in the number of its mentions in both the prime minister's parliamentary statements as well as his speeches outside the National Assembly: he alluded to this issue over 20 times in parliament, and on 38 occasions elsewhere.

In the face of such an onslaught of government communication, other players were also forced to react to it. As five different laws concerning the utility cost reduction went into effect in the first year of the policy, the opposition raised its shortcomings in interpellations. Before 2010, the issue of utility price costs had never been at the forefront of the opposition's work. In 2013, however, the number of interpellations focusing on this issue suddenly surged to 10, which was a substantial increase.

In addition to parliament, the press also covered widely the proposal. Magyar Nemzet, which had close ties to the government, but the issue on its cover page nine times, despite the fact that previously utility costs had rarely figured that prominently in the newspaper. Nevertheless, despite its rapid rise, the preeminent role of the utility cost issue faded very quickly, within a year. While it had dominated the agenda in 2013, after the 2014 election there was a significant decline in the attention on the issue in the respective agendas of the executive power, the opposition, and the media. And although the issue never completely lost its impact (it still figures in colored highlights on utility bills) from 2014 on the government pivoted to another issue: migration.

Migration Policy and the Policy Agenda of Fully Fledged Illiberalism
The issue of migration policy confronted Europe with one of its major challenges from 2014 on. Due to multiple wars in the Middle East (Afghanistan, Syria, Lybia, etc.) the flow of migrants from these and other countries in the region (as well as Africa in general) surpassed historic records. Although the countries of the European Union adopted

a wide variety of different stances on the issue, Fidesz's pronounced anti-immigration communication and decisions (such as for example the border fence erected at the southern border in 2015) quickly divided EU membership. The government, however, turned the international situation to its advantage in domestic public opinion, portraying itself as the protector of Hungarians and using the issue to shore up its public support. The government's communication (see Metz, 2017) and strategy-making were structured around this issue for multiple years, which ended up impacting the entire Hungarian political space, like the utility price issue had before.

In the second half of the 2010s, migration policy emerged as one of the most contentious issues between the European Commission and Western European countries in general (except the United Kingdom) and Hungary, and their confrontation over this issue drew massive international attention especially with respect to EU relocation planned related to Italian and Greek refugee camps. In addition to portraying immigration as an immediate threat to the security of Hungarians, Fidesz also cast the issues of family support and increasing domestic birthrates via social policy as antipoles to immigration (Bartha et al., 2020). At the same time, the government media began to cast George Soros, an American businessman of Hungarian origins, as a new enemy; he was portrayed as the main financial sponsor of migrants coming to Europe and as a financial speculator who was forging a global alliance against Hungary.

By putting migration at the fore of its communication, the government reacted to international events. This strategy seemed successful, and the government invested tremendous amounts of energy and resources into keeping the issue on the agenda (in 2015, they even launched a national consultation entitled *National Consultation on Immigration and Terrorism (2015)*). Thus, unsurprisingly, this area featured most prominently in the speeches given by the prime minister during these years. Viktor Orbán referred to immigration in over one hundred sentences of his parliamentary statements, while in his speeches outside parliament, he mentioned the issue over 500 times.

This relentless focus on the issue was also translated to public policy. Migration also became increasingly prominent in the text of decrees: the year 2016 saw 13 decrees on immigration, and another 11 were issued in 2017. Furthermore, in light of the opposition's agenda, migration also had an impact on the contents of interpellations. Thus, for example, this issue was also addressed in 17 interpellations in 2016.

Yet despite its meteoric rise, and similarly to the utility cost issue before, immigration, too, quickly lost its dominant place on the agenda. Although it continues to serve as one of the pillars of the government's communication in 2020, its influence on the political space has diminished significantly. Its impact on policymaking is far lower than it was in the year when it first burst onto the agenda. The trend of decline started in 2017, when migration still ranked among the top issues, but its values fell below the level we measured in the foregoing two years.

CONCLUSION

In this chapter we investigated the overall trends and structural breaks in post-regime change Hungarian policy agendas. We presented the radically different policymaking institutions and culture of the first period (1990–2010) marked by liberal democracy, and the post-2010 era of illiberalism. We first showed how the policy process underwent a fundamental change in the democratic structure that replaced the socialist regime. The regime-changing parties arrived at the new institutional structures and economic pillars for democracy and market economy in a way which was built on compromises and allowed for the processing of information from the private sector and civil society. And although the challenges of the transition period and the higher intensity of conflicts between the parties led to an increasingly bitter polarization between the left-liberal and right-wing forces, the policymaking process in particular was marked by efforts at reconciling the conflicting interests and engaging in social dialogue.

As is typical in democracies, in addition to the government, the opposition, too, had a real impact on the decision-making and the outcome of policy reforms. The increased involvement of the opposition in the decision-making process, along with the active presence of interest organizations, which also expressed their views, led to a deliberate (and sometimes: unorganized) legislative process. However, even as in many cases it took months or even a year for reforms to take on the final form in which they were ultimately adopted, it also had a beneficial impact on the quality of laws.

The most prominent policy areas during the time of liberal democracy included macroeconomics and government operations, which covered the economic and institutional pillars of the regime, as well as international affairs—both because of Hungary's desire to converge toward Western democracies and the desire to increase cooperation with the neighboring countries—as well as areas affiliated with public services. The rapid surge in the 2000s in the focus on transportation and health policies is illustrative of the latter; after the change in government in 2010, these issues did not experience such a surge.

After the electoral victory in 2010 of Viktor Orbán, his new ruling party enacted policies that led to major changes across the spectrum of issues and institutions. In addition to the institutional changes introduced by the illiberal regime, we also saw major changes in the policymaking processes. These processes became increasingly closed, and the voices and organizations that were critical of the government exerted only minimal influence on the legislation generated during this period.

Parliament turned into a factory for producing laws, while the proposals emanating from the government were often adopted and promulgated without any changes, in many cases within the span of a few hours. There was an increase in the share of bills sponsored by individual representatives (thus avoiding ex ante impact assessment), while the number of promulgated laws that had been initially proposed by the opposition dropped to a minimum. The government did not exhibit an interest in the preliminary debate of bills. However, even as parliament's role as one of the constituent elements in the system of checks and balances weakened, interpellations continued to figure prominently in the opposition's arsenal for questioning the measures taken by the government.

Drawing on the powers concentrated in his hands, the prime minister built his own personal power base in government; membership in his coterie was not based on the professional expertise of the persons involved but on their loyalty. In the centralized system that emerged, the government also transformed media relations. In addition to the efforts at undermining the position of opposition media and making their continued operations challenging or downright impossible, the governing party set out to build a government-friendly media empire that would focus exclusively on issues that serve to shore up the government's public support. The issue of public services, which had been central in liberal democracy, was relegated to the background and replaced by heavily politicized issues that strengthened the government's power as well as its efforts at propagating the idea that Hungary was facing enemies.

On the whole, we can assert that the formal framework of policy-making as it was first designed in the liberal democratic regime continued to prevail during the period investigated. Both regimes theoretically afforded citizens the freedoms of assembly, association, speech, and press, and they both held competitive elections. However, while in the liberal democratic phase the ongoing processes fostered the emergence of consensus-oriented decision-making and veritably fair elections, in the illiberal regime players outside the government saw their actual influence diminish.

Institutions of checks and balances were rendered hollow, the electoral system became gerrymandered and campaigns imbalanced in the favor of government might. Carefully crafted wedge issues dominated the agenda which became more centralized and polarized in the process. In this the policymaking of illiberal democracy became increasingly reminiscent of the top-down and manufactured logic of authoritarian regimes that came before it.

References

Bakos, G. (1994). Hungarian transition after three years. *Europe-Asia Studies, 46*(7), 1189–1214.

Bartha, A., Boda, Zs., & Szikra, D. (2020). When populist leaders govern: Conceptualising populism in policy making. *Politics and Governance, 8*(3), 71–81.

Bíró-Nagy, A., & Galgóczi, E. (2018). Brüsszel hatása: A magyar törvények és az Európai Unió (2006–2014). *Politikatudományi Szemle, 27*(3), 35–57.

Böcskei, B. (2015). Rezsicsökkentés: a közpolitikai változás, mint politikai innováció. *Politikatudományi Szemle, 24*(4), 94–114.

Boda, Zs., & Patkós, V. (2018). Driven by politics: Agenda setting and policy making in Hungary 2010–2014. *Policy Studies Journal, 39*(4), 402–421.

Bozóki, A. (2015). Broken democracy, predatory state and nationalist populism. In P. Krasztev & J. Van Til (Eds.), *The Hungarian patient: Social opposition to an illiberal democracy* (pp. 3–36). Central European University Press.

Bozóki, A., & Hegedűs, D. (2018). An externally constrained hybrid regime: Hungary in the European Union. *Democratization, 25*(7), 1173–1189.

Bräuninger, T., & Debus, M. (2009). Legislative agenda-setting in parliamentary democracies. *European Journal of Political Research, 48*(6), 804–839.

Enyedi, Zs. (2015). Plebeians, citoyens and aristocrats or where is the bottom of bottom-up? The case of Hungary. In H. Kriesi & T. S. Pappas (Eds.), *European populism in the shadow of the great recession* (pp. 229–244). ECPR Press.

Enyedi, Zs. (2016). Populist polarization and party system institutionalization. *Problems of Post-Communism, 63*(4), 210–220.

Enyedi, Zs., & Tóka G. (2007). The only game in town: Party politics in Hungary. In P. Webb & S. White (Eds.), *Party politics in new democracies* (pp. 147–178). Oxford University Press.

Ferge, Zs., & Juhász, G. (2004). Accession and social policy: The case of Hungary. *Journal of European Social Policy, 14*(3), 233–251.

Green-Pedersen, C., & Mortensen, P. B. (2010). Who sets the agenda and who responds to it in the Danish Parliament? *European Journal of Political Research, 49*(2), 257–281.

Jennings, W., Bevan, S., Timmermans, A., Breeman, G., Brouard, S., Chaqués-Bonafont, L., et al. (2011). Effects of the core functions of government on the diversity of executive agendas. *Comparative Political Studies, 44*(8), 1002–1029.

John, P., & Bevan, S. (2012). What are policy punctuations? Large changes in the legislative agenda of the UK government, 1911–2008. *Policy Studies Journal, 40*, 89–108.

Jones, B. D., & Baumgarten, F. R. (2005). *The politics of attention: How government prioritizes problems*. University of Chicago Press.

Körösényi, A. (2001). Parlamentáris vagy "elnöki" kormányzás?: Az Orbán-kormány összehasonlító perspektívából. *Századvég, 6*(20), 3–38.

Körösényi, A. (2015). A magyar demokrácia három szakasza és az Orbán-rezsim. In. Körösényi A. (Ed.), *A magyar politikai rendszer – negyedszázad után* (pp. 401–422). Osiris Kiadó.

Körösényi, A. (2017). Weber és az Orbán-rezsim. Plebisziter Vezérdemokrácia Magyarországon. *Politikatudományi Szemle, 26*(4), 7–28.

Körösényi, A. (2019). The theory and practice of plebiscitary leadership: Weber and the Orbán regime. *East European Politics and Societies, 33*(2), 280–301.

Lengyel, G., & Ilonszki, G. (2010). Hungary: Between consolidated and simulated democracy. In H. Best & J. Higley (Eds.), *Democratic Elitism: New theoretical and comparative perspectives* (pp. 153–171). Brill Academic Publishers.

Metz, R. (2017). Határok nélkül? Orbán Viktor és a migrációs válság. In A. Körösényi (Ed.), *Viharban kormányozni: Politikai vezetők válsághelyzetekben* (pp. 240–264). MTA TK Politikatudományi Intézet.

Mihályi, P. (2000). Corporate governance during and after privatization: The lessons from Hungary. In E. F. Rosenbaum, F. Bönker, & H.-J. Wagener (Eds.), *Privatization, corporate governance and the emergence of markets* (pp. 139–154). Palgrave Macmillan.

Molnár, C. (2018). A magyar törvényhozás napirendje a XVIII. századtól napjainkig. In Zs. Boda & M. Sebők (Eds.), *A magyar közpolitikai napirend. Elméleti alapok, empirikus eredmények* (pp. 204–223). MTA TK Politikatudományi Intézet.

Patkós, V. (2019). *Szekértáborharc - Eredmények a politikai megosztottság okairól és következményeiről.* Napvilág Kiadó.

Pócza, K. (2015). Az Alkotmánybíróság. In A. Körösényi (Ed.), *A magyar politikai rendszer – negyedévszázad után* (pp. 159–182). Osiris Kiadó.

Pócza, K. (Ed.) (2019). *Constitutional politics and the judiciary: Decision-making in Central and Eastern Europe.* Routledge.

Sebők, M. (2019). *Paradigmák fogságában - Elitek és ideológiák a magyar pénzügyi kapitalizmusban.* Napvilág Kiadó.

Sebők, M., Dobos, G., & Oross, D. (2013). Az ígéretteljesítés kutatásának módszertana. In G. Soós & A. Körörösényi (Eds.), *Azt tették, amit mondtak?: Választási ígéretek és teljesítésük, 2002–2006* (pp. 109–127). MTA TK Politikatudományi Intézet.

Sebők, M., Gajduschek, G., & Molnár, C. (2020). *A magyar jogalkotás minősége: Elmélet, mérés, eredmények.* Gondolat Kiadó.

Sebők, M., Kubik, B. G., & Molnár, C. (2017). A törvények formális minősége: Empirikus vázlat. In Zs. Boda & A. Szabó (Eds.), *Trendek a magyar politikában 2. A Fidesz és a többiek: pártok, mozgalmak, politikák* (pp. 285–310). Napvilág Kiadó.

Sebők, M., & Végh, P. P. (2018). Költségvetések. In Zs. Boda & M. Sebők (Eds.), *A magyar közpolitikai napirend: Elméleti alapok, empirikus eredmények* (pp. 152–163). MTA TK Politikatudományi Intézet.

Sólyom, L., Brunner, G., & Breyer, S. G. (2009). *Constitutional judiciary in a new democracy: The Hungarian constitutional court.* University of Michigan Press.

Szomszéd, O. (2005). Államfői jogkörök alkalmazása a gyakorlatban. *Politikatudományi Szemle, XIV*(3–4), 131–147.

Walgrave, S., Lefevere, J., & Nuytmeans, M. (2009). Issue ownership stability and change: How political parties claim and maintain issues through media appearances. *Political Communication, 26*(2), 153–172.

PART IV

Discussion

CHAPTER 9

The Effect of Regime Types on Policy Agendas in Hungary

Zsolt Boda, Tamás Barczikay, and Zsanett Pokornyi

The present volume started out from the assumption that policy-making varies according to political regimes. In the previous chapters, we presented the institutions as well as practices of policymaking in five different regimes across 150 years: the (proto-)democracy of the Austrian-Hungarian Monarchy, the authoritarian parliamentarism of the

Z. Boda (✉)
Centre for Social Sciences, MTA Centre of Excellence, Eötvös Loránd Research Network,
Budapest, Hungary
e-mail: boda.zsolt@tk.hu

T. Barczikay
Centre for Social Sciences, MTA Centre of Excellence, Eötvös Loránd Research Network, Budapest, Hungary
e-mail: barczikay.tamas@tk.hu

Z. Pokornyi
Centre for Social Sciences, MTA Centre of Excellence, Eötvös Loránd Research Network, Budapest, Hungary
e-mail: pokornyi.zsanett@tk.hu

© The Author(s), under exclusive license to Springer Nature Switzerland AG 2021
M. Sebők and Z. Boda (eds.), *Policy Agendas in Autocracy, and Hybrid Regimes*, Comparative Studies of Political Agendas,
https://doi.org/10.1007/978-3-030-73223-3_9

Horthy-regime between the two World Wars, the socialist autocracy from 1956 to 1989, the new democracy after the regime change, and the hybrid regime of Viktor Orbán after 2010.

In this chapter, we revisit our theoretical framework put forth in Chapter 2 in light of our empirical results. We also conducted additional time-series analyses to tease out long-term trends. With an eye toward generalization to other country cases with multiple regime changes, we discuss our findings along with the core concepts of policy content, policy process and discourses. The joint analysis of empirics related to these concepts yields a comprehensive picture of the effect of regimes on policy dynamics.

Policy Dynamics

Our initial theoretical expectation was that policy dynamics is characterized by more punctuations in non-democracies because of the higher friction rooted in a more centralized policy process, the lack of effective accountability mechanisms as well as the restricted flow of information (Jones et al., 2019). The analysis of the budgetary data of our databases corroborates this expectation. Sebők and Berki (2018) already demonstrated that punctuation in Hungarian budgets, measured by the so-called leptokurtosis scores of the year-on-year distributions of the changes in budgetary categories, is less accentuated in the post-1989 democratic era than during any other political regimes since 1867. This is in line with our theory. However, Sebők and Berki also found that the L-kurtosis score of the budgets of socialist autocracy is actually lower than those of the partly free regimes before World War II, suggesting that the degree of policy punctuation is not a linear function of the oppression level of regimes.

Since the authors did not distinguish between the liberal democracy of 1990–2010 and the post-2010 illiberal democracy of Viktor Orbán—that we labeled as a partly free political regime—we calculated the L-kurtosis values accordingly. We found that the score of the budgets after 2010 is considerably higher (0.48) than for those between 1990 and 2010 (0.33). The difference is strikingly high, especially if we take into consideration that it is still highly debated whether the Orbán-regime can or should be considered non-democratic or partly free, and if so from when. For instance, V-Dem classified the Orbán-regime free until 2017; Freedom House, while tracking a continuous decline in democratic quality, downgraded Hungary from "Consolidated democracy" into

"Semi-consolidated democracy" only in 2015. That is, the difference in the democratic quality before and after 2010 alone cannot explain the difference in policy punctuation.

Our finding suggests two, mutually non-exclusive hypotheses. The first hypothesis is that hybrid regimes indeed exhibit peculiar patterns of policymaking captured in terms of policy dynamics: that is, the difference of the policymaking in hybrid regimes compared to both democracies and autocracies might not simply be a matter of degree, but of quality. The second is that contextual factors may enter into an interaction with regime characteristics, yielding sometimes surprising results. More research is certainly needed in order to scrutinize and better understand these patterns, but our qualitative analyses point to possible explanations that could serve as hypotheses for future studies. It seems, for instance, that the strength of political legitimacy as well as ideological rigidity of the regime should be considered as an important factor explaining policy dynamics in different regimes.

Concerning the former: we posited an interaction between democratic quality and the strength of legitimacy in a way that legitimacy disproportionally increases the probability of policy punctuations under non-democratic conditions. As for the latter: we assumed that ideological rigidity may constrain large policy shifts. This may help to explain the counter-intuitive findings on hybrid regimes, as they are typically less ideologically oriented than "pure" autocracies. Our case studies show the merit of these assumptions.

The Orbán-regime between 2010 and 2018 enjoyed high popular support and a strong legitimacy stemming from a series of consecutive electoral victories since 2010 (including three national, three local–regional, and two European elections). The Fidesz party managed to secure a constitutional majority in parliament for all three National Assembly elections of the period. The political left practically collapsed due to a series of moral scandals, policy fiascos and the dramatic social consequences of the 2007–2009 economic crisis. Viktor Orbán was a highly divisive, but charismatic leader who remained unchallenged by contenders from the opposition. Macroeconomic conditions constantly and noticeably improved between 2012 and 2018.

Under these circumstances, Fidesz had a high degree of freedom to implement their policy agenda which was aimed at breaking up the policy consensus of the previous decades (Boda, 2020). Policymaking under Orbán has been described as highly pragmatic bricolage, with no strong ideological commitments (Körösényi & Patkós, 2017). The legitimacy of Fidesz also made it possible to dismiss the extant system of policymaking, including its actors, and to centralize the decision-making process (Boda, 2020).

At the same time, the hybrid character of the regime meant that elections still had some stakes and Fidesz used populist tactics in order to ensure continuous popular support (Bartha et al., 2020). Especially before the elections, the government either came up with policy innovations proposing generous allocations to families (e.g. Böcskei, 2016) and/or took strong policy positions in divisive issues (such as immigration or LMBTQ rights) in order to align their supporters and mobilize them against the "enemies" (migrants, George Soros, the EU itself, etc.). All these developments contributed to high levels of policy punctuation after 2010.

In contrast, the socialist autocracy that we classified as a not free regime constantly struggled with its fragile legitimacy. The revolution of 1956 forcefully demonstrated the weakness of the regime and instilled a constant fear among the rulers about a possible new popular revolt since the sheer existence of the Kádár regime depended on the presence of the Soviet Red Army in Hungary. Therefore, output legitimacy was an important means to gain allegiance from the people. The regime strived hard to constantly increase welfare provisions and avoid unpopular measures. The deficient performance of the economy became a festering problem already in the 1960s, but the regime found a temporary shield in the form of massive levels of foreign debt (which allowed for muddling through instead of radical reforms or austerity).

Radical reforms were also unfeasible due to the ideological rigidity of the regime: the market-oriented measures of the late 1960s were soon stopped by ideological hardliners of the party. Although the communist dictatorship of the early 1950s obviously implemented a radical systemic change in terms of policies as well, the consolidated socialist autocracy was frozen into its ideological frame which constraint fundamental reforms. In sum, although socialist autocracy was the least free of the Hungarian regimes we studied, the political logic of fragile legitimacy combined with a relatively high ideological rigidity pointed toward policy stability and moderate punctuations.

Our conclusion from this brief overview of policy dynamics in five different regimes is that studying policy punctuations is a fascinating challenge. It is a strong concept, which can be measured in a relatively simple way through the leptokurtosis score of the distribution of policy changes. However, simple as it may seem, it also hides complex phenomena related to the politics of policymaking. Jones et al. (2019) forcefully pointed to some of those phenomena, including centralization and the availability of information to decision-makers. We suggest that further elements should also be considered, including the legitimacy and the ideological rigidity of the regime in question. Data about the Hungarian regimes of over 150 years support the theory that democracies are characterized by lower levels of punctuations—but raise further questions concerning the meaning and implications of the degree of policy punctuations.

POLICY CONTENT

The theoretical framework presented in Chapter 2 implies that the content of policies may vary according to regime types. We expected democracies to provide more public goods and services, implement more redistributive policies, and focus less on the military and the police; to refrain from making large-scale policy reforms as a general rule of policymaking; and with better policy quality. We also assumed that while the preferences of the majority are all-important in a democracy, the rights and needs of minorities are also taken into account.

Is there a difference in policy decisions and attention concerning public services across regimes? Redistribution or, more precisely, the centralization of income was the highest during socialist autocracy. The share of the combined social welfare, health, and labor expenditures in the national budgets increased from 2.6% for the Dual Monarchy, to 18.1% for the Horthy regime, 22.6% for socialist autocracy, 43.1% in the liberal democracy, and 46.2% in the illiberal democracy. This shows a seminal trend, which is both associated with the emergence of the modern, post-World War II state with its multitude of responsibilities as well as the aging of the population and the shrinking of working-age cohorts.

We also analyzed long-term trends in terms of key public goods-related policy areas in terms of their share of attention on the agenda of parliament. We investigated the topic of health, labor, education, transportation, social welfare, and housing, all associated with the emerging welfare state, for both interpellations, the most consequential form of parliamentary questions, and law-making (see Fig. 9.1). The abovementioned seminal trends are reflected in the data for health and social welfare.

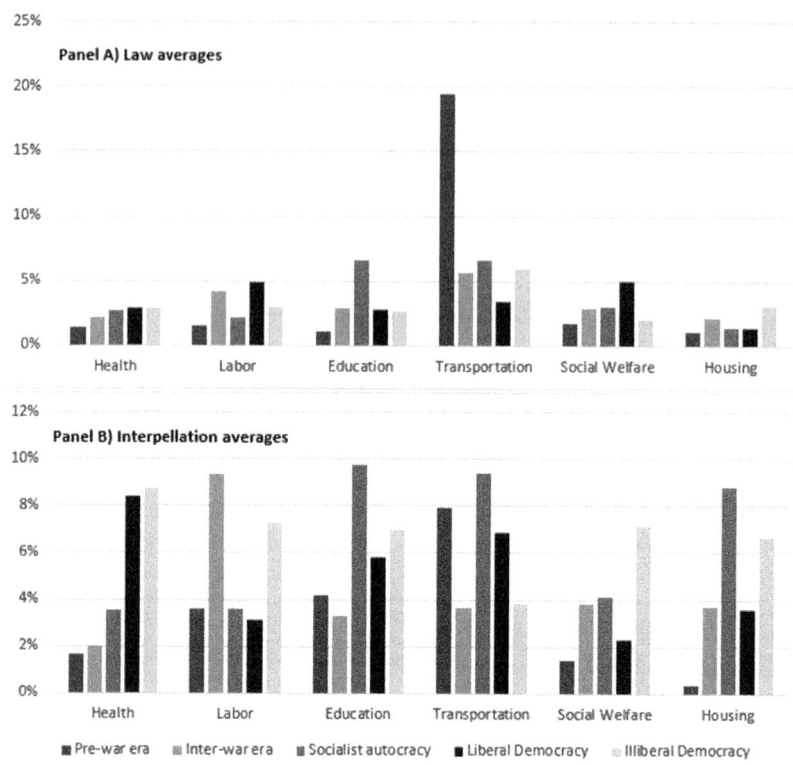

Fig. 9.1 Regime averages for laws and interpellations for welfare state-related topics

In the case of labor policy, we found a low (3%) presence of this issue on the interpellations agenda during the Dual Monarchy, which surged to 9% during the Horthy era; this surge owed to the economic crisis. As a result of the crisis, the issues of employment policy and job creation, along with the relevant problems in these areas, moved to the fore. Although the share of laws (4%) also rose somewhat as compared to the values we found in the Dual Monarchy, this increase is far less pronounced.

The low values we observed for labor policy under socialist autocracy (2% of laws and 3% of interpellations) roughly match the relevant figures of the period near the end of the 1800s. Here, it is notable that in that regime, full employment was sanctioned by law ("no one can be out of work in Socialism") and, therefore, labor policy was considered a taboo. As a consequence, unemployment was "kept behind the closed doors" of the major industrial conglomerates which dominated the economy in that era.

In the liberal and illiberal regimes following the 1989 transformation, the issue received a slightly stronger emphasis once again, but its share never reached 5%, neither with respect to interpellations nor in the case of laws. Thus, with the exception of interpellations in the Horthy period, it did not feature preeminently on the policy agendas of any of these regimes.

Education policy shows a more varied picture especially in the context of interpellations. The most striking trend was that interpellations and laws followed an antithetical trajectory between regimes. At the time of the Dual Monarchy, for example, when the share of education-related laws was negligible (1%), the policy area's share of interpellations was 4%. The modernization of education and the attempts at eliminating illiteracy were also prominently featured in the parliamentary debates at the time (see Chapter 5). Furthermore, the influential efforts of long-time religious affairs and education minister Kunó Klebelsberg (Chapter 6) contributed to a slight increase in the share of the laws dedicated to this policy area (3%). As compared to the period of the Dual Monarchy, however, the share of education-related interpellations was lower at 3%.

The socialist regime led to a massive change in the role of education on the agendas. As compared to the earlier regimes, we saw a surge both with respect to laws (7%) and interpellations (9%). The efforts of the State Party at creating an education system, which stood at the center of its ideology impacted the work of parliament in that period. In the post-1989 liberal and illiberal regimes, the issue declined once again in importance. Nevertheless, this drop was not considerable as debates surrounding the organizational structure of general public education as well as those related to tuition fees in higher education led to its 6% share of interpellations and to a 3% portion of laws.

The issue of transportation tended to produce high values with respect to both laws and interpellations. Legislation on transportation experienced a surge during the Dual Monarchy, with almost 20% of the laws at the time being devoted to this area. At 8%, its share of interpellations was also high at the time. The rapid progress of transportation, especially railways, in combination with the impact of industrialization, increasingly focused the attention of the decision-makers on transportation. The previously high share of transportation policy dropped massively during the Horthy era, however. Only 5% of the laws at the time concerned this issue, while interpellations regarding transportation fell to under 3%.

Another interesting fact is that as socialist autocracy consolidated **its power**, interpellations became a key policy venue for airing local grievances **on a parliamentary level**. Interpellations presented during the liberal and illiberal regimes also widely featured this topic owing to the expansion of Hungary's public road network initiated by the Gyurcsány government.

The role of social welfare as a public policy area was very much affected by the gradual development of the welfare state from the late nineteenth century on. Hence, its weight on the agenda was least pronounced during Dual Monarchy, when despite debates in parliament about the issues surrounding the nascent social safety net on the whole social welfare remained a marginal area. During the Horthy era and socialist autocracy, it began to gain importance, making up 3% of laws and 4% of interpellations. In the interwar period, the presence of this issue on the agenda was boosted by the impact of the economic crisis, while during the Kádár regime the impetus for its growing importance stemmed from the various measures enacted by the regime to increase consumption. We also found similar values in the liberal and illiberal regimes. The policy area's share of the laws grew by one percentage point while in the interpellations it experienced a slight decline, which led us to conclude that the overall share of the agenda of social welfare had essentially stabilized.

An interesting feature of the social welfare policy area is that apart from two years with extraordinary values, we did not find any exceedingly low or high values in the time-series data for laws. At the same time, the data at our disposal show that starting in 1975, the share of social expenditures as a percentage of budget spending began to increase. This trend persisted until 1988, the year just before the regime transition, when 40% of all budgetary spending was devoted to this category. This clearly shows the last-ditch efforts of the socialist regime to fend off public dissatisfaction in an era of mounting debt and fiscal distress.

The area of housing policy shows contrasting agenda share with respect to laws and interpellations. In terms of the legislative agenda, housing was marginal throughout all the periods we investigated, fluctuating between 1 and 2%. The share of related interpellations, however, shifted dynamically from time to time. While during the Dual Monarchy the attention on this issue was negligible, it gradually increased in the Horthy era (3% off interpellations) and soared further under socialist autocracy (9%). While its role declined substantially in the liberal and illiberal regimes that followed, its value nevertheless stabilized at 5%.

On the whole, and when it comes to public goods provision, the investigated policy areas paint a diverse picture of the regimes we analyzed. While the attention on transportation (the Dual Monarchy) and health (liberal regime) tends to be pronounced in regimes on the freer end of the democratic spectrum, at various points labor, education, and social welfare emerged as focal issues in the periods of the Horthy-era, socialist autocracy and Orbán's illiberal regime. As a clear outlier, education received the highest level of attention during the Kádár era.

Our main takeaway from this comparative analysis is that it is a daunting task to draw general conclusions based on our five cases which span over 150 years. Policy attention to public services is defined, to a large extent, by seminal trends rather than the degree of freedom of the respective political systems. Transportation was a very important topic of the nineteenth century with the boost of railway developments and later the advent of the automobile era. During the Horthy regime, a charismatic politician, Kunó Klebelsberg marked the development of education policy in a country which—due to the loss of territories in the wake of World War 1—could no longer rely on the vast natural resources of the Hungarian Kingdom. During the same years, the Great Depression caused a rise in concerns about labor and social welfare issues. The self-identity of the socialist autocracy was a (relatively) generous provision of social services, including free education.

It is important to note that this analysis does not provide a straightforward falsification of our original theoretical expectations either. We could not find overwhelming evidence that non-democratic regimes would, in fact, focus more on welfare provision than democracies. Our results simply imply that historical contexts are more important than regime types in this respect. We also face methodological issues which prevent us from drawing clear conclusions. Military spending is a case in point.

In the theoretical chapter, we assumed that democracies spend less on the military and law enforcement. However, the military was not a national competence in the Austrian-Hungarian Dual Monarchy, the Horthy regime was prevented for years from building up a substantial military presence due to the terms of the peace deal and official spending on law enforcement during socialist autocracy looks suspiciously low. We have cause to believe that real spending was partly hidden in related line items and secret provisions (see Chapter 7). It is also apparent that external shocks, namely the impending World War II were spurring military expenditures. The historical data of Roser and Nagdy (2013) suggest that between the two Great Wars, regime type was not the main factor behind the size of military spending as nations, democracies, and non-democracies alike, around the world prepared for the inevitable.

Besides quantitative data, a qualitative analysis of policy agendas and institutions also sheds light on some major differences between the regimes in question which would have remained hidden in a purely quantitative research design. The proto-parliamentary regime of the Dual Monarchy was characterized by an extension of human rights. Although the collective rights of national minorities were not recognized (as basically nowhere in Europe at that time), individual rights were not curtailed, but developed. For instance, the legal emancipation of Jews happened during those years. In contrast, the persecution of Jews was a governmental policy in the Horthy regime, the Communist Party was banned and its members imprisoned. Yet, from a general perspective, both regimes were classified as partly free, and with good reason.

The socialist autocracy, by definition, did not allow the political opposition to be organized. Although imprisonment for political activities became less and less prevalent with the moderation of the regime, dissidents were still forced to leave the country or were marginalized and stripped of their basic citizen rights. There was a systemic discrimination against the members of the pre-war middle class—for instance, admission to universities was conditioned on proper ideological profiles and family background.

The new liberal democracy after 1990 institutionalized human rights and the protection of minority interests not only in politics, but in several social fields. However, the illiberal turn after 2010 started an opposite movement: the political opposition and unpopular minorities (LMBTQ people, immigrants, Gypsies) came under pressure either formally (enacted in policies and laws) or informally (through institutional and political practices). This brief qualitative overview of just one major aspect of our theoretical treatment of what makes a democracy from a policy agendas perspective points to the importance of mixed-methods research and the role of in-depth case studies in the understanding of regime effects on policy dynamics.

PROCEDURES AND ACTORS

The most evident consequences of regime types on policymaking are related to the procedures and the actors involved. Autocratic regimes, by definition, limit the autonomy of social and political actors by controlling, and even banning, their activities. Their system of governance is more closed, more centralized than in democracies and they limit the number of policy venues available for citizens and stakeholder groups. In Chapter 2, we referred to this phenomenon as constraints on both the "demand side" and the "supply side" of political participation and as the truncated policy capacities of society.

Our analyses suggest that this is especially true for the socialist autocracy which was a "not free" regime. Although a large number of pseudo-organizations were active in this period, they were all under the direct command of the Socialist Party. Policy venues were also closely controlled up to a point that even the one-party parliament was not deemed to be dependable enough: real decision-making mostly happened inside the intransparent bodies of the Party. The media was rigorously censored. However, even autocracies need information and inputs: highly secretive opinion surveys were organized and academic research also enjoyed some degree of freedom (Kuczi & Becskeházi, 1992).

In the partly free Dualism, the Horthy regime as well as the post-2010 illiberalism, the number of policy actors was larger with more access to the policy process. The Horthy regime was the least free in this respect: some media outlets, parties and civil organizations were openly banned and the governing party made several attempts to tighten its grip on policymaking. The post-2010 Orbán-regime made also deliberate steps to take over or shut down media outlets, menace social actors (e.g., human rights NGOs) with retaliation. While consultations formally still existed, the practice of policymaking was about increasing centralization (Boda, 2020). Dualism was maybe the most liberal of the partly free regimes in terms of policy procedures and policy actors: the media was more or less free and civil society thrived. The institution of petition provided an opportunity for any organization, group or even individual to reach out to the legislators and ask for specific policies.

One of the consequences of limited policy venues and actor activity in autocracies is that policy decisions are less responsive to bottom-up initiatives which, in turn, translates into higher policy punctuations. Other consequences include less diversity in the thematic composition of policy agendas, and a lower level of association between the composition of different policy agendas. We will return to the former issue in the next subsection on policy discourses. In the following, we will focus on the association between different agendas which is a simple, yet powerful indicator of the responsiveness of policymaking.

Association Between Agendas

Boda and Patkós (2018) argue that the media agenda did not have an effect on the policy agendas during the first four years of Orbán's illiberal democracy, while, on the other hand, the symbolic policy agenda influenced the thematization of the media to a large degree. This is in stark contrast with findings from Western European democracies where the media have a small, but significant effect on policy agendas, while the latter do not predict what the media are talking about (Vliegenthart, et al., 2016). Due to data constraints, we will examine one specific relationship only: the one between the composition of the symbolic policy agenda (through interpellations) and decisions (laws).

Among the policy actors, we should consider the political opposition in the legislation as well. The opposition can influence the agenda by raising new issues; it can channel expert opinions or interest group inputs in the policymaking process; and it can also influence policy formulation. In non-democratic and hybrid regimes, by contrast, the course of decision-making is dominated by those in power. In this closed policymaking process, the opposition is marginalized and its impact on policies is heavily constrained (see Boda & Patkós, 2018; Böcskei & Szabó, 2019).

We analyzed the role of the opposition in the policymaking process through the degree of association between the thematic composition of interpellations and laws. We assumed that in the period of the Dual Monarchy, which was not extremely undemocratic by the standards of the age, as well as in the liberal democratic regime that emerged in the aftermath of regime transition in 1990, the opposition had a greater influence on the legislative process than in the Horthy era, in socialist autocracy, or the post-2010 illiberal regime. Our expectation was that in democracies, interpellations tend to move strongly in tandem with laws, which suggests that the opposition plays a substantial role in shaping legislation. Under non-democratic conditions, by contrast, the respective trends of laws and interpellations should diverge significantly.

We examined this expectation by comparing the changes of agendas in three policy areas of major importance throughout the regimes: macroeconomics, international affairs, and government operation. We performed our analysis based on a comparative review of the opposition's work in parliament (interpellations), along with the trends in legislative activity (laws). The general pattern is the same for each of the policy areas: the association between the composition of interpellations and laws varies according to regimes in a way that corroborates our expectations.

While in the Dual Monarchy and in the liberal democracy we found a rather harmonious joint movement of laws and interpellations, in the Horthy, Kádár, and Orbán eras, the values in the data series analyzed diverged strikingly. Below we illustrate the point with the topic of macroeconomics (Fig. 9.2). In the age of the Dual Monarchy, a time when many of the democratic features that were common in that period also applied to Hungary, the respective trends in the topics of interpellations presented by the opposition and of the laws adopted tended to move in the same direction. However, while the share of macroeconomic interpellations was very low (on average around 5%), nearly every fifth promulgated law (15–20%) pertained to macroeconomics. Thus, industrialization and the

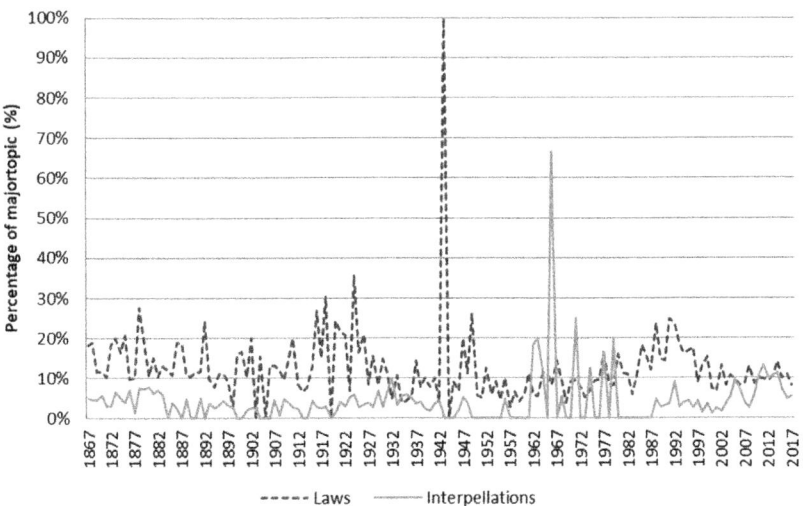

Fig. 9.2   Representation of major topic of macroeconomics

flourishing capitalism in Hungary at the time also had an impact on the content of the laws, but the issues surrounding the political structure and the Monarchy ended up diverting the opposition's attention from economic matters.

In the regime that prevailed between 1990 and 2010, we detected a similar dynamics of change as we noted for the Dual Monarchy. In the first years after regime change and the period of transition, the shifts in the thematic distribution of interpellations moved jointly with that of laws. However, while the emerging capitalist structure and the economic reforms pushed the topic of macroeconomics into the foreground in terms of the thematic distribution of laws (on average, 15% of laws pertained to this area), the relevant ratio with respect to interpellations was substantially lower, ranging from 5 to 10%. In 2007, as a result of the crisis of confidence engulfing the Gyurcsány cabinet in power at the time, as well as the controversies surrounding its health reforms, the share of macroeconomics in interpellations dropped to a low of 1%. However, the relevant figure started to rise again owing to the Global Financial Crisis of 2008.

While in the Dual Monarchy and in the liberal democracy the various agendas appeared to move roughly in tandem, in the other three regimes the time-series data for the respective policy venues tended to move in antithetical directions. We also found massive differences between the regimes investigated. In the Horthy period, for example, we saw the impact of the Great Depression in the rising number of laws concerning macroeconomics (thus, in 1927 almost 40% of the laws concerned macroeconomic issues), but the dynamics of interpellations did not track this change; their share was between 5 and 10%. In the 1930s, the trend shifted, with a drop in the share of laws on macroeconomic issues and a slightly rising trend in the mentions of this issue in interpellations.

Only one law was adopted in all of 1943, and since that legislation pertained to macroeconomics, in that particular year this major topic made up 100% of the agenda. However, the standout value of 1943 constitutes a watershed moment, visibly dividing two eras with very different volatilities in the share of macroeconomic legislation. Prior to 1943, the time series was characterized by higher volatility than in the post-World War II era. The gap between the relevant values of laws and interpellations was most pronounced during socialist autocracy.

During the harshest period of the communist dictatorship of the early 1950s, the share of macroeconomics of the interpellation agenda was not exceedingly high (15–20%). During the era of the socialist autocracy, however, the role of macroeconomics become more pronounced in legislation, too, as a consequence of the regime's efforts at modernizing Hungary and on account of external influences. The latter also had an impact on interpellations. Standout figures were observed during the period from 1962 to 1979, when the slowdown in the global economy and successive oil crises pushed concerns related to the economy to the fore.

Since 2010, both laws and interpellations have moved in a similar direction. However, the temporal order of observations is a key issue. While in liberal democracy interpellations impacted reforms through the debates *before* the relevant laws were adopted, in the illiberal regime it was more typical for the debate to take place *after* the reform had been adopted. Our results suggest that in the Dual Monarchy and in liberal democracy, the opposition had a broader array of possibilities to influence the relevant processes than under the Horthy-era, the socialist autocracy and illiberal democracy, since there seems to be a closer association between the symbolic agenda of the opposition (interpellations) and the policy agenda of laws. This illustrates that during the past 150 years of Hungarian history, regime type has had a major impact on the constitution of the range of societal players who had a say in the policy decision-making process.

The close association between the executive agenda and the legislative agenda may signal something different: the strength of "political governance" (Aucoin, 2012) or top-down policymaking that limits the influence of policy actors. In Chapter 8, we presented our analysis of prime ministers' speeches and the legislative agenda. We argued that before 2010 the association between the two was loose, while during the illiberal era it became particularly strong: the issues raised by Prime Minister Orbán in his speeches were shortly translated into policy proposals and bills.

The Speed of Legislation and the Use of Decrees

In Chapter 2 we also suggested that the speed of policymaking is faster in autocracies—this was called "institutional efficacy' by Baumgartner et al. (2017). The underlying causes are the lower number of policy actors and their limited consultation possibilities as well as the lower level of institutionalization of the decision-making process. In autocracies, the decision-maker may circumvent the institutional procedures which may not even be set in a rigorous manner. For instance, in Chapter 6, we discussed that in the Horthy regime, individual MPs could in principle sponsor bills—however, in practice the bills proposed by the opposition were not allowed on the agenda of the full session of the House. In Chapter 7, we presented how in the socialist autocracy there were two parallel decision-making "pyramids": the formal executive-legislative structures and the organs of the Party. The rules of the latter were not transparent yet decisions were binding even to officeholders in Parliament or the cabinet through their party membership.

Available data also support our expectation concerning the speedier policy process in autocracies: the number of days between the introduction of a bill to Parliament and its final vote was on average 17.6 in the hard communist dictatorship of the 1950s; 53.7 during the soft socialist autocracy of the 1970s; 87.3 in the liberal democracy of the 1990s; and 45.4 in the illiberal democracy of the 2010s. Autocracies often make deliberate efforts to change the rules of decision-making in order to render them more flexible: for instance, at the beginning of the Horthy regime, the Standing Orders of the legislation were changed in order to speed up legislation. During the first-government cycle of the illiberal Orbán government about one-third of its bills was proposed in the form of individual motions, which allow for the circumventing of standard procedures such as the conduction of impact assessments.

The lower level of institutionalization and faster decision-making in autocracies also goes hand in hand with government by decree: the decree/law ratio increases in non-democratic regimes (the only outlier is the illiberal democracy after 2010). The ratio was 5.9 in the Dual Monarchy, 14.8 in the autocratic Horthy regime, 36.3 in the socialist autocracy (including decree-laws), 6.4 during the liberal democracy, and 4.9 in the illiberal democracy of the Orbán government. The low value of the latter case is probably due to the fact that governing Fidesz party had a constitutional majority in Parliament and party discipline turned government MPs into rubber stampers of government proposals.

Policy Discourses

In Chapter 2, we suggested that—besides policy content and process—regime characteristics may influence the features of policy discourses. Policy discourses would be more diverse in democracies, because policy actors all bring their arguments into the policy debate, while in autocracies the policy discourse is dominated by the rulers who focus on their own agenda. Democratic policy discourse is supposed to be more contextual, focusing on the specific policy issues while in autocracies the dominant ideology may shape the discourses of different policy subsystems. We also assumed that policy discourses in democracies manifest high and positive valence, while autocracies may rely more on adversarial and crisis narratives as well as scapegoating. Finally, we suggested that autocracies may use discursive governance, that is, governing by words, as opposed to formal policy instruments, more often than democracies.

Our case studies and additional quantitative research support these claims. In the following, we first present a qualitative assessment of prime ministers' speeches over the five regimes examined. Second, we conduct a quantitative analysis of the diversity of symbolic policy agendas across the periods in question. Our findings show that each of the "not free" and partly free regimes is characterized by a dominant political discourse, which pervades policy discourses and guides policy decisions.

Ideological Discourses

In the case of the Horthy regime, the dominant discourse was centered around Christian values, the nationalist tradition, and the rejection of the Trianon Peace Treaty that stripped Hungary of extensive territories and forced millions of ethnic Hungarians to live as minorities in neighboring countries. The topoi of Christianity, nation, and Trianon were present in all of the prime ministers' speeches in the period. It is also clear that the reference to Christianity served as coded anti-Semitism, while the nationalist discourse was often accompanied by adversarial narratives about cosmopolitanism either in relation to Soviet Communism or liberal democracies. These recurrent discursive elements are in close connection with the content of policies concerning the discrimination of Jews, the close ties with the Catholic Church, and the political orientation of foreign policy including the goal of territorial revision.

However, some other data sources did not corroborate these findings. We found that party manifestos of the Horthy regime contained more policy content than those during the proto-parliamentary system of the Dual Monarchy. This may seemingly run against our expectations but an alternative explanation is equally viable: during the early years of democracy, parties used more rhetorical and less substantial—or at least: public policy-oriented—elements in their manifestos. We also have to note that the partly free Horthy regime was less ideological than the fully fledged autocracy of the Kádár era.

During socialist autocracy, the speeches of both the prime ministers and the first secretary were deeply permeated by communist ideology. The global fight between Capitalism and Communism was a recurrent theme. A Manichean worldview was obviously reflected in foreign policy: the rhetoric of the prime minister's speech in 1962 focused on the arms race between the Soviet Union and the United States, presenting the latter as a potential aggressor. This binary structure of opposition was present in internal politics as well where the hegemony of the socialist party and the social benefits of its rule was pitted against the threat of dissidents and anti-state agitators. Adversarial narratives and crisis communication were especially characteristic of the speeches at the hardline beginnings of the era. The tone softened with time: pragmatic topics and positive thematization gained ground.

As for the period of post-2010 illiberalism, we found significant differences in the rhetoric of Viktor Orbán inside and outside parliament. Orbán did not talk much in the National Assembly and if he spoke, his message was brief and the tone mostly pragmatic. The content of these speeches was typically devoid of ideology, crisis communication, or adversarial narratives. However, his speeches outside parliament show a different picture. His weekly briefings at the public broadcasting corporation or his grand lectures at events organized by his followers were more ideologically loaded. In those speeches, Orbán contextualized his politics in broader interpretive frames, identified time and time again the main enemies of the Hungarian people (which also changed every now and then) and regularly came up with ideological buzzwords and short, easy-to-understand slogans.

In a 2014 speech, he announced that Hungarian democracy is not liberal which gained him notoriety both in domestic politics and abroad. In 2019 he coined the term "Christian freedom." Just as during the interwar period a reference to Christianity was an implicit opposition to both Communism and Judaism, Christianity in Orbán's rhetoric is an implicit negation of multiculturalism and the Islam culture of immigrants. The notion of freedom may have been used as a counterweight to the negative connotations of illiberalism and referred to something valuable that should be preserved (hence "freedom" was juxtaposed with "liberalism").

Orbán regularly depicted himself as a "freedom fighter" who stood up against extremist liberalism and protected the traditional values of nation, family, and church. Since 2015 immigration became the dominant frame in his rhetoric. Immigrants were portrayed as the main threats to Hungary, along with actors—the European Union and Hungarian-American philanthropist George Soros—who allegedly would have opened the gates to mass immigration and coerced Hungary to give up its closed doors policy. The fight against immigration also enjoyed a prominent place in the government's communication campaign for generous natalist family policies, which targeted the crucial voting bloc of upper-middle-class families.

In sum, political discourses in non-democratic and partly free regimes were ideologically framed as a general rule and their policy discourses were in stark opposition with the more pragmatic public debates and government communication of the post-regime change period of liberal democracy. During the two decades starting in 1990, policy debates were not as heavily loaded with ideological content as in other regimes (and certainly not as a general characteristic of all policy subsystems). Debate participants in parliament and the media evoked contextual values more often than general interpretive frames.

Diversity of Policy Discourses

Besides the above qualitative analysis, we also used quantitative tools to determine the thematic diversity of policy agendas. Our expectation in Chapter 2 was that as competing discourses are suppressed and centrally organized campaigns flooded policy venues in "not free" and "partly free" polities one would expect less diversity. Drawing on international literature on this topic, we performed the relevant calculations by using the Shannon Diversity Index (H).[1]

---

[1] "$H = -1 \sum (x_i) \ln p(x_i)$, where the value of diversity (H) is estimated as the negative sum ($p(x_i)$) of all topics in the probability function. The x_i in the function denotes the

Diversity here refers to the diversity of policy topics on a specific policy agenda. It can take a value between 0 and 3, where a value of 0 means that the agenda is dominated by a single policy topic. In such a situation, the given policy agenda—such as parliamentary questions—is defined by a single policy issue, say macroeconomics. When the value of H is 3, then the dynamic between the various policy topics is completely balanced, in other words all policy areas receive equal attention (high diversity).

Our hypothesis was that the distribution of interpellations by policy areas would be more diverse in liberal democracy than in other regimes. It harks back to the logic we discussed in the theoretical chapter regarding the dominance of government thematization vis-á-vis any other policy actors. Our results indicate that the agenda was more diverse in democratic regimes, while in the Horthy era, in socialist autocracy, and in illiberal democracy it was more focused. The diversity of interpellations during the first phase of the Dual Monarchy was rather high, taking on values between 1.8 and 2.5. This means that toward the end of the 1800s, the representatives who interpellated the government touched on many policy areas at once. In the early 1900s, this diversity was interrupted by a growing focus of the agenda. The constitutional controversies of the Monarchy increasingly crowded out a substantial portion of other public policy topics.

The thematic distribution of interpellations during the Horthy regime was just as diverse as the first period of the Dual Monarchy, and this trend prevailed throughout the entire Interwar period. During the socialist regime, by contrast, the agenda became focused once again, and the content of interpellations was dominated by the issues that were seen as reinforcing the power of the ruling party. This focus was then disrupted by the high diversity we saw in the liberal regime following the transition in 1990. Drawing on their expanded privileges, the parties referred to a broad array of issues in their interpellations. After 2010, under the illiberal regime, the interpellations agenda became more concentrated again.

On the whole, our analysis of the diversity of the policy areas raised in interpellations reveals major differences between Hungarian regimes. The high level of agenda diversity in the proto-parliamentary and the liberal democratic era was disrupted by the growing focus on some issues in the

individual units of analysis (in the case at hand, that means the paragraphs in the prime minister's speeches) which are devoted to the given topic i, which is then multiplied by the natural log of the probability" (Jennings et al., 2011: 10).

Horthy-era, in the Kádár regime, and in the illiberal democracy. These results support our hypothesis that the opposition's expanded privileges in liberal (and nineteenth century) parliamentarism allow parties to present their views concerning the widest possible array of policy areas; to hold the government accountable; and to offer a competitive alternative to the government's policies.

CONCLUSION: THE EFFECT OF REGIMES ON POLICY DYNAMICS

In this chapter, we revisited the theoretical claims made in Chapter 2 on the possible effects of political regimes on policymaking in terms of policy dynamics, policy content, policy procedures and discourses. We built on our regime case studies of Part III and presented additional quantitative and qualitative analyses based on the data of the Hungarian Comparative Agendas Project.

We found that in autocracies there are fewer actors involved in policymaking and this is reflected in the less diverse policy agendas and discourses found under non-democratic conditions. The institutionalized processes of policymaking are often emptied, the venues are constrained and the opposition (if any) has a smaller effect on policies. This is illustrated by the weaker association between the symbolic legislative agenda (interpellations) of the opposition and the substantive policy agenda (laws). Policymaking is faster in autocracies and makes more use of governmental decrees as opposed to laws. Autocracies generally use a more ideological political discourse which is translated into policy discourses as well.

Policy dynamics is a complex issue that deserves more attention in the future, yet some of our findings are notable in the context of the effect of regimes on policy-making. Our data supports the hypothesis—tested in other contexts—related to higher punctuations under non-democratic regimes. However, we did not find clear evidence that democracies would devote more attention and resources to public services and less to law enforcement. Besides the problems of missing reliable data, the main reason for some of our equivocal findings is related to the starkly differing historical context of the regimes that render any direct comparison difficult. Also, we have to take into account the peculiarities of the regimes as all "partly free" polities are not all alike.

Socialist autocracy built its legitimacy on the idea that people were provided the basic welfare (which, according to the Marxist ideology, was not the case in capitalist societies). The Horthy regime of the interwar period was a partly free (hybrid) regime, which could not utterly discard the popular demands, on the one hand; and faced the challenge of rebuilding Hungary after a lost war and the loss of large territories and population, on the other. The latter task spurred an investment into physical infrastructure as well as—to a lesser extend though—human capital. These, and similar contextual factors play a major role in defining the policy choices and policy practices of different regimes.

What lessons can we draw from our study for future research? Both the merits and the limitations of our approach stem from the very essence of our endeavor which was based on comparing a limited number of political regimes across 150 years of history. Although the databases of the Hungarian Comparative Agendas Project offer a rich resource for quantitative analysis, we combined them with a qualitative approach in order to unfold the peculiarities and the contextual embeddedness of the regimes which influence their policymaking. Some of those peculiarities are rooted in specific historic events—like the abovementioned challenge of rebuilding the country after a lost war.

These are important takeaways for anyone with an interest in understanding specific political regimes and their social, cultural, and economic underpinnings; but they can only be generalized with great caution. Such an effort could build on our case studies which pointed to some features that may be used as explanatory variables in further analyses. More specifically, we suggest that the role of regime legitimacy, ideological orientation, leadership style, formal and informal norms may be important for analyzing other non-free regimes. These concepts have seldom been used in policy studies, especially in the context of analyzing the effects of regime characteristics on patterns of policymaking.

We referred above to the potentially important role of regime legitimacy in shaping policy choices and policy practices both in terms of its strength and its strategies used by the rulers. For instance, autocratic regimes with weak legitimacy may make serious efforts to increase the quality of their policies in order to ensure output legitimacy. Hybrid regimes may scrutinize public opinion and inflate policy bubbles around issues with high valence, but neglect less exposed policy areas. Our cases provide insights into how legitimacy strategies work and how they affect policymaking and policy dynamics, but further research is needed to untangle these complex interactions.

The ideological character of a regime, especially of hybrid and autocratic regimes, may also substantially affect policymaking. Radical ideologies may prescribe paradigmatic policy changes and thematic foci that may lead to high punctuations on a few, or occasionally on a number of fields. For instance, the rise of extreme right-wing ideology in Hungary in the 1930s led to the emergence of a new policy field that was labeled "the Jewish question": how to administer Jewish citizens, limit their freedoms, strip them of their rights in education, journalism, business—an obsession that tragically led to the mass extermination of Jews with surprisingly high administrative efficiency.

The hardline communist regime established after World War II installed a completely new economic and social system in which private property was almost completely abolished, civic autonomy eliminated. This caused a major change in many policy areas with new policy objectives and practices. However, the very same ideology acted as an impediment to further change and contributed to policy stability during the consolidated socialist autocracy when the regime was seeking for ways to improve its policy effectiveness. When and how ideologies contribute to policy change or policy stability are questions worth further study.

The concept of leadership and that of leadership styles are understudied in political science in general, let alone in policy studies. We couldn't deal with this problem in detail, but our case studies highlight its relevance. During the socialist autocracy, János Kádár's style and image as a puritan and pragmatic leader had a role not only in the symbolic legitimacy of the regime, but the political and policy choices made during this period. For instance, as we discussed in Chapter 7, Hungary started radical economic reforms already in the 1960s, and although they were ultimately stopped by the party's conservative communist wing, they started over in the 1980s when Hungary became the first country in the Soviet bloc to integrate into the global market economy and apply for a membership in the International Monetary Fund. Low-key privatization policies were also started in this period along with the licensing of the operation of the first multinational companies in the country.

Viktor Orbán, the architect of the post-2010 illiberal democracy also had a very distinct leadership style rooted in his personal charisma, his ability and willingness to control a wide array of political processes and his combative attitude. His style was certainly a major factor behind a number of policy choices and the emerging patterns of policymaking, like a penchant for heterodox policy solutions, the extreme centralization of the policy process, the sidelining of policy actors (which turned into veritable witch hunts when it came to human rights NGOs—Boda, 2020).

We are inclined to think that leadership style is especially important under non-democratic conditions when the role of formal institutions is less prevalent. However, phenomena like the spread of populist governance (Bartha et al., 2020), presidentialization and the rise of "political governance" (Aucoin, 2012) warn us that leaders play an increasingly important role in democracies as well, therefore the effect of their style on governance should be investigated in more depth. The distinction between formal and informal norms as well as the significance of the latter is well-known in public administration and policy studies (Peters, 2019). We suggest that informal norms are especially relevant in the context of non-democracies where the design of formal institutions and their actual use might significantly diverge. Our cases provide several illuminating examples in this regard.

The most striking one of those is the parallel decision-making structure of socialist autocracy. Besides parliament and the cabinet, the Central Committee and the Politbüro of the party dealt with the most important issues. Even the reliability of formal documents, such as budgetary data, casts a doubt on the importance of formal processes as illustrated by the suspiciously low military spending of the era. In a less accentuated manner, but such a parallel decision-making system was in place in post-2010 illiberal democracy as well. Evidence suggests that Viktor Orbán as Prime Minister holds the only real decision-making power and the role of the parliament or other veto player institutions (like the Constitutional Court) is barely more than symbolic.

Finally, let us come back to the question of policy dynamics which is at the very heart of the punctuated equilibrium theory that we used as our theoretical starting point. Our data supports the theoretical claim by Jones et al. (2019) that punctuation is more moderated in democracy. Our cases provide evidence of the factors listed by the authors—namely, higher friction rooted in centralization, lack of leadership motivation and information disadvantage. These were indeed at play under non-democratic conditions.

However, as we suggested above, other factors, like patterns of legitimacy, ideology, or even informal institutions and leadership style, might also contribute to higher punctuations in autocracies. They may also explain differences in punctuations, which do not necessarily reflect the differences in regime characteristics and democratic quality. The question of which factors influence policy punctuations and how they interact with regime characteristics is still open.

While we defined our volume as a contribution to the literature on policymaking under different regimes, our research brought up just as many, or even more, questions for further study than it was able to address. We find solace in that some would consider this to be a hallmark of a successful research project. All in all, our results speak to the importance of in-depth case studies and that of historical context besides the illuminating quantitative analyses associated with the Comparative Agendas Project. We believe that future research based on such a mixed-methods approach will yield further advances in our understanding of how political regimes define policymaking.

References

Aucoin, P. (2012). New political governance in Westminster systems: Impartial public administration and management performance at risk. *Governance, 25*(2), 177–199.

Bartha, A., Boda, Zs., & Szikra, D. (2020). When populist govern. Conceptualizing populism in policymaking. *Politics and Governance, 8*(3), 71–81.

Baumgartner, F. R., Carammia, M., Epp, D. A., Noble, B., Rey, B., & Yildirim, T. M. (2017). Budgetary change in authoritarian and democratic regimes. *Journal of European Public Policy, 24*(6), 792–808.

Boda, Z. (2020). *Ki dönt? Kormányzási stílusok és közpolitikai változás Magyarországon 2002–2014.* Gondolat.

Boda, Z., & Patkós, V. (2018). Driven by politics: Agenda setting and policymaking in Hungary 2010–2014. *Policy Studies, 39*(4), 402–421.

Böcskei, B. (2016). Overheads reduction: Policy change as a political innovation. *European Quarterly of Political Attitudes and Mentalities, 5*(3), 70–89.

Böcskei, B., & Szabó, A. (Eds.). (2019). *Hibrid rezsimek. A politikatudomány X aktái.* Napvilág Kiadó.

Jennings, W., Bevan, S., Timmermans, A., Breeman, G., Brouard, S., Chaqués-Bonafont, L., Green-Pedersen, C., John, P., Mortensen, B. P., & Palau, M. A. (2011). Effects of the core functions of government on the diversity of executive agendas. *Comparative Political Studies, 44*(8), 1001–1030.

Jones, B. D., Epp, D. A., & Baumgartner, F. R. (2019). Democracy, authoritarianism, and policy punctuations. *International Review of Public Policy*, *1*(1), 7–26. https://doi.org/10.4000/irpp.318.

Körösényi, A., & Patkós, V. (2017). Variations for inspirational leadership: The incumbency of Berlusconi and Orbán. *Parliamentary Affairs*, *70*(3), 611–632.

Kuczi, T., & Becskeházi, A. (1992). *Szociológia, ideológia, közbeszéd/Szociológia és társadalom-diskurzus*. Scientia Humana.

Peters, B. G. (2019). *Institutional theory in political science: The new institutionalism*. Edward Elgar Publishing.

Sebők, M., & Berki, T. (2018). Punctuated equilibrium In democracy and autocracy. An analysis of Hungarian budgeting between 1868 and 2013. *European Political Science Review*, *10*(4), 589–611. https://doi.org/10.1017/S1755773918000115.

Vliegenthart, R., Walgrave, S., Baumgartner, F. R., Bevan, S., Breunig, C., Brouard, S., Bonafont, L. C., Grossman, E., Jennings, W., Mortensen, P. B., Palau, A. M., Sciarini, P., & Mortensen, P. B. (2016). Do the media set the parliamentary agenda? A comparative study in seven countries. *European Journal of Political Research*, *55*(2), 283-301.

APPENDICES

A1

The Main Features of Regimes and Party Systems (1867–2018)
Csaba Molnár
See Tables A1 and A2.

Table A1   Main characteristics of Hungarian regimes (1867–2018)

Year/period (periods discussed in separate chapters in bold)	Historical classification	Inputs	Policy process	Outputs
1867–1918	**Austro-Hungarian Compromise (Dualism, Dual Monarchy): partly free**	Freedom of assembly, association, speech, and press Pluralistic media Strong and active interest groups and NGOs Competitive elections but census voting and open ballot	Constitutional monarchy Parliament with symmetrical bicameralism Government accountable to parliament and king Monarch with absolute veto Local self-governance Separation of powers Joint foreign policy and military affairs institutions with Austria	Important role of laws Decrees rise in importance during World War I Two distinct budgets for Hungary and the Austro-Hungarian Monarchy, respectively
1918–1919	First Republic: partly free	In the wake of WWI freedom of assembly, association, speech, and press are limited in scope, but they do exist Pluralistic media No elections were held	Republic No operating parliament The government is accountable to the National Council, which is made up of the governing parties Temporary, ad hoc solutions, non-institutionalized and unconsolidated regime	Governance by decree (even the "laws of people" are decrees in reality)
1919	Soviet Republic: not free	Civil rights severely constrained The media are controlled by the state Liquidation of independent interest groups and NGOs Non-competitive elections	Party state Unicameral parliament Unstable institutions Merging state and party administration Unity of power branches	A predominance of decrees over legislation by parliament

(continued)

Table A1 (continued)

Year/period (periods discussed in separate chapters in bold)	Historical classification	Inputs	Policy process	Outputs
1919–1944	**Horthy Regime: partly free**	Freedom of assembly, association, speech, and press do prevail, but they are limited in scope Limited, but pluralistic media Active interest groups and NGOs but in many cases limited by government interventions Competitive elections, but census voting and open ballot Persecution of anti-system organizations and persons (or those regarded as such)	Constitutional monarchy without a king Unicameral parliament until 1926, then asymmetrical bicameral parliament The government is accountable to both parliament and the regent The regent initially wields limited powers, but these are expanded over time Local self-governance Separation of powers	Central role of parliament The adoption of decrees becomes more prominent during the second phase of this period Enabling acts
1944	German Occupation: not free	Civil rights do not prevail State control over the media Liquidation of independent interest groups and NGOs No elections are held	German tutelage, military occupation, plenipotentiary Bicameral parliament which rarely convenes German puppet government Passive regent who is removed when he tried to assert himself	A predominance of decrees over legislation by parliament
1944–1945	National Socialist Regime: not free	Civil rights do not prevail Media are subject to state control Liquidation of independent interest groups and NGOs No elections are held	Party state Barely function bicameral parliament The "Leader of the Nation" serves as both head of state and government Parallel party and state administration Unity of power branches	A predominance of decrees over legislation by parliament

(continued)

Table A1 (continued)

Year/period (periods discussed in separate chapters in bold)	Historical classification	Inputs	Policy process	Outputs
1944–1946	Transitional Regime: partly free	Freedom of assembly, association, speech, and press do prevail, but they are limited in scope Pluralistic media Strong and active interest groups and NGOs Not fully competitive elections Persecution of anti-system organizations and persons (or those regarded as such) Increasing compliance with Soviet instructions	Form of government unclear Unicameral parliament Government is accountable to parliament Collective head of state (High National Council) Absence of local self-governance Separation of powers Tutelage of Allied Commission	A predominance of decrees over legislation by parliament
1946–1949	Second Republic: partly free	Freedom of assembly, association, speech, and press are increasingly subject to restrictions and then ultimately eliminated Massively diminishing media pluralism Liquidation of independent interest groups and NGOs Elections with limited competition Persecution of anti-system organizations and persons (or those regarded as such) Increasing compliance with Soviet instructions	Republic Unicameral parliament Government is accountable to parliament Weak president Absence of local self-governance Separation of powers, followed by increasing influence of the communist party in all areas Tutelage of Allied Commission until 1947	Important role of laws

(continued)

Table A1   (continued)

Year/period (periods discussed in separate chapters in bold)	Historical classification	Inputs	Policy process	Outputs
1949–1956	Rákosi Regime: not free	Civil rights and liberties are not respected by the state Media are controlled by the state Pseudo-NGOs Non-competitive elections Compliance with Soviet instructions	Single-party state Unicameral parliament Collective body exercises the responsibilities of the head of state (Presidential Council) Merging state and party administration Unity of power branches	Very little legislative activity performed by parliament The Presidential Council performs most of the activities in the authority of parliament (decrees laws) Major role of party decisions
1956–1990	**Kádár Regime: not free**	Civil rights and liberties are not respected by the state Media under state control Pseudo-NGOs Non-competitive election Compliance with Soviet instructions	Single-party state Unicameral parliament Collective body exercises the responsibilities of the head of state (Presidential Council) Merging state and party administration Unity of power branches	Very little legislative activity performed by parliament The Presidential Council performs most of the activities in the authority of parliament (decrees laws) Major role of party decisions
1990–2010	**Third Republic: free**	Freedom of assembly, association, speech, and press Pluralistic media Strong and active interest groups and NGOs Competitive elections	Republic Unicameral parliament Government is accountable to parliament Weak president Local self-governance Separation of the branches of power	Central role of laws adopted by parliament Increased adoption of decrees by the government

(continued)

Table A1 (continued)

Year/period (periods discussed in separate chapters in bold)	Historical classification	Inputs	Policy process	Outputs
2010–ongoing	**Orbán Regime: partly free**	Freedom of assembly, association, speech, and press Pluralistic media landscape Strong and active interest groups and NGOs competitive elections	Republic Unicameral parliament Government is accountable to parliament Weak president Local government stripped many of its policy responsibilities and incomes Separation of powers, but increasing concentration of power	More intense legislative activity by parliament Diminished intensity in the drafting and adoption of decrees

Table A2 Hungarian political regimes and party systems, 1867–2018

Year/period	Historical classification	Government party	Opposition	Main cleavages
1867–1918	**Austro-Hungarian Compromise (dualism): partly free**	Predominant party or grand coalition. Sixty-Sevener government parties: Deák Party (1867–1875), Liberal Party (1875–1906), National Party of Work (1910–1918) Highly diverse coalition from 1906 to 1910 and between 1917 and 1918.	Slight support, extremely fragmented Main ideological streams: • Forty-Eighter (Center-Left Party, Far-Left Party, Independence Party, Ugron Party, Justh Party, Kossuth Party) • conservative (Far-Right Party, Right-wing Opposition, United Opposition, Moderate Opposition, National Party, Constitutional Party) • Catholic (People's Party) agrarian-(Farmer Party, Independent Socialist Farmers' Party) • national minority (e.g., Slovakian National Party, Saxon Party, Romanian National Party, Serbian National Radical Party) • social democratic (Social Democratic Party of Hungary)	Public law: Those who support the union with Austria (Sixty-Seveners) and those who oppose it (Forty-Eighters) Liberals (Sixty-Seveners and Forty-Eighters)—conservative (conservative and Catholic parties) Catholic (People's Party)—protestant/secular Employers—employees (Social Democratic Party of Hungary) Urban-rural (agrarian parties) Hungarian—national minorities (national minority parties)

(continued)

Table A2   (continued)

Year/period	Historical classification	Government party	Opposition	Main cleavages
1918–1919	First Republic: partly free	Coalition of left-wing parties: Independence and Forty-Eighters (Károlyi) Party, Social Democratic Party of Hungary, Civic Radical Party, later National Smallholders' Party	A rapidly surging polarized opposition: • left-wing anti-system (Communist Party of Hungary) • right-wing anti-system organizations (Hungarian National Defense Organization) • center-right parties (Independence and Forty-Eighter Party, Hungarian Civic Party, National Smallholders' Party, Christian Social People's Party)	Democracy (governing parties, center-right parties)– dictatorship (left-wing and right-wing anti-system parties) Capitalism (center-right parties, National Smallholders' Party) – socialism (Hungarian Party of Communists, Social Democratic Party of Hungary) Agrarian (National Smallholders' Party)—industrial (Communist Party of Hungary, Social Democratic Party of Hungary)
1919	Soviet Republic: not free	Single party system; state party: Socialist Party of Hungary, then Party of Socialist-Communist Workers in Hungary	No legal opposition was allowed to operate. Active illegal right-wing organizations (but not parties)	Single-party system, no cleavages

(continued)

Table A2 (continued)

Year/period	Historical classification	Government party	Opposition	Main cleavages
1919–1944	Horthy Regime: partly free	A grand coalition until 1922, then a heterogeneous but mainly conservative government party as the predominant party in the regime: Unity Party (1922–1932), Party of National Unity (1932–1939), Party of Hungarian Life (1939–1944) Usually joined by a smaller right-wing coalition partner	Extremely fragment, many parties with small support Main ideological outlooks: • agrarian (Independent Smallholders' Party, etc.) • Christian (Andrássy-Friedrich Party, Christian Economy and Social Party, National Legitimist People's Party, etc.) • social democratic (Social Democratic Party of Hungary, etc.) • liberal (National Democratic Party, United Left Party, United Liberal Democratic Party, Civic Freedom Party, etc.) • radical right-wing (Hungarian National Independence Party, etc.) • national socialist (Hungarian National Socialist Party, Party of National Will, Party of People's Will, United Hungarian National Socialist Party, Arrow-Cross Party, etc.)	Agrarian (agrarian parties)—industrial (social democratic parties) Urban (liberal and social democratic parties)–rural (agrarian parties, governing parties) Employer–employees (social democratic parties) Religious (Christian parties)—secular (liberal and social democratic parties) Anti-Semitic (right-wing radical and national socialist parties)– Filosemitic (liberal and social democratic parties) Parliamentarian (governing parties, agrarian, Christian, social democratic, and liberal parties)– anti-parliament (right-wing radical and national socialist parties)

(continued)

Table A2 (continued)

Year/period	Historical classification	Government party	Opposition	Main cleavages
1944	German Occupation: not free	A coalition of Party of Hungarian Life, pruned of its anti-Nazi elements; the Hungarian National Socialist Party, and the Party of Hungarian Renewal (the latter was part of the coalition until August)	Left-wing and anti-Nazi parties banned. With the exception of the pro-German politicians of the former governing parties (the Party of Hungarian Life and the Transylvanian Party), as well as the far-right parties (Party of Hungarian Renewal, Arrow Cross Party, Hungarian National Socialist Party) only the opposition conservative Christian People's Party was allowed to operated, subject to certain restrictions	There were no cleavages, as of August 1944 no parties could operate legally any longer
1944–1945	National Socialist Regime: not free	Emerging single-party system led by the Arrow Cross Party, but a few other far-right parties (remnants of the Party of Hungarian Life, Party of Hungarian Renewal, Hungarian National Socialist Party) also delegate ministers into the government	No legal opposition was allowed to operate, no party outside the Arrow Cross Party was officially allowed to exist; the operations of other far-right parties are subject to major restrictions	Practically a single-party system, with no cleavages

(continued)

Table A2   (continued)

Year/period	Historical classification	Government party	Opposition	Main cleavages
1944–1946	Transitional Regime: partly free	Grand coalition (Independent Smallholders' Party, Social Democratic Party, Hungarian Communist Party, National Peasant Party); as a result of Soviet pressure, cabinet portfolios are not distributed on the basis of the election results. From the very beginning, the Communist Party sought to eliminate the other parties, and to that end it removed several smaller groups from the Smallholders' Party	Grand coalition featuring all relevant political forces, no major opposition left. Very weak opposition parties: • Hungarian Radical Party: radical liberal party of intellectuals • Civic Democratic Party: intellectual party comprising conservative and liberal politicians	agrarian (Independent Smallholders' Party, National Peasant Party)—industrial (Social Democratic Party, Hungarian Communist Party) Religious (Independent Smallholders' Party, Civic Democratic Party)—secular (Social Democratic Party, Hungarian Communist Party, Hungarian Radical Party) Capitalism (Independent Smallholders' Party, Civic Democratic Party)—socialism (Social Democratic Party, Hungarian Communist Party, National Peasant Party)

(continued)

Table A2 (continued)

Year/period	Historical classification	Government party	Opposition	Main cleavages
1946–1949	Second Republic: partly free	Coalition government comprising the Hungarian Communist Party, the Social Democratic Party, the Independent Smallholders' Party, National Peasant Party. In 1948 the Hungarian Communist Party and the Social Democratic Party are merged.	The operations of the divided right-wing (Democratic People's Party, Hungarian Independence Party, Camp of Christian Women, Independent Hungarian Democratic Party) and liberal (Hungarian Radical Party, Civic Democratic Party) opposition are subject to increasing restrictions By 1949, the opposition parties are mostly eliminated, its politicians are arrested, and forced either into passivity or emigration. Some of them become communist fellow travelers	Religious (Democratic People's Party, Camp of Christian Women)—secular (Social Democratic Party, Hungarian Communist Party, Hungarian Radical Party) Agrarian (Independent Smallholders' Party, National Peasant Party)—industrial (Social Democratic Party, Hungarian Communist Party) Capitalism (Independent Smallholders' Party, right-wing and liberal opposition)—socialism (Hungarian Communist Party, Social Democratic Party, National Peasant Party)

(continued)

Table A2 (continued)

Year/period	Historical classification	Government party	Opposition	Main cleavages
1949–1956	Rákosi Regime: not free	Single-party system, state party: Hungarian Working People's Party	A legal opposition was not allowed to operate	Single-party system, no cleavages applied
1956–1990	Kádár Regime: not free	Single-party system, state party: Hungarian Socialist Workers' Party	A legal opposition was not allowed to operate; they only began to form from 1988	Single-party system, no cleavages applied
1990–2010	Third Republic: free	Alternation in government of center-right and left-wing-liberal coalitions. A single-party government between 2008 and 2010 (but with external support of the previous coalition partner)	A gradual increase in the concentration of the party system, from a moderate pluralism to a two-and-a-half-party system • center-right (conservative, Christian democratic, liberal) parties: Hungarian Democratic Forum, Christian Democratic People's Party, Fidesz from 1993, Independent Smallholders' Party until 1992) • radical right: Party of Hungarian Justice and Life, Independent Smallholders' Party after 1992 • liberal: Alliance of Free Democrats, Fidesz until 1993 • social democrats: Hungarian Socialist Party	Urban (Alliance of Free Democrats, Party of Hungarian Justice and Life)–rural (Independent Smallholders' Party, Christian Democratic People's Party, Fidesz after 1998) Religious (Christian Democratic People's Party, Independent Smallholders' Party, Hungarian Democratic Forum, Fidesz after 1998)—secular (Alliance of Free Democrats, Hungarian Socialist Party Fidesz until 1993) Post-communist: (Hungarian Socialist Party)—anti-communist (everyone else)

(continued)

Table A2   (continued)

Year/period	Historical classification	Government party	Opposition	Main cleavages
2010–ongoing	**Orbán Regime: patly free**	Predominant party system: government composed of the heterogeneously right-wing Fidesz (and its satellite party, Christian Democratic People's Party)	Extremely fragment opposition with low level of support. Major ideological affiliations: • social democratic (Hungarian Socialist Party, Democratic Coalition) • radical right (Jobbik) • green/left radical (Politics Can Be Different, Dialogue) • liberal (Together, Momentum Movement)	Urban (left-wing parties)–rural (Fidesz, Jobbik) Religious (Christian Democratic People's Party)–secular (Hungarian Socialist Party, Democratic Coalition) GAL (Politics Can Be Different, Dialogue)—TAN (Jobbik, Fidesz, Christian Democratic People's Party) Post-communist (Hungarian Socialist Party, Democratic Coalition)—anti-communist (Fidesz, Jobbik, Christian Democratic People's Party, Politics Can Be Different)

A2

The Machine Learning Approach to the Policy Classification of Newspaper Articles
György Márk Kis

This research note applies the novel approach developed by Sebők and Kacsuk (2020) to classify frontpage articles by their policy content from a prominent Hungarian political newspaper, Magyar Nemzet. It presents the methodology undergirding much of the media analysis presented in this book. We present how a manually classified training set of 21,700 articles can be leveraged to assign a high-confidence tag in five rounds to 17,854 "virgin" articles. Based on our results, this approach promises to significantly reduce the workload on human coders tasked with annotating large corpora of textual data with the Comparative Agendas Project policy topics codes, and possibly beyond.

Analyzing media corpora has long been a task which required immense human workpower due to the sheer size of these datasets.[1] This study presents an attempt to use machine learning in order to classify the policy content of frontpage articles of a Hungarian print daily using a novel method presented by Sebők and Kacsuk (2020). The study elaborates on the methodological choices, the algorithm itself, and the results of the policy topic coding workflow.

Support Vector Machines (SVM) are popular tools in classifying documents: Google Scholar lists approximately 17,400 hits for the search "svm text classification" just for the first six months of 2020. The method itself is used with a variety of tuning parameters and other attributes, and is renowned to work effectively in high dimensional feature spaces (such as Document-Term Matrices which serve as the basis for much of quantitative text analysis research).

The text classification literature started taking its modern form in the 1990s, with enough experimentation done to be surveyed by Yang (1999). The author states that most methods used nowadays have been extensively applied to the famed Reuters datasets throughout the 1990s

---

[1] This research note presents the results of the Hungarian Comparative Agendas Project research team realized under the direction of Miklós Sebők. The author acknowledges Sebők and Kacsuk (Sebok & Kacsuk, 2020) as the source of the methodology and workflow presented in this note. The data provided by CAP and the coordinating efforts of Orsolya Ring of the human validation process is also much appreciated.

(ibid, 71–72). The thorough application of Support Vector Machines was undertaken by Joachims (1998) and Dumais (1998). The seminal work of Joachims (1998: 140–142) described SVMs as not only new (presented in its current form only in 1995) but robust over several applications and providing improvements over other, state-of-the-art solutions. Joachims argued that the advantages of SVMs in text classification contexts are the ability to handle very high dimensional feature spaces, handle sparse document vectors, work unsupervised without the need for constant parameter optimization, and work similarly regardless of the domain.

Dumais (1998) compared popular classification methods with Linear SVM on the Reuters dataset in terms of accuracy, learning speed, and classification speed. The learning speed for SVM was shorter by a factor of 2–73, while classification time did not differ substantially. Multiclass accuracy, precision, and recall were several percentage points better for overall performance and the most frequent categories as well. SVM generally proved to be better at any point on another oft-used metrics of cost-benefit for machine learning, the so-called ROC curve.

Active Learning, a supplementary learning method used in our approach, appeared only a few years after the aforementioned works. Tong and Koller (2001) introduced an algorithm which SVMs can use to request new instances. Similarly to Dumais, they also compared their solution to known Active Learning methods, showing that it outperforms them. These works quickly established SVM as not just a new contender, but the champion of text classification to be defeated. The advantages of SVMs listed above are timeless: robustness and the ability to deal with tens of thousands of features are always required, while computational complexity is still a major hurdle for most researchers.

The Dataset
The dataset used in our research project originally consisted of 57,858 front-page articles from the Hungarian political daily *Magyar Nemzet* (abbreviated as MN, translated as "Hungarian Nation"). The dataset includes articles from 1990 to 2014. This newspaper was in circulation between 1938 and 2018 and then from 2019 on and had started out as an anti-Nazi, right-leaning paper initially financed by Jewish industrialists. During the decades of socialist autocracy MN—though controlled as all publications were—retained its status as a forum for foreign politics,

culture, and opinion pieces not necessarily adhering strictly to party directives. It conserved its right-leaning, conservative outlook after the regime
change of 1989.

These 57,858 text files were created by an Optical Character Recognition method from digitized front pages and are considered to be the
most complete dataset available for this particular newspaper. The dataset
in itself is unique in that it was created not by scraping or crawling from a
text database, but parsing through images of front pages originally printed
on paper. The OCR algorithm was tuned to accommodate layouts and
their changes through time. Therefore, our workflow does not presup-
pose a digitized version of the analyzed newspapers, only scans of prints
(or prints themselves) which are generally available in most state library
systems.

In their purest form, text files consist of a name, created by concate-
nating the publication year, month, day, and the given number of the
article on that day, with the title, subtitle, and text enclosed in the UTF-
8 encoded text file. With algorithmic solutions, one can extract different
date attributes, frequencies, and categorize the texts according to year,
month, political regime, prime minister, etc.

21,700 of the original 57,858 files received major topic codes in our
research process after validation by two separate human coders. Expert
human coding is seen as the gold standard of such tasks, the manual
coding thus created a reliable training set. (Previous experiences in the
Hungarian Comparative Agendas Project [CAP] with coding parliamentary documents, such as interpellations and bills, revealed an intercoder
reliability of 85% when all items were coded by two experienced human
coders, working separately.) The remaining 36,158 texts were collectively
used as a test set for the first run of the algorithm.

Data Preparation
Before separating the data into training and test sets, several preparation
methods needed to be conducted. No text file exhibited an unusually low
or high character count, and no duplicates were found. The preparation
consisted of the following steps:

1. Removing numbers and punctuation
2. Stripping whitespace
3. Conversion to lowercase
4. Removing stopwords

5. Stemming
6. Removing stopwords.

Text data preparation or preprocessing is a way of standardizing the textual data for the algorithm. Numbers and punctuation do not carry an inherent meaning which could be analyzed by frequencies. Whitespaces are non-visible spacing characters created by errors in the typography, OCR, or the cleaning algorithm. Removing them ensures the "word-space-word-space-word" pattern in the texts. Changing everything to lower case creates non-ambiguity: unless stated otherwise, character strings "Christmas" and "christmas" are different ones for computers, while they generally share the same meaning, especially if considered in frequency analysis.

Stopwords are words which have no individual meaning and can only be given one in contexts, such as pronouns. There is no definitive list of these—in our study we used the one provided by the R package "tm" (Feinerer & Hornik, 2020). Stemming is the most important part of data preparation. It reveals the stem of the words, making it possible to equate the same word, even if it appears in different grammatical forms throughout the data set.

Support Vector Machines
The motivation of a Support Vector Machine is to find a set of hyperplanes that best separate the data points in binary formulations, i.e., cut through the data with linear or nonlinear cuts. Best separation is generally achieved by maximizing the margins between the hyperplane and the data points closest to the hyperplane—these points are called support vectors (akin to the notion as they are supporting or stretching out the specific hyperplane, like columns would support a heavy roof). The requisitive binary setting can be achieved either in "one-vs-one" (macroeconomics vs. defense) and "one-vs-rest" (macroeconomics vs. anything else) formulations of multiclass data sets and applications.

For our textual data, we extracted term frequencies from the documents into a Term-Document Matrix, known as a TDM. The TDM takes all terms encountered in the dataset and counts them per document. This yields a matrix in which rows are terms, columns are documents and cell values are counts. Thus every column is a vector representation of a document in a correspondingly high dimensional space. The SVM takes these vectors as features (independent variables) and constructs hyperplanes accordingly.

There are several weighting methods for frequency-based analyzes, such as term frequency-inverse document frequency (TF-IDF), logarithm, unit normalization, or entropy. Weighting during data preprocessing is considered to be advantageous, especially if the weighting conforms to the technique used. TF-IDF weighting takes term frequencies and inversely weights them as a function of their prevalence (Spark, 1972). Terms that appear in most documents frequently bear no relevance for information retrieval in the aspect of classifying and unique content, while rare terms usually carry distinguishable information. We have used this weighting throughout the classification.

Active Learning, Ensemble Voting and Bagging
In the algorithm, we have used the concepts of active learning, ensemble voting, bagging, and undersampling. In *active learning*, the algorithm asks for user input periodically. The motivating idea behind this is the hypothesis that machine learning algorithms will work substantially better if they are allowed to ask for input on predetermined terms, such as most ambiguous cases, and be the most effective possible, as they are asking for minimal input, in exchange for maximum marginal improvement (Miller et al., 2018).

Ensemble voting is an approach where several classifiers are used to categorize data, but instead of labeling the data and moving on to the next point, they cast their votes on the label. This can be binary or probabilistic, as several different methods can be used at the same time. A decision can be reached through majority or unanimous voting. Ensemble voting is generally reserved for a collection of different algorithms. However, in this study, we use it to denote aggregated voting from several runs of the same algorithm.

During the analysis of this paper, we have chosen to only accept unanimous voting and let the active learning method query labels only when there were *multiple* unanimous votes throughout the rounds. The motivation behind this was to reach the best possible results no matter the size of the resulting number of labels. In this sense, the method will only work on part of the unlabeled articles, but it will rival expert-based manual coding within that set (as discussed later).

Bagging (shorthand for bootstrap aggregating) is a technique, where *n* number of new samples are generated from the original training set, with the same number of observations, and with replacement (Hastie et al., 2009: 282–288). Then n models are fitted to the bootstrapped samples, and, in the end, an aggregation method is used on the results. (In this paper ensemble voting fulfilled this role.) The method prevents overfitting, as the multiple models make it harder for dominant features to overtake model building.

Finally, *undersampling* is a process where the ratios within a sample are controlled, based on the ratios in the population (Choi, 2010: 7–9). Under- and oversampling can be used to force a sampling algorithm to select certain categories less (or more) than a random sampling would. This balances a set where certain features seem overly strong, as the forced ratios will help prevent overfitting.

The Methodology of the Research Process

The methodology used in this paper is a slightly modified version of the one presented by Sebők and Kacsuk (2020), called the *Hybrid Binary Snowball* process. This starts by taking the manually coded articles and creating a preprocessed training set out of them. The algorithm then fits a Support Vector Machine on five undersampled samples, in five rounds of training and prediction for each sample, hence an article from the test set needs 25 (unanimous) votes to be successfully classified. The classification is done in one-vs-all settings, breaking down the multiclass problem into binary problems. (This is a well-known method for SVM, which can only be used for binary problems.) Classified articles are then sampled for human validation, and the boundary cases ask for input as part of the active learning component. If a sampled major topic reaches the round-specific accuracy threshold (Round 1—85%, Round 2—80%, Round 3 and on—75%), it is considered to be successfully classified, and is pooled into the training set.

Major topics (in our case: policy areas such as healthcare and defense) below the accuracy threshold are left in the test set with their labels deleted. Sampled articles, which were considered as misclassified by the human coder, were marked with negative information, not to let the SVM classify it in the same topic again. The active learning set is pooled into the training set after human validation. The number of classified articles is monitored between the rounds, and an expert opinion is formed whether diminishing returns are larger than the computational needs of another round. According to our experiences, newly classified articles flatten out between 3 and 5 rounds.

Our method hinges on several parameter choices. The utilized Spark Linear Support Vector Classifier requires an upper limit on iterations and a regularization parameter. The iteration parameter sets the maximum number of iterations for the algorithm to find the hyperplane (in the case it doesn't converge before this), using the regularization parameter as a rule for how serious of a problem misclassifications are. The larger the parameter, the stricter the algorithm becomes. For both, the default values of 10 and 0.1 were chosen, respectively.

These parameters could be refined by testing (such as a grid search or random search on a parameter space), but the computational needs made it very hard to go into extended optimization for the sake of possibly trifling gain in our selected measures (One round finished in roughly 8 hours with the computational capacity available for this project), and human validation takes several hours (not counting data and project management, etc.). A grid search of only 100 possible iteration-regularization pairs on a grid of 10 by 10 would have resulted in several months of work with no guarantees of increased accuracy, precision, recall, or F1-score. Another choice made was related to the number of samples and cycles within a round. Based on our experiences, any whole number between (and containing) 3 and 7 gives appreciable results. We chose 5 as a sort of middle ground between the boundaries.

Results

The algorithm ran for three rounds, with the author monitoring performance after each round with human validation. After the third round, the classification process was stopped due to the diminishing returns compared to computational and validation needs, as newly classified articles dropped from tens of thousands to hundreds (Fig. A1).

During the three rounds 17,584 documents were kept with finalized labels. This resulted in 39,284 cases in the training set, meaning 17,584 classified and validated texts from the original test set were classified permanently, resulting in a 48.6% classification rate after three rounds. It is important to keep in mind that this rate was reached with the given accuracy thresholds and the unanimous voting requirement. Relaxing these would have made it possible to reach higher final classification rates, albeit at the cost of decreasing final accuracy which would not be, as good as in the case of expert human coders (the gold standard for such tasks).

During the human validation process, 36 texts were identified as anomalies, meaning they were products of errors in the OCR process,

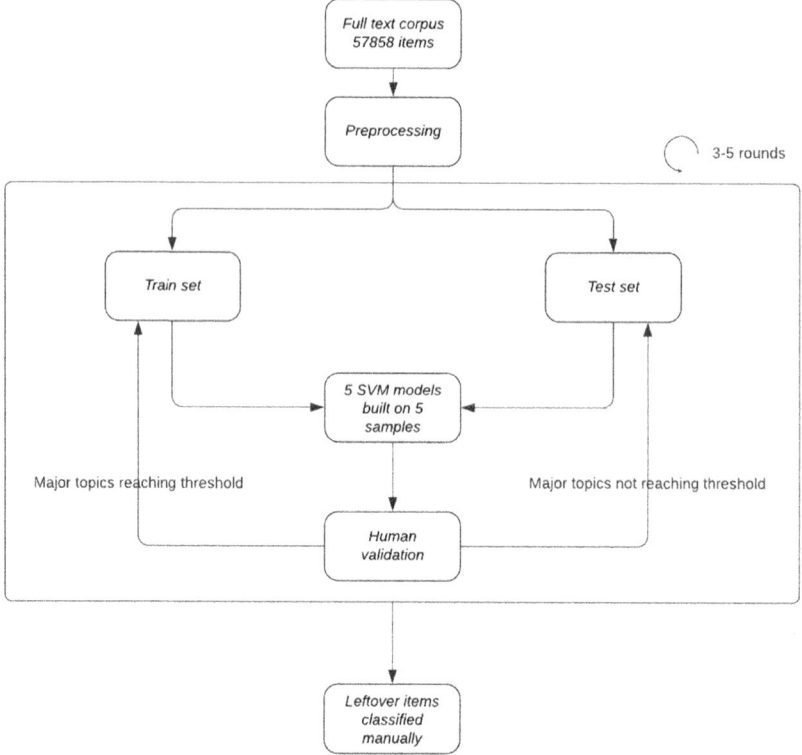

Fig. A1   Rough process chart of the classification

giving us two articles pasted together. These were extracted after identification, to be manually dealt with later. The final number of 17,584 was reached by manually validating 5657 decisions, therefore the reward to labor ratio (automatically classified text without validation vs. validated texts) was 2.1.

The aggregated precision of the method based on the validated samples was 82.8%. Major topics showed considerable variation around this average, partly due to wide-ranging sample sizes for different policy topics (topic 9—"immigration" and 18—"foreign trade" were not classified at all (despite being present in the training set), while topic 21—"public lands" had only two classified (and positive), as seen in Fig. A2.

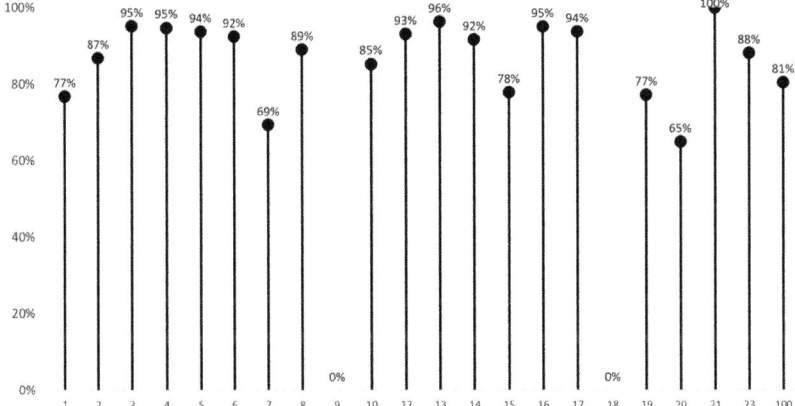

Fig. A2 Aggregated precision per major topic

Recall in itself can only be estimated as a *pseudorecall* until all the documents from the corpus are classified. For the pseudorecall, we used the major topic distribution found in the training set and assumed that this was representative of the complete data set. As seen in Table A3, the difference between the training set distribution and the final pooled training set distribution is the increased prevalence of code 19 (international affairs) and 100 (media codes, such as weather, sports, etc.). The pseudorecall for these major topics could go above 100% since the actual and complete distribution was unknown. The aggregated pseudorecall of the remaining major topics was 70.8%. From these measures a pseudo-macro-F1 score could be calculated, resulting in 0.763.

Generally major topics were dominated by code 19 (international affairs) and code 100 (media codes), especially in the first government cycle. A qualitative analysis of newspaper front pages in the era lends face validity to this finding.

A plot is provided both with or without the two outlier codes (see Figs. A3 and A4, respectively).

Discussion

Our database yielded useful insights into the media policy agenda beyond the distribution of major policy topics. A frequency analysis of the writing style throughout the decades of democracy reveals a sharp drop in median

Table A3 Performance measures per major topics

MT	precision (%)	pseudorecall (%)	pseudo-Fl
1	77	80	0.78
2	87	61	0.72
3	95	89	0.92
4	95	84	0.89
5	94	97	0.95
6	92	65	0.76
7	69	58	0.63
8	89	69	0.78
9	0	55	0.00
10	85	72	0.78
12	93	71	0.81
13	96	84	0.90
14	92	67	0.77
15	78	64	0.70
16	95	68	0.79
17	94	77	0.84
18	0	57	0.00
19	77	116	0.93
20	65	65	0.65
21	100	57	0.73
23	88	76	0.82
100	81	155	1.06

word count and mean characters per article (see Table A4). (These two features correlate almost perfectly since mean and median character count per word constantly hovers around 8.) Front-page articles tended to be much longer right after the regime change of 1990, even after discounting a large number of unusually long texts. This shows a rebalancing of front-page structure starting from 2002.

As Fig. A5 shows, outliers have been featured less as a trend, making us able to hypothesize the supremacy of small to medium information bits on the front page in contrast to large pieces after the first cycle.[2] This may be more related to typesetting and business decisions as opposed to some grand strategy on behalf of editors.

In late 1990, long front-page articles were supplemented by a vertical bar containing short previews of articles inside. From 1991 to 1993, more

[2] The anomaly on April 30, 2004 was a large frontpiece about the European Union one day before Hungary officially joined it.

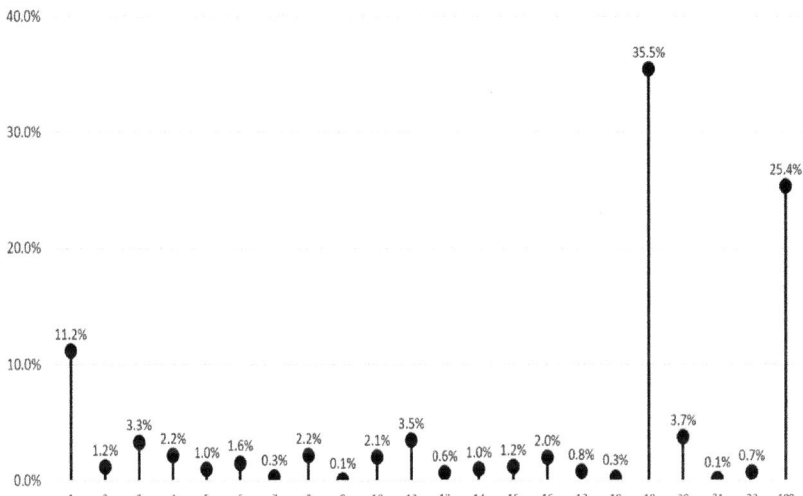

Fig. A3 Major topic distribution for all topics

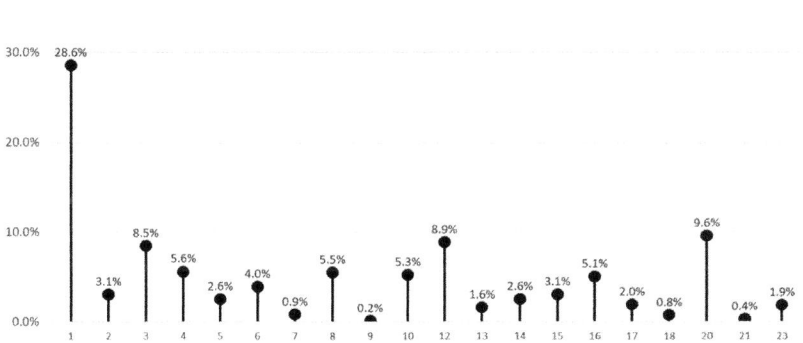

Fig. A4 Major topic distribution without topic 19 and 100

and more articles were fit on the front, sometimes even previewing the next day's large opinion pieces and cultural articles. From 1994 on a new style was adopted: front-page articles with the goal of previewing instead of informing, and generally several pictures, drawings. Adverts started

Table A4 Stylistic attributes per government cycle

Cycle no#	Median characters per article	Median words per article	Number of articles
1	1254	151	2948
2	786	95	4853
3	812	109	5019
4	553	72	9462
5	507	65	7837
6	568	74	9165

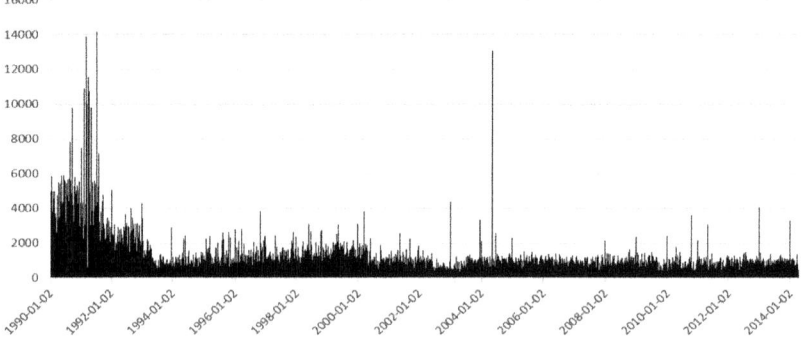

Fig. A5 Mean article lengths per day

appearing on front pages the same year. In October of 2000, the front page employed a new style and the main attributes of the layout stayed the same until the end of the period in question.

Do these changes have a bearing on the policy topic composition of front-page articles? Is the fragmentation of front pages accompanied by a greater heterogeneity of policy content or does it only mean more occurrences of the same few policy areas? These questions can be answered by using the chi-square analysis, which highlights the differences between expected and observed counts. In the contingency tables associated with this method the cell values reflect observed counts, while row and column sums (marginals) can be used to calculate expected counts. Conventionally chi-square tests show an aggregated deviation from expectations.

Applying this approach to the major topic distributions by government cycles, the chi-square statistic with a Monte Carlo simulation was 5338.6, which exhibits the Cramer's V value of 0.165 for our 6 by 22 table (p-value of 0.0005), which is considered a medium effect size according to Cohen (2013). This means that the major topic distributions deviate considerably from expectations in their counts. An analysis of the standardized residuals coming from a chi-square test reveals large heterogeneity among government cycles and topics, with a few outstanding residuals. These residuals show deviations from the topics' own expected rates, meaning the topic in that specific cycle was over-represented compared to the expectations based on marginals—we can consider it as a more detailed analysis of an aggregated chi-square test.

The first cycle after regime change was dominated by international affairs. The 2002–2006 government cycle was hallmarked by the topic of macroeconomics. This finding is in line with our qualitative overview of the era in Chapter 8. The same is true of the 2006–2010 electoral period when healthcare was not only a major reform issue in the MSZP-SZDSZ coalition but it had a notable impact on MN front pages as well.

We have to keep in mind that the deviations certain major topics exhibit does not mean these topics trump all others. If a very much under-represented topic overperforms expectations, it might still mean further underrepresentation, but still show us, that in those topics some kind of attention punctuation happened.

As a final mini analysis we looked at the techniquality of language usage in our corpus through the lens of Zipf's law. This states that in a natural language corpus the frequency of any word is inversely proportional to its rank in the frequency table. Deviations from this distribution inform us about the richness and technicality of the words used in the examined corpus. In our dataset, the Zipf plot (see Fig. A6) shows considerable deviation from the expected distribution for the top 100 thousand ranked tokens. For our case, it means that the vocabulary of our text corpus possesses smaller frequencies for the top-ranked words than expected, hinting at a rich vocabulary and a usage of technical language.

Conclusion

In this research note we have presented a method based on the Hybrid Binary Snowball workflow for using artificial intelligence to code policy topics in newspaper articles. Originally proposed by Sebők and Kacsuk

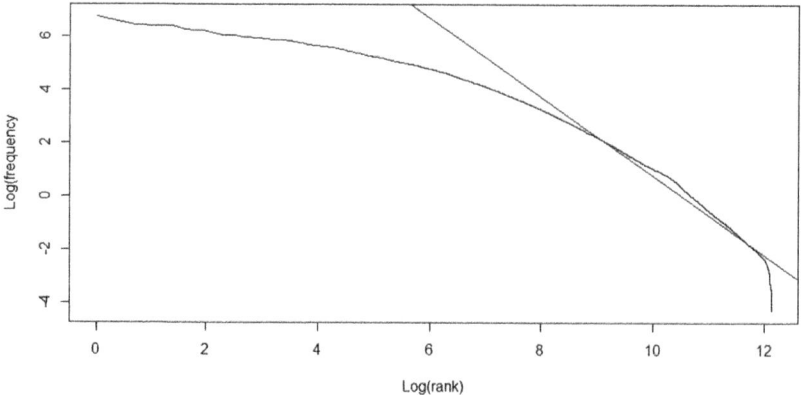

Fig. A6 Zipf plot of Magyar Nemzet vocabulary and expectation line

(2020), this method was used on a Hungarian daily newspaper's front-page articles for extracting policy content based on word frequencies using Support Vector Classification. The method worked with reasonably high precision, one similar to the intercoder reliability we've experienced for human coders, albeit on a limited portion of the test set. The unanimous voting rule of the workflow ensured high precision, but in this case only let 48.6% of the test set be classified by our standards.

There are several ways by which the method could be improved. The first one is kernel optimization. The SVM was built with a linear kernel, meaning that the data points were mapped in a linear space. Optimization can take place by testing other kernels, such as polynomial or radial basis functions. Another way of improving classification is parameter optimization. The regularization parameter (and others possibly needed by nonlinear kernels) should be tested for improvements in precision and recall. A third way of optimizing is using different weightings for the word frequencies.

In terms of computational complexity, apart from improving the hardware side of the equation, a feature extraction technique called non-negative matrix factorization (NMF) could be used. NMF generally makes it easier to work with matrices (especially large ones as in text mining) as it decomposes the Term-Document Matrix into a matrix with linear combinations of the features, and another with the corresponding weights. As proposed by Guduru (2006) the SVM combined with NMF has the potential to decrease the number of features tenfold while dropping less in accuracy.

REFERENCES

Choi, J. M. (2010). A selective sampling method for imbalanced data learning on support vector machines. *Graduate theses and dissertations*, 11529. Iowa State University. https://doi.org/10.31274/etd-180810-2653.

Cohen, J. (2013). *Statistical power analysis for the behavioral sciences*. Academic Press.

Dumais, S. (1998). Using SVMs for text categorization. *IEEE Intelligent Systems*, *13*(4), 21–23.

Feinerer, I., & Hornik, K. (2020). *tm: Text mining package*. R package version 0.7–8. https://CRAN.R-project.org/package=tm.

Guduru, N. (2006). *Text mining with support vector machines and non-negative matrix factorization algorithms*. University of Rhode Island.

Hastie, T., Tibshirani, R., & Friedman, J. (2009). *The elements of statistical learning: Data mining, inference, and prediction*. Springer Science & Business Media.

Joachims, T. (1998). *Text categorization with support vector machines: Learning with many relevant features*. Paper presented at the European conference on machine learning.

Miller, B., Linder, F., & Mebane Jr, W. R. (2018). *Active learning approaches for labeling text*. Technical report, University of Michigan, Ann Arbor, MI.

Sebők, M., & Kacsuk, Z. (2020). The multiclass classification of newspaper articles with machine learning: The hybrid binary snowball approach. *Political Analysis*, *29*, 1–14. https://doi.org/10.1017/pan.2020.27.

Spark, J. K. (1972). A statistical interpretation of term importance in automatic indexing. *Journal of Documentation*, *28*(1), 11–21.

Tong, S., & Koller, D. (2001, November). Support vector machine active learning with applications to text classification. *Journal of Machine Learning Research*, *2*, 45–66.

Yang, Y. (1999). An evaluation of statistical approaches to text categorization. *Information Retrieval*, *1*(1–2), 69–90.

Index

Printed by Printforce, the Netherlands